Decision-Aiding Software and Legal Decision-Making

Recent Titles from Quorum Books

Export Strategy
Subhash C. Jain

The Protectionist Threat to Corporate America: The U.S. Trade Deficit and Management Responses
Louis E. V. Nevaer and Steven A. Deck

Environmentally Induced Cancer and the Law: Risks, Regulation, and Victim Compensation
Frank B. Cross

Legal and Economic Regulation in Marketing: A Practitioner's Guide
Ray O. Werner

Smoking and the Workplace: Issues and Answers for Human Resources Professionals
William M. Timmins and Clark Brighton Timmins

Private Pensions and Employee Mobility: A Comprehensive Approach to Pension Policy
Izzet Sahin

Group Decision Support Systems for Effective Decision Making: A Guide for MIS Practitioners and End Users
Robert J. Thierauf

Deregulation and Competition in the Insurance Industry
Banks McDowell

Chemical Contamination and Its Victims: Medical Remedies, Legal Redress, and Public Policy
David W. Schnare and Martin T. Katzman, editors

Statistics for Real Estate Professionals
Rebecca F. Guy and Louis G. Pol

DECISION-AIDING SOFTWARE AND LEGAL DECISION-MAKING

A Guide to Skills and Applications Throughout the Law

Stuart S. Nagel

QUORUM BOOKS
New York • Westport, Connecticut • London

Library of Congress Cataloging-in-Publication Data

Nagel, Stuart S., 1934-
Decision-aiding software and legal decision-making : a guide to skills and applications throughout the law / Stuart S. Nagel.
p. cm.
Bibliography: p.
Includes index.
ISBN 0-89930-382-X (lib. bdg. : alk. paper)
1. Information storage and retrieval systems—Law—United States.
2. Law offices—United States—Automation. I. Title.
KF242.A1N237 1989
343.73'0999—dc19
[347.303999] 88-39911

British Library Cataloguing in Publication Data is available.

Library of Congress Catalog Card Number: 88-39911
ISBN: 0-89930-382-X

First published in 1989 by Quorum Books

Greenwood Press, Inc.
88 Post Road West, Westport, Connecticut 06881

Printed in the United States of America

The paper used in this book complies with the Permanent Paper Standard issued by the National Information Standards Organization (Z39.48-1984).

10 9 8 7 6 5 4 3 2 1

To the many innovative members of the legal profession
who are using or contemplating using decision-aiding software
to improve their law practices and the legal system

Contents

PART II: SPECIFIC LAWYER SKILLS

Preface

The field of microcomputers as decision aids in law practice is improving so rapidly that it is now time for the second book on the subject, even though the first book was published as recently as 1987. The earlier book was mainly concerned with speculating about ways in which decision-aiding software could be used by lawyers for judicial prediction, litigation strategy, allocating scarce resources, and negotiation-mediation. This book is mainly concerned with describing how those speculative ideas can be and are being actually implemented by decision-aiding software for lawyers.

The first book reflected ideas that were mainly developed in 1985 for a conference on "Using Personal Computers for Decision-Making in Law Practice" sponsored by the Committee on Continuing Professional Education of the American Law Institute and the American Bar Association (ALI-ABA). This book reflects ideas that were mainly developed in 1988 for a follow-up short course on "Legal Decision-Making and Microcomputers," also sponsored by the ALI-ABA. In the intervening time period, the author had approximately three years of experience working with the Policy/Goal Percentaging software (abbreviated P/G%), which is designed to process (1) a set of alternative cases or decisions that relate to legal matters, (2) a set of criteria for explaining differences among the cases or for choosing among the decisions, and (3) a set of relations between the alternatives and the criteria in order to explain or choose the best alternative, combination, allocation, or predictive decision-rule.

The book is divided into three parts covering general developments, specific lawyer skills, and applications to all fields of law. The main general development is that since 1985 there have been a number of events indicating that decision-aiding software is catching on. These developments include relevant newsletters, bar journal articles, law review articles, judicial articles, books, software, surveys of law firms, conferences, and training courses. Part I of the book also provides a preview of various uses of decision-aiding software to practicing lawyers, including a general discussion of the actual and potential benefits of such software.

Part II is the largest, containing 8 of the 13 chapters. It deals with specific lawyer skills. The most basic skills are those that relate to applying law to specific situations and disputes (Section A). In that context, chapter 3 discusses computer-aided counseling, and chapter 4 discusses computer-aided mediation. A key aspect of such counseling relates to helping clients make decisions with decision-aiding software. That includes decisions that are not strictly legalistic decisions, such as whether to get a divorce or how to allocate an estate. A key aspect of computer-aided mediation relates to enabling the conflicting sides to come out ahead of their best expectations by facilitating arrangements whereby each side gives on some criteria that are not so important to it, but receives on other criteria that it considers more important.

Section B under specific lawyer skills relates to the law-making activities of lawyers. These activities do not occur as much in most law practices as law-applying does. Such activities are, however, frequently considered to be the highest form of lawyer activity because they help shape the law that will be applied in future situations. Section B helps to emphasize that microcomputers can be helpful in lawyer decision-making at various levels in the legal system. The law-making material is divided into legal policy evaluation and computer-aided advocacy. The evaluation material emphasizes analyzing (1) alternative legal policies on the rows of a spreadsheet, (2) societal or other goals on the columns, (3) relations between the policies and the goals in the cells, (4) overall scores at the far right for each policy, and (5) an ability to determine what it would take to bring a second-place or other-place alternative up to first place. The computer-aided advocacy material emphasizes simulating the alternatives, goals, and perceptions of the decision-makers in order to be able to better influence them in a desired direction.

Section C of Part II deals with law-prediction skills. These are important skills since one can neither apply law nor make law if one cannot say something meaningful about the effects of one application or another, or one proposed law or another. In the practicing lawyer context, one can talk about predicting appellate court decisions or other decisions from prior cases. One can also talk about predicting trial court decisions or other decisions from factual elements. These are two kinds of predicting that are especially relevant to lawyers, but the methodology is applicable to prediction in general.

Section D deals with law administration. A firm cannot so effectively apply law or participate in making law if it is not so well administered. It needs to have some efficiency concerning its ability to get things done without excessive costs. In that context, we are not talking about the use of microcomputers to enable people to type faster or to be able to avoid typing completely. We are instead talking about efficiency in lawyer decision-making that affects the benefit/cost ratio of law firm activities. One specific recurring example is the division of labor among lawyers and other personnel in a law firm—an especially important factor in determining productivity. Another recurring example is the problem of how to sequence activities. This can be a crucial factor in productivity, as illustrated by the sequencing system developed by Admiral Hyman Rickover for building nuclear submarines.

Part III of the book is concerned with applications to all fields of law. Chapter 11 deals with relations among private citizens. This includes (1) contracts, such as law firm partnership contracts, or a contract designed to provide for consumer protection; (2) property law, including estate allocation and housing for the poor; (3) family law, including divorce issues and the desirability of no-fault divorce; and (4) tort law, including predicting who will win in civil cases and evaluating alternative liability systems. Notice that for each field of law there is a law-applying example and a legal policy example.

Chapter 12 deals with public law relations between the government and the people. This includes (1) criminal law with data for predicting a conviction or an acquittal and data for developing crime-reduction policies; (2) constitutional law, including equal protection case analysis and the desirability of judicial review; (3) economic regulation, including welfare proceedings and legal policy for dealing with unemployment-inflation; and (4) international law, including case prediction where the United States is a party and choosing among alternative forms of arms control.

Chapter 13 deals with procedural law. The first part is on criminal procedure, using plea bargaining as a law-application example, and using right to counsel alternatives as a law-making example. The second part is on civil procedure, using personal injury negotiations as a law application, and evaluating the use of juries in civil cases as a legal policy evaluation.

Chapter 14 is entitled "Legal Ethics and Microcomputers." It could have been entitled "Legal Ethics and Microcomputers as Decision Aids in Law Practice." It is specifically concerned with applications from the previous 13 chapters that raise questions of individual ethics and professional responsibility. The individual ethics questions relate to the fact that decision-aiding software encourages decision-makers to be more explicit about the goals they are seeking to achieve than they otherwise would be. That raises questions as to whose goals should be pursued and to what degree in terms of the client, the lawyer, the other side, other lawyers, the court, and society. The professional responsibility questions that are discussed relate to how decision-aiding software is relevant to the representation of the poor and the unpopular by the legal profession. Raising those representation questions provides an opportunity to review how the software can be applied to evaluating a set of alternatives in light of various societal or other goals.

In drafting acknowledgments, thanks are often given to institutions, publishers, and individuals. The key institution in this context is the American Law Institute, including Paul Wolkin, Mark Mendenhall, Alex Hart, Nancy Kane, and Kevin O'Connor, all of whom played a part in either the 1985 or the 1988 short course dealing with microcomputers and the law. The key publisher in this context is the joint publishing firm of Greenwood, Praeger, and Quorum, including Eric Valentine, Mildred Vasan, and James Sabin, all of whom played a part in publishing the books relevant to those short courses. The key individuals include John Long, who worked with me in developing the software; Miriam Mills, who coauthored some of the material; Madelle Becker, who helped in assembling the materials; and especially Joyce Nagel, who participated in numerous stages of the process of developing this and other books.

Special credit is due to the many members of the legal profession who have been trying and using decision-aiding software partly so others could benefit from their experiences. It is hoped that this book will stimulate many more members of the legal profession to do so to the benefit of their clients, themselves, and the legal system.

PART I

General Developments

CHAPTER 1

Preliminary Examples

The purpose of this chapter is to provide a few specific examples of applications of decision-aiding software in law practice. The first three examples deal with the practicing lawyer in private law practice. The fourth relates to legal policy evaluation. This combination of examples relates to private law firms and traditional common law practice, as well as government law work and the legal aspects of public policy. These examples occur throughout the book.

PRIVATE LAW PRACTICE

After the 1985 ALI-ABA short course on "Using Personal Computers for Decision-Making in Law Practice," many of the lawyers in the short course reported using the methods in their law practice activities. The three examples below all involve such applications.

Choosing Arbitrators in Medical Malpractice

The first example is E. Fremont Magee, a partner in the firm of Piper and Marbury of Baltimore, Maryland. He uses the P/G% or LawChoice software to help in deciding among candidates for arbitration panels in medical malpractice claims. Before a medical malpractice matter can be tried in court in Maryland, it must first be submitted to a statutory three-member arbitration panel. Each side is given resumes for five potential candidates to serve as the panel chair. All the candidates are attorneys. There are also five candidates to serve as the one lay member on the three-person panel, and five candidates for the one health care provider. The plaintiff's and the defendant's sides each have the opportunity to strike two candidates from each of the three lists. The most important list is the lawyers because it determines who will chair the panel. The biographical information for the lawyers indicates (1) year of birth, (2) type of practice, (3) years of trial experience, (4) frequency of trials, (5) medical malpractice experience, (6) relation with health care providers, (7) arbitration experience, (8) undergraduate college, (9) law school, and (10) year admitted to the bar.

In deciding whom to recommend for the chair of an arbitration panel, Magee prepares a 5 by 10 matrix with 5 candidates on the rows and 10 characteristics on the columns, or vice versa, as is shown in table 1-1. In the cells are words or numbers indicating how each candidate scores on each characteristic. He then converts the words into numbers, generally using 1-10 scales. He also gives different weights to the 10 criteria to indicate their relative importance in terms of what he is looking for in an ideal panel chairperson. He gives a weight of 3 to criteria 3, 4, 5, and 7, a weight of 2 to criteria 2 and 6, and a weight of 1 to criteria 1, 8, 9, and 10. A negative weight is given to year of birth and year admitted to the bar in order to indicate that a low score is more desirable than a high score. For example, one would prefer a chairperson who was born in 1920 over one who was born in 1960 on the theory that older attorneys are more experienced and more capable of exercising authority. The number 1,920 is, however a lower number than 1,960, but the number −1,920 is higher than the number −1,960.

He then converts the raw scores into percentages by dividing each raw score by the highest score received on its characteristic, as is shown in table 1-2. This percentaging enables each candidate to have a meaningful overall summation score even though the criteria are measured in a variety of ways, such as years for age, number of cases for arbitration experience, and a 1–10 scale for law school prestige. In giving each candidate an overall score based on the 10 criteria or characteristics, Magee takes into consideration the relative importance of the criteria by using them to multiply the percentages. Thus each candidate receives an overall score that is the sum of 10 products, where each product is the weight of the characteristic multiplied by the percentage score of the candidate on the characteristic.

The next step is to observe the rank order of the overall scores for the five candidates. The rank order is arbitrator A, then E, B, C, and D. Arbitrator A receives a score of 30% on a scale that goes from 0 to 100%. Arbitrator E receives a score of 23%, and so on. One could do an analysis with the software to show what it would take to bring Arbitrator E up to a tie with or ahead of Arbitrator A. Any one of A's 10 characteristics could theoretically change for the worse to make a tie, or any of B's 10 characteristics could theoretically change for the better to make a tie. Likewise, any one of the weights could change to make a tie. Most, if not all, of those changes would be unreasonable, given the large gap between A and B of 30% versus 23%. Thus A has a firm hold on first place.

If Magee were in control of the selection of a chair, he would recommend the person with the highest overall score. This, however, is an arbitration panel, and there must be agreement between Magee and the other side. Magee might therefore recommend his second choice first in anticipation that the other side will reject whoever Magee mentions first. Magee can then come forward with

Table 1-1
Criteria for Chairs of Medical Arbitration Panels

CRITERIA / ARBITRATOR	Year of Birth w = -1	Type of Practice w = 2	Years of Trial Experience w = 3	Frequency of Trials w = 3	Medical Malpractice Experience w = 3	Relation-ship with Health Care w = 2	Arbitration Experience w = 3	Under-graduate College w = 1	Law School w = 1	Year Admitted to Bar w = -1
A	'30	Insurance Defense 7	20	Frequent 4	All the time 8	Wife is Physician 7	4 cases 5	Jones 2	Jones 2	'50
B	'50	Plaintiff's Personal Injury 4	2	Occasional 3	All the time 8	None 1	4 cases 5	Howard 7	Howard 7	'75
C	'40	General 3	10	Occasional 3	None 1	Brother is Physician 4	4 cases 5	Wilson 4	Smith 6	'65
D	'44	General 3	10	Seldom 2	None 1	Pension Work for physicians 6	None 1	West 9	West 9	'75
E	'10	Workmen's Comp. 4	40	Frequent 4	None 1	Brother is M.D. 4	None 1	West 9	West 9	'30
Totals	174	21	82	16	19	18	17	31	33	424

Table 1-2

Converting the Scores into Percentages

CRITERIA / ARBITRATOR	Year of Birth w = 1		Type of Practice w = 2		Years of Trial Experience w = 3		Frequency of Trials w = 3		Medical Malpractice Experience w = 3		Relation-ship with Health Care w = 2		Arbitration Experience w = 3		Under-graduate College w = 1		Law School w = 1		Year Admitted to Bar w = 1		Weighted Sums	
	%	x w	%	x w	%	x w	%	x w	%	x w	%	x w	%	x w	%	x w	%	x w	%	x w	Σ	Σ/16
A	17	-17	33	67	24	73	25	75	42	126	32	64	29	88	6	6	6	6	12	-12	426	30
B	29	-29	19	38	2	7	19	56	42	126	5	9	29	88	23	23	21	21	18	-18	321	20
C	23	-23	14	29	12	37	19	56	5	16	18	36	29	88	13	13	18	18	15	-15	255	16
D	25	-25	14	29	12	37	12	38	5	16	27	55	6	18	29	29	27	27	18	-18	206	13
E	5	- 6	19	38	49	146	25	75	5	16	18	36	6	18	29	29	27	27	7	- 7	372	23
Totals	100	-100			100	200	100	300	100	200	100	200	100	100	100	100	100	100	100	-100	1600	100

his first choice as if he were making a concession. A better approach would be for Magee to develop a second 5 by 15 matrix with the same candidates and characteristics, but with weights that reflect the relative importance of the criteria from the perspective of the other side's decision-making. The second set of overall scores might be very helpful in arriving at a chair that would be high on Magee's list but also would be likely to be acceptable to the other side.

Simulating the other side would also give Magee insights into the perceptions and values of the other side that could be useful in trying to convince them to accept Magee's first choice. That kind of reasoning can be facilitated by software that can indicate what it would take to bring a second or other choice up to first place. Magee's first choice might be the other side's third choice. The threshold analysis can inform Magee what it would take in terms of changing the other side's perceptions and values to make that third choice into an acceptable first choice. Magee could then concentrate on seeking to change the perceptions and values that come closest to the threshold figures, and are thus easier to change than those perceptions or values that are far from the threshold figures. For example, the other side's third-place choice might become its acceptable first-place choice if Magee can convince the other side to put more weight on arbitration experience, or if Magee can convince the other side that the third-place candidate has had more relevant arbitration experience than the other side perceives.[1]

Choosing a Law Firm Location

The second example is C. Howard Thomas, Jr., a partner in the firm of Saul, Ewing, Remick, and Saul of Philadelphia. He presented two interesting uses of P/G% made by his law firm at the Legal Tech '86 Conference in Philadelphia. One use involved deciding where to move the offices of a firm that had to move because it needed larger quarters. There were about five key places to choose among, and there was considerable emotion in arguing over the five places. The partners decided to be explicit on the criteria the firm was seeking to achieve and how each place scored on each of those criteria. By doing that, the emotional subject could be handled more rationally. The analysis showed a certain place to be the tentative winner. A sensitivity analysis was then performed to see what changes in the relative weights of the criteria and in the scores of the alternatives on the criteria would be necessary to bring each other place up to the same desirability level as the first-place alternative. It was decided that all of the needed changes were unreasonable. The partners then felt pleased they had made the right choice as to where to move the law firm. The firm has also made use of P/G% in deciding whether to litigate or settle out of court. The analysis in at least one big case was shared with the client to convince the client that accepting the settlement was a wise decision.[2]

Predicting Case Outcomes

The third example is Karen S. Dickson and John Finan of the Akron University Law School. They analyzed a dozen key cases that involved the issue of whether a worker is an employee or an independent contractor. The analysis involved scoring each case on seven criteria as to whether the criterion was present or absent. Each case was given a summation score by adding its points on the criteria. The cases in which the total points were nine or more consistently found the worker to be an employee. The cases in which the total points were eight or less consistently found the worker to be an independent contractor. That consistent pattern was established after noting the need to give extra weight to whether the principal has control of the details of the agent's work, as compared to the other criteria. Dickson and Finan thus used the P/G% prediction methodology inductively to operationalize the concepts of employee and independent contractor more clearly than the courts had previously verbalized those concepts.

Table 1-3 shows the Dickson-Finan analysis. There are 12 cases on the rows and 7 criteria on the columns. The scoring on each criterion is 2 for yes and 1 for no. That scoring applies to all the criteria except the first one on controlling details. That criterion involves 4 for yes and 2 for no to indicate that it is considered twice as important or at least more important than the other criteria. One could achieve the same effect by scoring the first criterion on a 1–2 scale, but giving it a multiplier weight of 2. The last column labeled "Outcome" shows how the cases were decided. A 2 means the court found the individual to be an independent contractor and thus less capable of binding the person who was probably being sued. A 1 means the court found the individual to be an employee of the defendant or other person involved in the case.

If one adds across the whole numbers for each row to arrive at the totals given in the column labeled "Old Sum," then one can see that all the cases that add to 9 points or more resulted in a finding of an independent contractor being present. All the cases that add to 8 points or less resulted in a finding of an employee being present. That consistency would not occur if one did not recognize that controlling the details of the agent's work is an especially important predictive variable.

The numbers that have decimal parts represent averages on each criterion. They have been inserted where no other information was available. If blanks were left in those cells, that would be the equivalent of zero scores, which could distort the results. The average score for each column or predictive criterion was determined by adding the whole numbers on the column to obtain the total for each column. That total was then divided by the quantity of numbers on each column to obtain the average. Those averages were then inserted into the blanks on the assumption that each case for which there was unknown information was probably at the average on that criterion for want of any better information.

If one adds both the whole numbers and the decimal numbers across for each row, then the new sums show that a score of 12 or more results in an independent

Table 1-3
Predictive Criteria in Cases Involving a Distinction Between Employees and Independent Contractors

CRITERIA / CASE	Control of Details	Employee in Distinct Business	Tools and Place of Work	Length of Employment	Method of Payment	Regular Business of Employer	Belief of Parties	Old Sum	New Sum	Out-Come
Daily Sun	4	1	1	1.57	1	1.67	1.33	7	11.57	1
News-Journal	2	1	1	1.57	1	1.67	1.33	5	9.57	1
Hoeft	2	1	1	1	1	1.67	1.33	6	9.00	1
Southhard	2	1	1	2	1	1.67	1.33	7	10.00	1
Kiamesha-Concord	2	1	1	2	1	1.67	1	8	9.67	1
U.S.	2	1	2	2	2	1.67	1.33	9	12.00	2
Pure Oil Co.	2	1	1	1	1.00	1	1.33	6	8.33	1
Bureau Co-Op	2	1	1	1	1	1.67	1.33	6	9.00	1
Consolidated	4	2	1	1.57	1.00	2	2	11	13.57	2
X	4	2	1	2	1	1.67	1	11	12.67	2
Charles Journal	4	2	1	1.57	2	1.67	1.33	9	13.57	2
Express	4	2	1	1.57	1	2	1.33	10	12.90	2
Total	34	16	13	11	12	5	4	95	131.85	17
Average	2.83	1.33	1,08	1.57	1.00	1.67	1.33	7.92	10.99	1.42

contractor finding, and a score of less than 12 results in an employee finding. That method is more accurate because it relies on more complete information. It is possible that an independent contractor case could otherwise receive an unduly low score because of lack of information, not because it was inconsistently decided.[3]

GOVERNMENTAL LAW PRACTICE

The Basic Problem

Table 1-4 provides an example of using the P/G% software to arrive at a conclusion as to what policy ought to be adopted in light of a set of goals to be achieved. The subject matter is how should illegally obtained evidence be treated by the courts in criminal cases. The four alternatives listed consist of (1) the good-faith exception to excluding the evidence; (2) the suspension-dismissal exception to excluding the evidence from *Bivens v. Six Unknown Agents*, 403 U.S. 388 (1971); (3) the prevailing rule of excluding illegally seized evidence from criminal proceedings from *Mapp v. Ohio*, 367 U.S. 643 (1961); and (4) the previous emphasis on the possibility of damage suits and prosecution to deter illegal searches from *Wolf v. Colorado*, 338 U.S. 25 (1949). The goals to be achieved include (1) decreasing illegal police searches, (2) not encouraging lying by the police, (3) decreasing crime occurrence, and (4) feasibility in being capable of being adopted.

Table 1-4 also shows how each alternative is scored on each criterion using a 1–3 scale, where 3 = relatively high on the goal, 2 = middling on the goal, and 1 = relatively low on the goal. On the goal of decreasing illegal police searches, the alternatives of suspensions-dismissals and damages-prosecution are the strongest deterrents if applied. On not encouraging lying, the good-faith exception does not do so well compared to the other alternatives. On decreasing crime occurrence, the good-faith exception scores highest because it allows the police the freest hand. On the matter of feasibility, the good-faith exception may be questionable as to its constitutionality. Suspensions-dismissals lacks legislative feasibility, and damages-prosecution lacks judicial feasibility.

If one adds across each alternative without giving different weights to the goals, then the scores of the alternatives are 5 for the good-faith exceptions and a three-way tie for the other three alternatives. Even with different weights for the goals to consider the liberal, neutral, and conservative positions, there is still a three-way tie between suspension-dismissal, the exclusionary rule, and damages-prosecution. The bottom-line conclusion is that the exclusionary rule is the best of the tied alternatives because it is the only one that passes the feasibility constraint. It is feasible in the sense that it has been widely adopted across the 50 states. The other three alternatives have not been widely adopted, and there is considerable doubt as to whether they ever could be.

Without the feasibility criterion, the exclusionary rule comes out third or

Table 1-4
Law Evaluation: Evidence Illegally Obtained

ALTERNATIVE POLICIES	GOALS TO BE ACHIEVED				OVERALL SCORES							
	Decrease illegal police searches (L)	Not encourage lying by police (N)	Decrease crime occurrence (C)	Feasi-bility	Liberal Score		Neutral Score		Conservative Score		Total	
					B	A	B	A	B	A	B	A
1. Good-faith exception	1	1	3	1	8	11	10	13	12	15	30	39
2. Suspension-dismissal	3	2	2	1	15	18	14	17	13	16	42	51
3. Exclude evidence	2	2	1	3	11	20	10	19	9	18	30	57
4. Damages-prosecution	3	2	2	1	15	18	14	17	13	16	42	51

NOTES:

1. The four alternatives are (1) allow the evidence in if the police testify they did not intend to engage in illegal behavior, (2) allow the evidence in if the state adopts a system of suspensions on the first offense and dismissal on the second offense, (3) exclude illegally seized evidence from criminal proceedings, and (4) emphasize damage suits and prosecution to deter illegal searches.

2. Conservatives are considered as giving the relatively conservative goals a weight of 3, neutral goals a weight of 2, and liberal goals a weight of 1. Liberals are considered as giving the conservative goals a weight of 1, neutral goals a weight of 2, and liberal goals a weight of 3. Neutrals are considered as giving all the goals a weight of 2. Feasibility is assumed to be worth a weight of 3 in view of its importance.

3. The scoring of the alternatives on the goals is done on a 1--3 scale. A 3 means conducive to the goal. A 2 means neither conducive nor adverse. A 1 means adverse to the goal.

4. An overall score is calculated by summing the products of the relation scores multiplied by the weights across each row or policy. For example, the liberal score of 8 is arrived at by summing (1 times 3) plus (1 times 2) plus (3 times 1), or 3 + 2 + 3 = 8.

5. The liberal, neutral, conservative, and total scores are shown before (B) and after (A) adding the feasibility criterion. Without that criterion, the exclusionary rule comes out third or fourth out of the four alternatives. With that criterion, the exclusionary rules comes out first on all four value systems.

6. The other three alternatives are relatively lacking in feasibility because (1) the good-faith exception has questionable constitutionality, since it may provide too little deterrence against illegal search and seizure; (2) a system of suspensions and dismissals would require approval by state legislators or police administrative boards, which is unlikely; (3) prosecution of police officers for illegal searches without physical violence is unlikely, and the probabilities are quite low of an innocent or guilty person suing for damages, winning, and collecting anything substantial.

fourth of the four alternatives. With that important feasibility criterion, the exclusionary rule comes out first on the liberal, neutral, and conservative value systems, although with a bigger margin under the liberal values in choosing between the exclusionary rule and the good-faith exception.

Adding Further Alternatives and Criteria

This example of how to deal with illegally obtained evidence lends itself well to showing how the P/G% spreadsheet perspective can be used to experiment with adding additional alternatives and additional criteria. For example, in 1986 the Supreme Court in effect added another alternative that is sometimes referred to as the blameless exception. The blameless exception says that the illegally obtained evidence should be admitted into court provided that the police are totally blameless in how the evidence was obtained. For example, if the search warrant that they executed contained a wrong address due to a mistake by the magistrate or the prosecutor with the police not being at fault, then the evidence should be admitted on the grounds that excluding the evidence cannot deter wrongful police behavior if there was no wrongful police behavior to be deterred.

Without the blameless exception if the criteria have equal weight, then we have a three-way tie among suspend/dismiss, exclude evidence, and sue/prosecute. If extra weight is given to the goal of feasibility, then excluding the evidence becomes the winning alternative. With the blameless exception under consideration, it becomes the winner. The before-and-after results are shown in table 1-5.

The blameless exception wins because it appeals to both liberals and conservatives. Liberals are willing to accept it because they hold that people should not be punished if they are not at fault, and sometimes they should not be punished even when they are at fault. Conservatives are willing to accept it because it is a retreat from excluding all illegally obtained evidence. In terms of the spreadsheet analysis, the blameless exception receives a roughly neutral 2 points on a 1–3 scale with regard to (1) decreasing illegal police searches, (2) not encouraging lying by the police, and (3) decreasing crime occurrence. On the fourth criterion, it receives 3 points because of its positive relation with feasibility. Thus it receives an overall score of 2 + 2 + 2 + 3 or 9 points, as shown in the bottom line of table 1-5.

One interesting aspect of the policy problem of dealing with illegally obtained evidence is the fact that it arouses so much emotion among liberals and conservatives. This is so even though there really does not seem to be much difference in the overall scores of the various alternatives. The similarity in overall scores is shown in the last column of table 1-4. Those scores would be even more similar if extra weight were given to decreasing crime occurrence, which would raise the overall score of the good-faith exception. The similarity is also shown in the

Table 1-5
Adding Additional Alternatives

BEFORE			AFTER		
Alternative	Combined Rawscores	%	Alternative	Combined Rawscores	%
1 GOOD FAITH EXCEP.	6.00	20.00	1 GOOD FAITH EXCEP.	6.00	15.38
2 SUSPEND/DISMISS	8.00	26.67	2 SUSPEND/DISMISS	8.00	20.51
3 EXCLUDE EVIDENCE	8.00	26.67	3 EXCLUDE EVIDENCE	8.00	20.51
4 SUE/PROSECUTE	8.00	26.67	4 SUE/PROSECUTE	8.00	20.51
			5 BLAMELESS EXCEPTION	9.00	23.08

NOTES:

1. The numbers on the before-side of table 1-5 come from adding the scores of each alternative on each criterion in table 1-4 giving each criterion equal weight. Thus the 6 points for the good faith exception come from adding 1 + 1 + 3 + 1 to equal 6.

2. The numbers on the after-side of table 1-2 are the same for the first four alternatives since their scores on the criteria have not changed as a result of adding a fifth alternative.

3. The fifth alternative of the blameless exception receives scores of 2 + 2 + 2 + 3 on the four criteria using a 1-3 scale for a total score of 9.

overall scores of table 1-5. One might therefore ask what additional criteria might there be that are not being included that could explain why liberals seem to give the exclusionary rule a substantially higher overall score than conservatives do. The answer may be seen in recognizing that emotional support of or attack on legal policies often relates to the symbolic nature of the policies more than the functional effects of the policies.

For liberals, excluding illegally seized evidence has important symbolic significance in indicating that the legal system places a high value on decreasing police harassment of innocent individuals who may be subjected to an illegal search, even if exclusion does not greatly decrease such searches. For conservatives, allowing the evidence to be used has important symbolic significance in indicating that the legal system places a high value on convicting guilty defendants even if admitting the evidence does not greatly decrease crime occurrence. Thus if we add the criterion of anti-harassment symbol and the criterion of anti-crime symbol, we obtain results like those shown in table 1-6.

The before-side of that table uses the liberal overall scores from table 1-4 after adding the feasibility criterion. It also uses the conservative overall scores. On the anti-harassment symbol, there is likely to be agreement that the good-faith exception would probably have an adverse effect. The other alternatives, if adopted, would have a positive effect in terms of the symbol even if they have a low likelihood of being adopted (in the case of alternatives 2 and 4), or even if they have little effect on actually changing police behavior (as with alternative 3). On the anti-crime symbol, the good-faith exception has a positive relation, whereas the exclusionary rule has a negative relation. The other two alternatives are relatively neutral on the anti-crime symbol in that they allow the incriminating evidence to be admitted, but they simultaneously involve punishing the police.

If the relation scores in the anti-harassment column are given a weight of 3 and those in the anti-crime column are given a weight of 1 in conformity with the liberal values, then the new overall scores are 17, 29, 30, and 29. If, on the other hand, the anti-harassment scores are given a weight of only 1 and the anti-crime scores are given a weight of 3 in conformity with the conservatives values, then the new overall scores are 25, 25, 24, and 25. The numbers that are especially important to compare in this context are (1) the overall scores of 20 and 18 between liberals and conservatives on excluding illegally seized evidence (before considering the symbolic criteria), which is only a difference of 2 points, and (2) the overall scores of 30 and 24 on excluding the evidence (after considering the symbolic criteria), which is a much more substantial difference of 6 points. Thus one can conclude that the sharp differences between liberals and conservatives on the exclusionary rule may be due more to symbolic criteria than they are to the more functional criteria of decreasing illegal police searches or decreasing crime occurrence. This example not only illustrates dealing with the adding of additional criteria, but also with trying to explain why some people choose one policy alternative or decisional alternative, rather than another.[4]

Table 1-6
Adding Additional Criteria

CRITERIA / ALTERNATIVES	BEFORE		AFTER			
	Liberal	Conservative	Anti-Harassment Symbol	Anti-Crime Symbol	Liberal	Conservative
1. GOOD FAITH EXCEP.	11	15	1	3	17	25
2. SUSPEND/DISMISS	18	16	3	2	29	25
3. EXCLUDE EVIDENCE	20	18	3	1	30	24
4. SUE/PROSECUTE	18	16	3	2	29	25

NOTES:

1. The numbers on the before-side of table 1-6 come from the liberal and conservative columns of table 1-4 before adding any symbolic criteria.

2. The relation scores on the after-side of table 1-6 are based on a 1-3 scale, where a 3 indicates a positive relation with the goal, a 2 indicates a neutral relation, and a 1 indicates a negative relation.

3. The overall scores on the after-side of table 1-6 come from adding the original scores to the two new scores taking into consideration liberals give a relatively higher weight to the anti-harassment symbol and a relatively lower weight to the anti-crime symbol, and vice versa for conservatives. Thus, the liberal 17 comes from adding 11 + 3 + 3. The conservative 25 comes from adding 15 + 1 + 9, and so on for the other overall after scores.

SOME GENERAL IDEAS

The idea of computer-aided law decisions is a law variation on computer-aided manufacturing (CAM) and computer-aided design (CAD), which are becoming increasingly important in the U.S. economy. Computer-aided law decisions have in common a systematic procedure for processing a set of (1) goals to be achieved or predictive criteria, (2) alternatives for achieving the goals or alternative situations, and (3) relations between criteria and alternatives in order to choose a best alternative, combination, allocation, or predictive decision rule.[5]

Computer-aided decisions thus differ substantially from computer-aided clerical work like word processing, file management, litigation support, document drafting, citation access, or law office bookkeeping.[6] At the other extreme, computer-aided decisions differ from the idea of computers making decisions in place of appellate judges, trial judges, legislators, legal counselors, law negotiators, lawyer advocates, judicial administrators, or law firm administrators.[7] Computerized clerical work is highly possible and useful, but it is not lawyer work. The concept of computers as decision-makers without judges, lawyers, and other legal personnel is probably not possible and of questionable value if it were possible.

Microcomputers can be helpful in processing goals, alternatives, and relations, especially for indicating what it would take to bring a second-place alternative up to first place, or what it would take to improve a predictive decision rule. The microcomputer software described in this chapter and book belongs in the general categories of multicriteria decision-making, expert systems, and artificial intelligence. The specific software is called Policy/Goal Percentaging because it relates policies or decisions to goals or criteria, and it uses part/whole percentaging to deal with the goals being measured in different ways.

The material that follows is designed to place lawyer-aiding software in a broad context of definitions, classifications, and software examples. After discussion of benefits and trends, the book proceeds through specific lawyer skills that relate to law applying, law making, law prediction, and law administration. It then proceeds to applications in all fields of private, public, and procedural law.

NOTES

1. On arbitration and other ways of resolving disputes, see Stephen Goldberg, Eric Green, and Frank Sander (eds.), *Dispute Resolution* (Boston: Little, Brown, 1985). On the relevance of the characteristics of judges to their decisions, see S. Nagel, *The Legal Process from a Behavioral Perspective* (Homewood, IL: Dorsey Press, 1969). On the methodology of choosing among discrete alternatives, see John Arnold, *The Art of Decision-Making* (American Management Associations, 1973).

2. On making locational decisions, see Charles Pinkus and Anne Dixson, *Solving Local Government Problems: A Practical Application of Operations Research in Cities and Regions* (London: Allen and Unwin, 1981). On law firm efficiency, see Bradford Hildebrandt and Jack Kaufman, *The Successful Law Firm: New Approaches to Structrue and*

Management (New York: Harcourt Brace Jovanovich, 1983). On decision-making under conditions of risk and litigation strategy, see Howard Raiffa, *Decision Analysis: Introductory Lectures on Choices under Uncertainty* (Reading, MA: Addison-Wesley, 1968).

3. On predicting future occurrences in light of past occurrences, see Spyros Makridakis, Steven Wheelwright, and Victor McGee, *Forecasting: Methods and Applications* (New York: Wiley, 1983). On the substance of independent contractors versus employees, see Harold Reuschlein, *Hornbook on the Law of Agency and Partnership* (St. Paul: West, 1981).

4. On legal policy evaluation, see S. Nagel, *Law, Policy, and Optimizing Analysis* (Westport, CT: Greenwood-Quorum, 1986). On the substance of search and seizure law, see Stephen Schlesinger, *Exclusionary Injustice: The Problem of Illegally Obtained Evidence* (New York: Marcel Dekker, 1977).

5. For general materials on multicriteria decision-making applied to the legal process, see S. Nagel, *Microcomputers as Decision Aids in Law Practice* (Westport, Conn.: Greenwood-Quorum, 1987). An earlier version is available from the Committee on Continuing Professional Education of the American Law Institute and the American Bar Association. On the general methodology, see S. Nagel, *Evaluation Analysis with Microcomputers* (Greenwich, Conn.: JAI Press, 1989); and the "Policy/Goal Percentaging" program, Decision Aids, Inc., 361 Lincoln Hall, University of Illinois, Urbana, IL 61801.

6. For discussions of computer-aided clerical work, see Mary Ann Mason, *An Introduction to Using Computers in the Law* (St. Paul: West, 1984); and Daniel Remer, *Computer Power for Your Law Office* (Berkeley: Sybex, 1983). Relevant software includes WordStar (word processing), DBase II (file management), Evidence Master (litigation support), Matthew Bender (document drafting), WestLaw and Lexis (access to citations and case excerpts), and Data Law (billing and bookkeeping).

7. For articles that optimistically, pessimistically, or jokingly view computers as partly replacing judges and lawyers, see Paul Bartholomew, "Supreme Court and Modern Objectivity," 33 *New York State Bar Journal* 157-164 (1961); Hugh Gibbons, "Using Computers to Analyze Legal Questions," in Thomas Rasmusson (ed.), *System Science and Jurisprudence* (Lansing, Mich.: Spartan Press, 1986); and Reed Lawlor, "Stare Decisis and Electronic Computers," in Glendon Schubert (ed.), *Judicial Behavior: A Reader in Theory and Research* (Chicago: Rand McNally, 1964).

CHAPTER 2

Decision-Aiding Software and the Law

This chapter will describe the nature, classifications, trends, benefits, and costs of the new decision-aiding software that relates to law practice and the legal process.

THE SOFTWARE

Definitions and Classifications

The essense of decision-aiding software is its ability to process a set of (1) law-related alternatives to choose among; (2) relevant criteria, goals, or rules for determining which alternative or alternatives are most appropriate or most likely to be chosen; and (3) the relations between each alternative and each criterion in order to choose or explain the best alternative, combinaton, or predictive decision-rule.

Any software can be helpful in making decisions such as information-retrieval software like Westlaw and Lexis, which provide relevant citations and excerpts. We are now also seeing information-retrieval software that emphasizes trial court decisions, especially in damages cases such as SettleMate and a forthcoming on-line version of the reports of the Jury Verdict Research Corporation. Even office practice software such as word processing, file management, and bookkeeping can be helpful in making decisions by providing relevant reports. To quality as decision-aiding software, though, it should deal with the five essential elements of alternatives, criteria, relations, tentative conclusions, and what-if analysis, either for prescribing what decisions ought to be reached or for predicting what decisions will be reached.

There are different kinds of decision-aiding software and different ways of classifying them. Some common categories include:

1. Decision-tree software for making decisions under conditions of risk such as whether to go to trial or accept a settlement. A decision tree is usually pictured as looking like a tree on its side with branches and subbranches. The branches generally represent alternative possibilities that depend on the occurrence or nonoccurrence of probabilistic events.
2. Linear programming software for allocating money, time, people, or other scarce resources to activities, places, tasks, or other objects to which the resources are to be allocated. In terms of form rather than function, linear programming involves maximizing or minimizing an objective function or algebraic expression subject to constraints generally in the form of inequalities like greater than or less than.
3. Statistical software for predicting how a future case is likely to be decided regarding liability, damages, guilt, sentence, or other judgment in light of past cases or expert opinions. Statistical software generally involves calculating averages or predictive equations in which decisions or other outcomes are related to legal or factual inputs.
4. Spreadsheet-based software in which the alternatives tend to be on the rows, the criteria on the columns, relations in the cells, overall scores for each alternative in a column at the far right, and a capability for determining what it would take to bring a second-place or other-place alternative up to first place.
5. Rule-based software that contains a set of rules for dealing with a narrow or broad field of law. The user gives the computer a set of facts, and the computer applies the rules to the facts in order to determine which alternative decision is likely to be decided. Such software is sometimes referred to as artificial intelligence (AI) or expert systems, but the other forms of decision-aiding software also have characteristics associated with AI and expert systems.
6. Other decision-aiding software that does not fit into the above categories but that does process alternatives, criteria, and relations to arrive at a prescription-evaluation or a prediction-explanation. This is often referred to as multicriteria decision-making (MCDM) software because it emphasizes multiple criteria, although it may also work with multiple alternatives.
7. Decision-aiding software that focuses on a specific field of law, as contrasted to the above software, which cuts across all fields of law. The fields of law in which specialized decision-aiding software seems to be most developing are personal injury law, estate planning, and taxation.
8. Software that is useful for generating alternatives, goals, or relations, but that does not process those elements in order to draw a conclusion.

Examples and References

There are many brand names that fit into each of these categories, including the following:

1. Decision-tree software includes Arborist, SuperTree, Clarence, Ondine, StrataTree, and RiskCalc. For an analysis of decision trees applied to law, see Morris Raker, "The Application of Decision Analysis and Computer Modeling to the Settlement of Complex Litigation," in Nyhart (1987); and S. Nagel, "Microcomputers" (1985).

2. Linear programming and related software includes Erikson-Hall, Lee-Shim, IFPS, Holden-Day, LP Master, Burns-Austin, LP Professional, and Vino-Gino-Lindo. A good comparative analysis of linear programming and related packages is Ramesh Sharda et al., "Mathematical Programming Software for Microcomputers" in Gass et al. (1986).
3. Statistical software like StatPal, Hall-Adelman, ABC, Stata, EpiStat, PsychoStats, Crosstats, Chao, SPSS, SAS, BDM, StatFast, and StatPac. A good comparative analysis of statistics packages is Dennis Lezotte, "Statistical Software for Microcomputers" in Gass (1986).
4. Spreadsheet software (especially if based on Lotus 1-2-3) includes Best Choice, What's Best, 1-2-Tree, Minitab, 1-2-3 Breakeven, PG Lotus, and GoalSeeker. For an analysis of some aspects of decision-aiding spreadheet software, see Deepak Bammi and Loren Padelford, "Using Spreadsheets for Decision Analysis" in Gass (1986). Also Nagel and Stanton, "Using Framework Spreadsheets" (1989).
5. Rule-based software for predicting or prescribing decisions could include Teknowledge, Expert87, ExSys, ESCA-DSS, MicroExpert, Ashton-Tate, and Texas Instruments. For a good comparative review of rule-based expert systems software, see Carl Grafton and Anne Permaloff (1986). Rule-based software that is specifically related to legal rules includes Judith, DataLex, Rubric, Hypo, Lex, Default, Oblog-2, Esplex, and LexVision. Many of those law-related programs are described in Hafner (1987).
6. The miscellaneous MCDM software includes such names as Lightyear, Confidence Factor, Decision Analyist, Expert Choice, Prefcalc, DecAid, Electre, Policy PC, P/G%, DecisionMaker, Decision, P-G Plato, Seriatim, Decision Making, Decide, Pairs, MASS, MOLP, MAUD, and MIDAS. For comparisons of MCDM software, see Humphreys and Wisudha (1987), Radcliff (1986), and B. Golden et al., "Decision Insight Systems for Microcomputers," in Gass (1986). Some of the software fits into more than one category, such as Best Choice or P/G%, which can perform the functions of all six categories, although it is mainly classified as spreadsheet-based software.
7. Relevant substantive legal software includes Determining Damages, Legal Analytics, SettleMate, InValve, ComproWise, TaxCalc, Aardvark, TaxMan, and Meldman.
8. Software that can help in generating alternatives includes the Idea Generator, the Brainstormer, and Trigger. Software that helps generate relations such as the probability of an alternative achieving a goal includes SPAT. Statistical software can also sometimes be used for generating relations, such as regression coefficients or average scores of an alternative on a criterion.

As for evaluations of the different kinds of decision-aiding software, useful comparative evaluations can be found in the articles that are cited above. Other relevant literature compares methodologies rather than software packages. That literature includes Hwang and Yoon (1981), Brightman (1980), and Nagel, *Evaluation Analysis* (1989). The category that is most versatile and user-friendly is probably the spreadsheet category, especially variations on Lotus 1-2-3. It can do most kinds of risk analysis, allocation analysis, and prediction analysis better than decision-tree, linear programming routines, or a statistical package.

ACTUAL AND POTENTIAL BENEFITS

As for the actual and potential benefits of decision-aiding software, they depend to some extent on the kind of software to which we are referring, but there are a number of cross-cutting benefits (as well as costs) worth mentioning:

Framing the Alternatives, Goals, and Relations

1. Encouraging lawyers to be more explicit about goals they are seeking to achieve, alternatives available for achieving them, and relations between goals and alternatives.
2. Being more explicit can generate an interesting ethical cost that Jim Sprowl (1986) has raised, namely that it forces lawyers to think more clearly about the goals they should be pursuing. That could be considered a benefit to improving the legal profession, even if it creates dilemmas for individual lawyers.
3. In listing some alternatives, criteria, and relations, the lawyer's creativity may be stimulated regarding the development of new alternatives. Decision-aiding software also stimulates creativity in the development of criteria and determining relations.
4. Working with multiple criteria can facilitate the adoption of alternatives or solutions in which one side comes out ahead on some criteria, and the other sides come out ahead on other criteria. Thus a multiple-criterion perspective can more easily lead to solutions in which one side wins and the other side loses.
5. Decision-aiding software can facilitate making changes in alternatives, criteria, relations, and other inputs in order to determine the effects of those changes on the tentative conclusions.

Overcoming Analytic Problems

6. Such software can be helpful in dealing with missing information by indicating how high a damage award, settlement offer, or other input has to be in order to bring a tentative second-place or other-place alternative up to first place. The software can thus change a question as to the numerical value of an item into the earlier questions of whether the numerical value is likely to be above or below a threshold, break-even, or critical value.
7. The software can be helpful in dealing with problems of how to combine goals or criteria that are measured on different dimensions.
8. The software can be helpful in making choices in mutually exclusive situations or in situations that allow for combinations of alternatives. In addition to choosing among alternatives, the software can also aid in allocating scarce resources to the alternatives or budget categories with or without a variety of constraints that need to be satisfied.
9. The software can simplify complicated problems by asking the user to supply only enough information to deal with the problem, and then outputting only enough information for the user to make a decision. This is without subjecting the user to the complicated processing that might occur between the input and the output unless the user wants it.

Diverse Users and Uses

10. Decision-aiding software is not only beneficial to practicing lawyers, it can be used by legal policy-makers to help evaluate alternative legal policies in light of various criteria.
11. The software can also be beneficial to legal scholars in obtaining a better understanding of why decisions are reached the way they are, and a better understanding of what decisions ought to be reached on a high level of generality.
12. Decision-aiding software has been applied with concrete examples to all fields of law, including contracts, property, torts, family law, constitutional law, economic regulation, criminal law, international law, civil procedure, and criminal procedure.
13. Decision-aiding software has been applied to all types of legal skills, including counseling clients, negotiating with the opposition, advocating a position in court, mediating disputes, generalizing from a set of cases, generalizing from a set of facts, evaluating alternative legal policies, assigning people to tasks, deciding the best order in which to process cases, and group decision-making.
14. Decision-aiding software can be useful in teaching law, since it can facilitate role playing with regard to how to handle and develop alternatives, criteria, and relations in order to arrive at decisions.

General Benefits

15. Decision-aiding software decreases the possibility of making clerical errors in keeping track of the inputs, doing arithmetic, and manipulating data.
16. Some decision-aiding software provides the benefit of encouraging users to inject their knowledge of the subject matter into the process, rather than have substance imposed on them. Some users, though, may prefer decision-aiding software in which they do not have to inject any substantial knowledge, although such software may not sufficiently consider specific situations.
17. Decision-aiding software can stimulate lawyers to become more receptive to doing systematic decision analysis even when the software is not available.
18. A cost involved in using decision-aiding software is the need to learn how to use it. That investment of time may be highly worthwhile in terms of the above-mentioned future benefits. The amount of time needed to learn decision-aiding software is becoming less as the software becomes more user-friendly and the documentation is improved.
19. In general, the benefits of decision-aiding software do seem to outweigh the costs substantially, especially if the software is considered to be a supplement to traditional perspectives rather than a substitute.

RELEVANT TRENDS

There are a number of trends that indicate that the time is appropriate for the adoption of decision-aiding software by law firms:

Journals and Books

1. An increasing mention of decision-aiding software in journals for practicing lawyers. For an example is the lead article by Burns and Hodde from the February 1988 *Attorney's Computer Report.* The article says: "The decision-making technique known as decision analysis can be a powerful tool for the lawyer familiar with its nature and use."
2. An increasing mention of decision-aiding software in the scholarly law reviews, such as Nagel's "Computer-Aided Law Decisions" (1987). It is the third article on that subject that the *Akron Law Review* has published in the last few years. The other two deal with judicial prediction and litigation strategy.
3. An increasing mention of decision-aiding software in the journals for judges. See, for example, Nagel and Barczyk, "Can Computers Aid in Dispute Resolution?" from *Judicature.* This is also the third article that *Judicature* has published on decision-aiding software in the last few years. The other two deal with sequencing cases and assigning judges to tasks.
4. An increasing publication of whole books devoted to decision-aiding software for lawyers, including Johnson and Mode (1985) and Nagel, *Microcomputers as Decision Aids in Law Practice* (1987).

Other Indicators

5. Increasing publication of relevant software such as "Determining Damages" by Shepard's McGraw-Hill, "SettleMate" by Lawyers Technology, Inc., "The Art of Negotiation" by Experience in Software, Inc., and "Best Choice" by Decision Aids, Inc.
6. Increasing mention by law firms of the use of decision-aiding software. This can be seen by comparing the Chicago-Kent surveys of the top 500 law firms in 1985 and 1986. They reveal a substantial increase in the use of spreadsheets for modeling purposes in that recent one-year period.
7. Increasing presentations of relevant papers at scholarly meetings and bar association meetings, including worldwide conferences like the Fourth Annual World Congress on "Law and Computers" held May 1988 in Rome.
8. Increasing inclusion of decision-aiding software in training courses and job descriptions for paraprofessionals, legal administrators, and related personnel, as indicated by journals like the *Legal Administrator* and *Legal Assistant Today.*
9. Increasing occurrence of relevant training institutes for continuing legal education programs as indicated by the ALI–ABA short courses on "Applying Decision Science to Law Practice" and "Using Personal Computers for Decision-Making in Law Practice."

What may be needed is the establishment of a Decision-Aiding Software Working Group with the Lawyers Technology Advisory Council of the American Bar Association. It could perform such functions as (1) making lawyers more aware of what decision-aiding software is, (2) stimulating the development of new and better decision-aiding software for lawyers, and (3) evaluating existing and future programs and packages designed to aid lawyers in reaching decisions from alternatives, criteria, and relations. Decision-aiding software does have a lot to offer in terms of making law practice more effective, efficient, and equitable. It is good to see law practice benefit as much as possible from new technology developments, including decision-aiding software.

PART II

Specific Lawyer Skills

SECTION A

Law Applying

CHAPTER 3

Computer-Aided Counseling

Chapter 3 will describe how microcomputers can aid in counseling clients as to the best action to take in order to achieve given goals. The idea of computer-aided counseling (CAC) is a law variation on computer-aided manufacturing and computer-aided design, which are becoming increasingly important to the U.S. economy.

Computer-aided counseling is a substantially higher level of computer usage than document drafting, which incorporates decisions into a form of a will, deed, lease, or other document after the key decisions have been made. Computer-aided counseling is designed to aid in making the decisions that may subsequently be incorporated into a document through the use of document-drafting software or more traditional drafting methods.

The most appropriate software for computer-aided counseling is probably software that enables one to process a set of (1) goals the decision-makers might have for reaching a decision, (2) the alternative positions they might take regarding the overall issue or subissues in the case, and (3) the relations between each position and each goal showing how conducive or adverse each position is to each goal. An example of such software is Policy/Goal Percentaging.

CHOOSING AMONG ALTERNATIVE DIVORCE DECISIONS

The basic decision in a typical domestic relations case might be whether or not to get a divorce. The *alternatives* to be inputted into the decision matrix might be:

1. Stay married as is.
2. Develop a mutually beneficial agreement to improve the marriage relation with or without marriage counseling or legal counseling.

3. Live apart but still married, like a trial divorce with or without a separate maintenance agreement.
4. A full divorce.

The *criteria* for deciding among those alternatives tend to be more specific than the alternatives are. Some relevant general criteria that may favor moving toward a divorce might be:

1. A desire to avoid a spouse who is an alcoholic or a drug addict.
2. A desire to avoid a spouse who is violent.
4. A desire to remarry in order to remedy a case of desertion.
4. A desire for greater privacy and independence.

Criteria that may favor staying married include:

5. A desire to preserve one's economic well-being.
6. A desire to look good in the eyes of one's colleagues or relatives.
7. A desire to provide parental and other benefits to one's children.
8. A desire to preserve whatever companionship the marriage provides.

Each of the alternatives could be *scored* on each of those criteria on a 1–5 scale. A 5 means highly conducive to the criterion or goal, a 4 means mildly conducive, a 3 means neither conducive nor adverse, a 2 means mildly adverse, and a 1 means highly adverse. The criteria can be given different weights to show their relative importance. One can also weigh all the criteria equally and observe the threshold analysis to see what changes in the weights would be necessary to bring the second-place alternative up to first place. There is no need to use percentaging in this example since all the goals are measured on the same 1–5 scale.

These basic ideas concerning the alternatives, criteria, and relations on whether to obtain a divorce are incorporated into table 3-1. That table, in effect, serves as a two-dimensional checklist with the alternatives on the rows and the criteria on the columns. One can then insert the relation scores into the cells for the specific case with which one is working. One can then obtain an *overall score for each alternative* by adding the relation scores across each alternative with or without multiplier weights. The alternative that receives the highest score is generally the one to recommend.[1]

ALLOCATING AN ESTATE AMONG BENEFICIARIES

The Input to the Counseling Decision

Table 3-2 provides an example of computer-aided counseling in the field of will drafting. There are computer programs available that will convert decisions

Table 3-1
Computer-Aided Counseling: Whether to Obtain a Divorce

1A. The Alternatives

1. Stay Married as is
2. Develop Agreement
3. Live Apart
4. Full Divorce

1B. The Criteria

Criterion	Meas. Unit	Weight
1. - Alcohol/Addict	1-5 Scale	1.00
2. - Violence		1.00
3. Remarriage		1.00
4. Privacy/Independence		1.00
5. Economic Status		1.00
6. Colleagues/Relatives		1.00
7. Children		1.00
8. Companionship		1.00

1C. The Relations

Alternative/Criteria Scoring

	- Alcohol	- Violence	Remarriage	Privacy/Ind.	Economic Status
Stay Married as is	0.00	0.00	0.00	0.00	0.00
Develop Agreement	0.00	0.00	0.00	0.00	0.00
Live Apart	0.00	0.00	0.00	0.00	0.00
Full Divorce	0.00	0.00	0.00	0.00	0.00

Alternative/Criteria Scoring

	Colleague/Relatives	Children	Companionship
Stay Married as is	0.00	0.00	0.00
Develop Agreement	0.00	0.00	0.00
Live Apart	0.00	0.00	0.00
Full Divorce	0.00	0.00	0.00

NOTES:

1. Each alternative can be scored on each criterion on a 1-5 scale where 5 means highly conducive to the criterion. 4 means mildly conducive. 3 means neither conducive nor adverse. 2 means mildly adverse, and 1 means highly adverse.
2. Each criterion can be given the same weight of 1.00, or the criteria can be given different weights depending on their relative importance.

concerning estate allocation into the proper legal form to serve as a valid will, such as the WillWriter program. Those programs, however, are not for helping the testator decide how to divide his or her estate. They assume such decisions have already been made. They are useful in providing checklists as to what decisions should have been made or need to be made.

In this example, the testator is trying to decide among three possible beneficiaries: his son, daughter, and wife. In using the P/G% program to aid in making such decisions, the lawyer and the testator together can list the possible beneficiaries. The testator with the aid of the lawyer can tentatively decide on a set of criteria for evaluating the potential beneficiaries. In this case, there are two criteria: need and deservingness.

Need is scored on a 1–5 scale. A 5 in this context means highly needy, and a 4

Table 3-2
Computer-Aided Counseling: Estate Allocation

2A. Scoring the Beneficiaries on Need and Deservingness

Alternative/Criteria Scoring

	Need	Deservingness
Son	2.00	4.00
Daughter	4.00	2.00
Spouse	5.00	3.00

NOTE: Table 2A shows that the alternative beneficiaries are a son, a daughter, and a spouse. The criteria for allocating are need and deservingness. Each beneficiary is scored on each criterion on a 1-5 scale. A 5 means highly conducive to the criterion. A 4 means mildly conducive. A 3 means neither conducive nor adverse. A 2 means mildly adverse, and a 1 means highly adverse.

2B. Allocating in Proportion to How Well the Beneficiaries Score on Each Criterion

Part/Whole %

	Need	Deservingness
Son	18.18	44.44
Daughter	36.36	22.22
Spouse	45.45	33.33

NOTE: Table 2B shows in the first column how the estate would be allocated if only need were considered. The son then receives 2/11 or 18%, the daughter 4/11 or 36%, and the spouse 5/11 or 45%. Likewise with the second column on deservingness.

2C. Averaging the Separate Allocations to Determine the Overall Allocations

Total Resources = $1000.00

	Alloc.	P/W%
1 Son	$313.13	31.31
2 Daughter	$292.93	29.29
3 Spouse	$393.94	39.39

NOTE: Table 2C averages the allocations based on need and deservingness to determine an overall allocation. Thus, the son gets 31% overall which is the average between 18% on need and 44% on deservingness. Likewise with the daughter and the spouse.

The averages in Table 2C are based on treating need and deservingness as having equal weight or importance. One could arrive at a weighted average for each beneficiary if the criteria had different weights or degrees of relative importance.

One can also specify minimum allocations for each beneficiary. If a beneficiary fails to receive the minimum percentage in step 2C, then give the beneficiary that minimum and reallocate the remainder to the other beneficiaries.

2D. What It Would Take to Bring a Second Place Alternative Up to First Place

	Son	Spouse	Weight
Need	3.60	3.00	0.407
Deservingness	6.00	1.86	2.455

NOTE: Table 2D shows the scores the son or spouse would have to receive on each criterion to justify the son receiving the same allocation as the spouse. It also shows that there would be a tie in the allocation if the weight of need were cut more than half from 1.00 to .41, or if deservingness were more than doubled from 1.00 to 2.46. A similar table could be generated for the daughter and spouse or for the son and spouse.

Table 2D can be helpful to someone who is advocating an increased percentage to one of the beneficiaries. It can also be helpful to the will-maker in deciding whether he or she really wants a certain beneficiary to have more or less than another beneficiary.

2E. The Weights at Which Each Criterion Dominates the Other Criteria

	Weight	
Need	5.00	Stopping difference set at:
Deservingness	5.00	5.1 percentage points

NOTE: Table 2E shows that if the weight of need is raised from 1 to 5, then the allocation percentages in Table 2C will be within 5 percentage points of the percentages on the left side of Table 2B. Likewise if the weight of deservingness is raised from 1 to 5, then the allocation percentages in Table 1C will be within 5 percentage points of the percentages on the right side of Table 2B.

means mildly needy. At the other extreme, a 1 means highly well-off or the opposite of highly needy, and a 2 means mildly well-off or the opposite of mildly needy. A 3 thus means neither needy nor well-off, but somewhere in the middle. On such a scale, the wife scores a 5. The daughter scores a 4, and the son scores a 2.

Deservingness is also scored on a 1–5 scale. A 5 in this context means highly deserving, a 4 means mildly deserving, a 3 means neither deserving nor undeserving, a 2 means mildly undeserving, and a 1 means highly undeserving. Deservingness can especially refer to how nice the potential beneficiary has been to the testator or refer to the good the beneficiary might do with the bequest, although those could be two separate criteria. On the deservingness scale, the son scores a 4. The wife scores a 3, and the daughter scores a 2.

The Outputs from a Counseling Decision

The object now is to use that jointly determined information to derive meaningful allocation percentages for each of the three beneficiaries. The most meaningful way to do that is to first allocate in proportion to the need scores as if need were the only criterion. That involves summing the need scores, which means 2 + 4 + 6 = 11. The son would then receive 18% of the value of the estate since 2/11 is 18%. The daughter would receive 4/11 or 36%, and the spouse would receive 5/11 or 45%. One can also determine the allocations if deservingness were the only criterion. Allocating in proportion to the deservingness scores means 44% to the son, 22% to the daughter, and 33% to the spouse. Those allocations are shown in table 3-2B.

The next logical step is to indicate what the allocations should be if one combines both need and deservingness. Those combined allocations simply represent the average between the two separate allocations, assuming need and deservingness are considered to be equally important. Thus the son gets 31% since that is the midpoint between 18% and 44%. One could also add 18% to 44% and divide by 2. The daughter gets 29% as the average between 36% and 22%, and the spouse gets 39%.[2]

Changing the Inputs to See the Effect on the Outputs

Those allocations, however, are only tentative. They represent a first cut or initial analysis, subject to change depending on what is revealed as a result of making changes in the inputs. An appropriate change to experiment with might involve additional beneficiaries, such as other relatives, friends, or charities. Doing so might suggest additional criteria, such as the extent to which the bequest might be appreciated, or might result in the testator receiving favorable publicity. One might also experiment with other ways of measuring need or deservingness besides a 1–5 scale, although the methodology changes if the criteria are measured on different scales.

An especially useful tool for analyzing the effects of changes in the scores is the threshold analysis shown in table 3-2C. It shows the changes in the scores that would have to occur to bring the son or daughter up to the allocation level of the wife, or to bring the wife down to the level of the son or daughter. This is useful where the testator is having doubts as to whether the beneficiaries should receive equal or different amounts. Table 3-2C shows that for the son to share equally with the wife, one of four scores or a combination would have to change, namely (1) the son's 2 on need would have to be 3.60, (2) the son's 4 on deservingness would have to be 6, which is impossible on a 1–5 scale, (3) the wife's 5 on need would have to drop to a 3 or be misestimated by that much, or (4) the wife's deservingness would have to be a 1.86 instead of a 3. If all those possibilities seem unrealistic, then one can feel more confident in giving the extra allocation to one's wife. The analysis also shows that the son should be given the same allocation as the wife if the testator values deservingness as being 2.46 times as important as need, or if need is considered .41 as important as deservingness. The same kind of analysis can be applied in determining what it would take to bring the daughter up to the same allocation as the wife.

Convergence analysis is a related form of sensitivity analysis designed to show the effects of changes in the inputs on the bottom-line allocations. It shows how high the weight of a criterion has to be raised in order for that criterion to dominate the other criteria. "Dominate" is defined in this context as generating bottom-line percentages that are within 5 percentage points of what they would be if the criterion in question were the only criterion. For example, table 3-2E shows that if the weight or relative importance of need was considered to be 5 times as great as deservingness, then the bottom-line allocation percentages of table 3-2C would be within 5 percentage points of the percentages shown on the left side of table 3-2B.

More specifically, if we indicate to the computer to give need a weight of 5 when deservingness has a weight of 1, then the allocation percentages will be 23% to the son, 34% to the daughter, and 43% to the spouse. Those percentages are each within 5 percentage points of the 18%, 36%, and 43% that would be obtained if need were the only criterion. Likewise, one can give a similar interpretation to the convergence weight of 5 for the criterion of deservingness. That kind of analysis usefully avoids arguments over whether one criterion is 2, 6, 10, or *N* times more important than another criterion. If the convergence weight is 3, there is no need to argue whether the weight given should be 6 or 10 since both will produce virtually the same result as if the weight were infinity.

SOME CONCLUSIONS

The P/G% program has other useful features for estate allocation or for any kind of allocation. It can deal with negative criteria such as keeping administrative costs down. It can work with 1–5 scales, dollars, percentages, years of service, or other measurement dimensions. It can work with missing information, especially by determining the threshold or convergence value of missing items. One can then decide whether the missing item is likely to be above or below the threshold or convergence value, which is easier to do than giving the exact value of the missing items. The software can also deal with problems in which the user is seeking to determine which alternative or combination of alternatives is best, rather than how to allocate scarce resources. It can also deal with minimum and maximum constraints on the alternatives or criteria, including conflicting constraints. The program can be used to help allocate partnership profits among the members of a law firm, to allocate time or money to various activities or places, and to allocate taxes to various governmental programs.[3]

From this analysis, one can see that legal counseling can be aided by multi-criteria decision-making software, which varies greatly in subject matter, quality, and level of intelligent activity. A key underlying feature, however, is the idea that the best decision-aiding software is the kind that captures the process of what good decision-makers do implicitly. It then converts the process into an algorithm or computerized routine. That computerized routine can then be used by other decision-makers to improve their decision-making.

The small incremental effort involved in learning how to use P/G% software can produce substantial incremental benefits. Those benefits include enabling a lawyer to provide better counseling on how to allocate a client's scarce resources, or how to choose among other alternative decisions.[4]

OTHER EXAMPLES

For additional examples relevant to computer-aided counseling, see the applications in chapters 11, 12, and 13. In those chapters, there are 18 applications not counting divorce issues and estate allocation, which have already been used in this chapter. If, for example, one looks to the private practice applications one could talk about:

1. Advising a partnership on how to divide its annual profits (see chapter 11).
2. Advising a damages client on the probability of winning in a civil case and the likely damages (see chapter 11).
3. Advising an arrested client on the probability of winning in a criminal case and the likely sentence if the prosecution wins (chapter 12).
4. Advising a civil rights litigant on the probability of winning, regardless of whether the litigant is suing or being sued (chapter 12).
5. Advising an administrative agency or a client who has business before administrative agencies as to the legality of a proceeding and the likelihood of being upheld on appeal (chapter 12).
6. Advising the State Department or the Department of Justice on the likelihood of the United States winning as a party in an international litigation (chapter 12).
7. Advising a client in a criminal case whether to go to trial or accept a plea bargain (chapter 13).
8. Advising a client in a civil case whether to go to trial or accept an out-of court settlement (chapter 13).

Likewise, if one looks to the legal policy applications, one could talk about:

1. Advising the Department of Commerce, the Federal Trade Commission, or the Consumer's Union about appropriate consumer protection legislation (chapter 11).
2. Advising the Department of Housing and Urban Development, a local planning commission, or a civil rights group about appropriate legislation designed to provide housing for the poor (chapter 11).
3. Advising a state legislative committee, the Department of Health and Human Services, or a women's group about no-fault divorce legislation (chapter 11).
4. Advising the ABA Litigation Section, a trade association of insurance companies, or a group of civil law researchers about the values of alternative tort systems (chapter 11).
5. Advising the local state's attorney's office, a foreign ministry of justice, or the American Civil Liberties Union about alternative forms of crime reduction (chapter 12).
6. Advising the framers of the constitution for a new nation, a judicial reform group, or a justice on the U.S. Supreme Court about the merits of alternative institutional arrangement for reaching decisions on constitutional interpretation (chapter 12).
7. Advising the AFL-CIO, the National Association of Manufacturers, or the president about alternative legislation in dealing with unemployment and inflation (chapter 12).
8. Advising the United Nations, the European Arms Control and Disarmament Agency, or the campaign manager of a U.S. senator interested in foreign affairs as to the meaningfulness of alternative arms control treaties (chapter 12).
9. Advising a state attorney general, the American Judicature Society, or the Legal Services Corporation concerning varying degrees and ways of providing counsel for the poor in criminal cases (chapter 13).
10. Advising the ABA Judicial Administration Section, the American Law Institute, or the U.S. Senate Judiciary Committee concerning the possible encouragement or discouragement of juries in civil cases (chapter 13).

NOTES

1. On computer-aided counseling from an expert systems perspective, see Charles Walter (ed.), *Computing Power and Legal Reasoning* (St. Paul: West, 1985). On the legal aspects of divorce counseling, see Homer Clark, *The Law of Domestic Relations in the United States* (St. Paul: West, 1968); and Harry Krause, *Family Law in a Nutshell* (St. Paul: West, 1977).

2. It makes more sense to average the two allocations (as is done in table 3-2C) than to add together the 1–5 scores. The latter method was used in an article by S. Nagel, "Computer-Aided Counseling, Negotiation, and Advocacy" in the *Connecticut Law Tribune* of January 5, 1987. Averaging the allocations is more in conformity with classical calculus optimization and is about as easy to do.

3. For further details on the application of multicriteria decision-making software to legal advocacy and other lawyer decisions, see S. Nagel, *Microcomputers as Decision Aids in Law Practice* (Westport, Conn.: Greenwood-Quorum, 1987). On allocating money or other resources to activities, places, or people, see S. Nagel, "Optimally

Allocating Money to Places and Activities,'' in Patrick Humphreys and Janos Vecsenyi (eds.), *High Level Decision Support: Lessons from Case Studies* (Amsterdam: North Holland, 1988).

4. Other microcomputer programs relevant to estate allocation include ''WillWriter'' of Nolo Press, 950 Parker Street, Berkeley, CA 94710; ''Fiduciary Accountant'' of the Institute of Para-legal Training, 1926 Arch Street, Philadelphia, PA 19103; and ''Estate Tax Planner,'' of Aardvark-McGraw-Hill, 1020 North Broadway, Milwaukee, WI 53202. None of the three specifically deal with how to divide an estate. The first one converts allocation decisions in a will; the second aids in probating and administering a will; the third makes tax calculations for various decisions.

CHAPTER 4

Computer-Aided Mediation

The purpose of this chapter is to describe the general nature of computer-aided mediation and how it can be applied to resolving public policy and litigation disputes. The chapter also seeks to answer a number of questions, both at the beginning and the end, which skeptics, cynics, and the intellectually curious might be likely to raise.

The essence of computer-aided mediation described in this chapter is reflected in the chapter's title. For a starter, CAM involves the use of computers, but that does not mean much; it is how they are used that counts. Computers could be used in dispute resolution to type the legal papers, which would be a rather mundane use that is not much more valuable than what a typewriter could provide. Computers could be used to keep track of complicated information for the various sides, but that is not much more valuable than what a filing cabinet can provide, along with a good indexing system. Computers could be used to calculate expected values and predicted outcomes in order to facilitate smashing the other side, who may not have such a calculating tool available.

The essence of what this chapter is interested in is expressed in the concepts of mediation and multicriteria. Mediation implies arriving at solutions in which both sides in some sense come out ahead, as contrasted to more traditional adjudication or arbitration in which there is a winner and a loser. Mediation does not necessarily require a third party. In a two-person negotiation, one or both of the parties could seek sincerely to bring about a mediation solution in which both sides come out ahead, as contrasted to using that mode as a pretense for getting the other side to make unreasonable concessions.[1]

The concept of multicriteria refers to the fact that if there is only one criterion or dimension involved, like a pie to be divided, then whatever one side gets, the other side loses. On the other hand, if there are multiple criteria involved, then it is possible for one side to give on some of the criteria that are not so important to it and receive on other criteria that it does consider important, and likewise with the other side. A computer can facilitate that kind of multicriteria dispute resolution better than individuals with pencil and paper or trying to work out of their heads. One can, however, do the kind of reasoning associated with computer-aided mediation without a computer, just as one can do mediation without a mediator.[2]

THE GENERAL NATURE OF COMPUTER-AIDED MEDIATION

The Federal District Court of the Northern District of Illinois experimented with computer-aided mediation for the first time in 1987. The experiment was reasonably successful, although subject to improvement. As a result of the experiment, the court decided to offer computer-aided mediation on a more general basis. Doing so involved drafting a flyer containing questions and answers that potential users of computer-aided mediation might raise. Those questions and answers are as follows:

Why Mediate Rather Than Litigate?

Litigation is expensive to the parties and the taxpayers. Litigation is risky in the sense that chance factors can cause a plaintiff or a defendant to lose everything. On the other hand, mediation costs considerably less in terms of money and time. It involves less risk because both sides are likely to achieve some of their objectives.

Why Use Computer-Aided Mediation?

Computer-aided mediation has advantages over ordinary mediation in being able to arrive at mutually beneficial solutions with less time and expense. It is especially capable of arriving at solutions in which each side gives on some issues that are not so important to it, but may be quite important to the other side. Doing so facilitates solutions in which each side can come out ahead of their respective best expectations, rather than merely ahead of their worst expectations.

What Is Computer-Aided Mediation?

Computer-aided mediation involves a mediator who helps develop a settlement arrangement that both sides can recognize as being substantially better than the probabilistic value of going to trial. Doing so involves working with a user-friendly program that enables each side to clarify the benefits and costs of settling versus going to trial. No prior knowledge of computers or computer-aided mediation is needed in order to be able to make constructive use of this type of procedure.

How Does the Software Facilitate Settlements?

The software is especially applicable to mediation and negotiation by facilitating the following important relevant activities:

1. Making predictions as to the probability or magnitude of events occurring, such as winning at trial and the level of damages.
2. Choosing among alternative approaches to presenting evidence, negotiating, mediating, or choosing among other alternative courses of action.
3. Allocating time, people, money, or other scarce resources to activities, places, or other people.
4. Determining what it would take to bring a second-place alternative (like accepting a settlement) up to the desirability level of a first-place alternative (like going to trial, taking strike action, or declaring war).
5. Developing and analyzing a number of criteria or components in a package settlement so that each side yields on items that are not so important but are important to the other side.
6. Dealing with nonmonetary goals like the stress or pleasure of going to trial, or like the regret one would feel as a matter of hindsight from wrongly rejecting a million-dollar offer on the grounds that the expected value of the case was more than a million dollars.
7. Dealing with missing information on future events by converting questions of what are the probability, benefits, or costs likely to be into questions as to whether they are above or below computer-calculated threshold, break-even, or critical values.
8. Dealing with conflicting constraints where, for example, there are various minimum demands that add to more than the maximum available.
9. Other problems involving predicting, choosing, allocating, what-if analysis, packaging criteria, multidimensional goals, missing information, conflicting constraints, or the need for simplicity in view of those numerous complications that can occur in realistic dispute resolution situations.

How Does One Arrange for Computer-Aided Mediation?

As of December 1987, computer-aided mediation is available in the Federal District Court of the Northern District of Illinois through the office of Judge Marvin Aspen. He has been a pioneer in the development of this new and useful form of alternative dispute resolution. He is working on this matter with Jack Cooley and Stuart Nagel. Mr. Cooley is a professional mediator, former federal magistrate, and professor of law at the Loyola University Law School. Stuart Nagel is a consultant and trainer in computer-aided legal decision-making, a former assistant counsel to the U.S. Senate Judiciary Committee, and a professor of political science at the University of Illinois.

Nagel and Cooley are in the process of training other lawyers to be computer-aided mediators in other federal and state courts. Some of the training is being conducted through the Committee on Continuing Professional Education of the American Law Institute and the American Bar Association. Most of the training is occurring by lawyers trying the relevant software and reading the relevant documentation, including this book.

What Are the Monetary Costs and Benefits?

There are no charges unless a settlement is reached. The charges are then only for expenses and a reasonable flat fee. As an example, a federal products liability case was recently settled for $375,000. It saved the defendant approximately $600,000 since there was $950,000 in liquidated damages. It saved the plaintiff $375,000 over what could have been a total loss, given the relatively low probability of collecting. The fee to the computer-aided mediators was only $1,500 plus $300 in expenses. Future fees will be approximately 1% of the estimated money saved by going to mediation rather than litigation, although with a provision for negotiating special circumstances. Monetary benefits also include the saving of litigation and time. Nonmonetary benefits include learning how microcomputers can be used for more effective negotiation and mediation in other cases.

RESOLVING LEGAL POLICY DISPUTES

Computer-aided mediation has at least two major uses in the legal process and possibly in human interaction in general. One use is for resolving disputes as to what policies or principles should be adopted for resolving future cases, or for dealing with policy, family, or other problems. A second use is for resolving an immediate dispute between individuals, groups, nations, or other entities. The first use is a rule-making use, and the second is an adjudication use employing the language from administrative law. The first use can be considered a policy-making or law-making use, and the second use a policy-applying or law-applying use, using the language of public policy analysis or law.

This section of the chapter will describe briefly an example of how computer-aided mediation might have been able to resolve a legal policy dispute if it had been applied. The dispute is relevant to illustrating an appropriate computer program and how policy disputes can be resolved by changing the alternatives, the criteria, or the relations between alternatives and criteria.

The Computer Program and the Disputes

The essense of the program in this context is its ability to show disputants quickly the effects of alternative proposals on their respective criteria. The program can also show the effects of changing the criteria, their relative weights, and the relations between alternatives and criteria. Showing those effects can facilitate arriving at dispute-resolving compromises, including optimizing compromises where all the disputants come out ahead of their original best expectations, rather than merely ahead of their worst expectations.

The program is designed to process a set of (1) goals to be achieved, (2) alternatives for achieving them, and (3) relations between goals and alternatives in order to choose the best alternative or combination for maximizing benefits minus costs of the disputants or other users. The program is called Policy/Goal

Percentaging because it relates policies (or alternatives) to goals (or criteria), and it often uses part/whole percentaging to deal with the occurrence where goals may be measured on different dimensions.

The concept of dispute involves persons, groups, ideologies, or other entities who are in conflict over how a matter should be resolved. A problem is not necessarily a dispute, since it may involve one person or entity trying to decide what to do. The major processes whereby disputes are resolved are through forms of negotiation, mediation, arbitration, or adjudication. In *negotiation,* the two or more sides interact to try to come to an agreement, which may be considered mutually desirable or may be forced by one party on the other through threats of negative sanctions. In *mediation,* a nondisputant tries to bring the disputants to an agreement. If the nondisputants have the power to impose a solution on the parties, then they are generally referred to as *arbitrators* (where chosen by the parties), or as judges (where the nondisputants are imposed on the parties). *Mediators* generally seek solutions that will be considered mutually satisfying by the parties. *Arbitrators* and judges seek solutions that are considered correct in accordance with a body of past practice, common sense, or rules, and the solutions may not be mutually satisfying. Arbitrators as compared with *judges* tend to place more emphasis on past custom and less on past recorded cases. They also place more emphasis on uncodified common sense and less emphasis on codified rules.

The kind of dispute resolution with which this part of the chapter is especially concerned is disputes over public policies for dealing with various social problems. For example, in the controversy over how to provide legal services for the poor, liberals and Congress advocate salaried government lawyers by way of the Legal Services Corporation. Conservatives and the Reagan White House advocate a program of volunteer lawyers serving the poor. Both sides agree that the key criteria for deciding among the alternative delivery systems are (1) inexpensiveness, (2) accessibility, (3) political feasibility, and (4) competence. There is also rough agreement that volunteers are better on inexpensiveness and political feasibility, whereas salaried government lawyers are better on accessibility and competence. The big dispute as to the inputs for arriving at a conclusion is over the relative weights of the goals. The liberals place a higher weight on accessibility and competence, whereas the conservatives place a higher weight on inexpensiveness and political feasibility.

Changing the Alternatives Being Considered

Perhaps the best way to resolve disputes over the relative weights of the goals (or for that matter over any disputed policy problem) is to try to find a new alternative that will please both sides in light of their differing weights, goals, perceptions, constraints, or other inputs. An example is working with the existing Legal Services Corporation, but requiring all Legal Services Agencies to use 10% of their budgets to improve the accessibility and competence of volunteer lawyers. Accessibility can be improved by bringing the volunteer lawyers to the agency offices to meet with relevant clients. Competence can be improved through training manuals, training workshops, and matching specialist lawyers with clients who relate to their specialties. Such a 10% system may be better than a pure Legal Services Corporation, even for those with liberal weights, because it provides a better benefit/cost ratio and greater political feasibility without decreasing accessibility or competence. Such a system is also better than the existing Legal Services Corporation from a perspective with conservative weights, because it represents an improvement on all four goals over the existing system. Also if volunteering becomes mandatory for license renewal, then the volunteers are likely to dominate the system.

Computer output for the legal service example is given in Table 4-1. Part A of the table shows how the two original alternatives and the new alternative score on the four criteria on a scale of 1–2, corresponding to "relatively no" and "relatively yes." Part B shows the same data, but with the scores on inexpensiveness and political feasibility doubled to reflect conservative values. Part C shows the same data as A, but with the scores doubled on accessibility and competence to reflect the liberal emphasis. The key item to note is that the optimizing compromise scores better than the favored alternative of either side using each side's own value system. Finding such optimizing compromises is facilitated by this kind of analysis.

Instead of adding an alternative, subtracting one might be helpful where more than two alternatives are involved. For example, by reducing three alternatives to two, we may have a clear-cut runoff where one of the two alternatives in effect gets an especially large portion of the votes or points that would otherwise go to the third alternative. Related to adding an alternative is the idea of consolidating two or more alternatives. Doing so in effect creates a new alternative. That new alternative may be a good compromise if there were only two alternatives at the time of the consolidation. If there were more than two alternatives, then consolidating can have the beneficial effect of reducing the number of alternatives. Related to consolidating (although in the opposite direction) is subdividing one alternative into two or more alternatives. Perhaps one of those newly created alternatives may be a compromise alternative on which the disputants can agree. If not, some of the newly created alternatives might be quickly eliminated as clearly inferior, thereby clarifying the situation although not reducing the number of alternatives. Each time there is an addition, subtraction, consolidation, or subdivision, the P/G% program can quickly show how the new alternatives compare in terms of their overall or summation scores on the criteria, with regard to either raw scores or percentaging scores.

Changing the Criteria

All of the above approaches to making changes in the alternatives can also apply to making changes in the criteria. For example, a dispute might be more

Table 4-1
An Example of Computer-Aided Mediation in Legal Policy Evaluation

	Inexpensiveness	Accessibility	Political feasibility	Competence
A. With unweighted criteria				
Volunteer	2.00	1.00	2.00	1.00
Salaried	1.00	2.00	1.00	2.00
Compromise	1.50	2.00	2.00	2.00
B. With conservative values				
Volunteer	4.00	1.00	4.00	1.00
Salaried	2.00	2.00	2.00	2.00
Compromise	3.00	2.00	4.00	2.00
C. With liberal values				
Volunteer	2.00	2.00	2.00	2.00
Salaried	1.00	4.00	1.00	4.00
Compromise	1.50	4.00	2.00	4.00

NOTES:

1. The alternative ways of providing legal counsel to the poor include:
   (1) Volunteer attorneys, favored by the White House
   (2) Salaried government attorneys, favored by the Congress
   (3) A compromise that involves continuing the salaried system, but requiring that 10 percent of its funding go to making volunteers more accessible and competent.
2. The criteria are inexpensiveness, accessibility, political feasibility, and competence. Each alternative is scored on each criterion on a 1-2 scale.
3. Conservative values involve giving a weight of 2 to inexpensiveness and political feasibility when the other criteria receive a weight of 1. Liberal values involve giving a weight of 2 to accessibility and competence when the other criteria receive a weight of 1.
4. With conservative values, the volunteer system wins over the salaried system 10 points to 8. The compromise is an overall winner with 11½ points.
5. With liberal values, the salaried system wins over the volunteer system 10 points to 8. The compromise is an overall winner with 11½ points.
6. The "10 percent compromise" is thus a super winner in being better than the original best solution of both the conservatives and the liberals.

capable of being resolved by adding a criterion that brings out that alternative B is clearly the winner, even though the two alternatives were originally tied. Likewise, subtracting a criterion could make alternative B clearly the winner. The same effect in terms of clarifying the winner can also occur as a result of consolidating two or more criteria or as a result of subdividing a criterion.

Unlike the alternatives, the criteria are subject to different weights to indicate their relative importance, although the alternatives are subject to different overall scores to indicate their relative importance. The overall scores of the alternatives, however, are outputs of the analysis, whereas the weights of the criteria are inputs of the analysis. By changing those criterion weights, alternative B may become the clear winner. Working with different weights when all the weights were originally the same can help resolve many disputes. Along related lines, one can work with the weights and criteria of just the first disputant, and then just the second disputant. Doing so generates two sets of overall or summation scores for the alternatives. One can average those overall scores in order to see which alternative might be the winner, or one can average the weights that the disputants assign to the criteria. The averaging can be a weighted average if one side of the dispute is considered to have more weight or to be entitled to more votes than the other sides or other disputants.

Working with minimum and maximum constraints is another approach that especially applies to the criteria, although it could apply to the alternatives. For example, the subject matter of a given dispute may cause the disputants to agree that a certain criterion is desirable, such as the age of the person to be hired, but only up to 70 years because of a relevant retirement rule. That could eliminate some alternatives as could a minimum requirement of age 21. Likewise, the subject matter of a given dispute may make it meaningful to have a maximum and/or minimum constraint on an alternative. Perhaps, for example, the original alternatives are (1) spending $100 on Activity P and $10 on Activity Q versus (2) spending $90 on Activity P and $30 on Activity Q. The alternatives under consideration may be reduced if there is a maximum budget of no more than $115, a maximum expenditure on an activity of no more than $95, or a minimum expenditure on an activity of no less than $20. The P/G% program allows one to determine quickly the effects of changing minimum and maximum constraints on criteria and alternatives, as well as changing the criteria and the alternatives themselves.

Changing the Relations Between Alternatives and Criteria

In resolving disputes, the third big area of change involves the relations between the alternatives and the criteria. What begins as a tie could possibly be resolved by changing the scores for some of the relations. One could also show the overall summation scores for the alternatives when all the relations are scored from a conservative perspective and a liberal or other perspective. One can then average those two or more sets of overall scores in order to arrive at a superoverall winner as was discussed in talking about conservative and liberal weights and criteria.

Along related lines, one can change the relations by providing for more refined measurement as when one goes from a 1–2 scale to a 1–5 scale, or less refined but clearer measurement as when one goes from a 1–5 scale to a 1–2 scale. One could change the measurement units from a 1–5 scale to a scale measured in dollars, years, miles, or another dimension. Changing the measurement scale may require shifting from a raw score approach to a percentaging approach if multidimensionality is introduced. For example, although one can add the raw scores on two criteria, both of which are measured on 1–5 scales, one cannot so meaningfully add the raw scores from a 1–5 scale to the scores from a scale measured in miles. It may, however, be meaningful to indicate how each alternative scores on each criterion in terms of the percentage relation of each raw score to the maximum raw score possible or to the total of the raw scores on a criterion. The P/G% program works especially well with such multidimensionality in view of the program's emphasis on working with part/whole percentages of raw scores converted into percentages of the total points on a criterion.

Steps or Options

In light of the above general principles and specific examples, one can conclude that microcomputers and the P/G% program can help facilitate negotiation and mediation leading to dispute resolution by proceeding in accordance with the following steps or options:

1. Determine the initial alternatives, the criteria, and the relations between the alternatives and the criteria in light of each side's values and perceptions. The P/G% input-format facilitates clarification of those dispute parameters.
2. Determine what it would take each side to convince the other side. The threshold, break-even, or tie-causing analysis of the P/G% program facilitates that determination. If each side could at least partly convince the other side, encourage them to do so, since the result may be a mutually acceptable alternative or compromise.
3. Experiment with a variety of additional alternatives, as contrasted to the original deadlocked alternatives. Use the P/G% program to determine quickly the overall or summation score for each alternative using the criterion weights of each side to the dispute. Look especially for new alternatives that could be endorsed by both sides more strongly than their original first choices. At least find an alternative that could be each side's second choice and thus serve as a compromise winner in a series of paired comparisons.
4. Try changing the alternatives by subtracting some, by consolidating two or more, or by subdividing some. Try doing the same things with the criteria. Use the P/G% program to determine the overall or summation scores of the new set of alternatives.
5. Try changing the criterion weights, or try averaging the alternatives in light of the different sets of weights that the conflicting disputants have.
6. Try working with reasonable minimum and/or maximum constraints on the criteria and/or the alternatives to see what difference that makes.
7. Try changing some of the relation scores and maybe the measurement units on which the scores are based. That may mean experimenting with the procedures in the P/G% program for dealing with criteria measured on multiple dimensions.

RESOLVING LITIGATION DISPUTES

Computer-aided mediation in litigation can be considered as having begun in November 1987, because that is when the first court case was known to have been settled at least partly as a result of computer-aided mediation.

A Civil Case Study

The case involved a U.S. insurance company suing a foreign electronics company in the Federal Court of the Northern District of Illinois. The subject matter of the case was products liability. The names of the litigants are confidential. Some of the facts have been simplified or made more general for methodological purposes. The case can be especially used to indicate how computer-aided mediation can facilitate superoptimum settlements or at least ordinary settlements.

Figures 4-1 and 4-2 illustrate what is involved in a superoptimum settlement. The plaintiff demands $700,000 as a minimum in order to settle. The defendant offers $350,000 as a maximum in order to settle. The object of a superoptimum settlement is to provide the plaintiff with more than $700,000 while simultaneously not having the defendant pay more than $350,000. In other words, the

Figure 4-1
Settle Versus Trial from the Plaintiff's Perspective

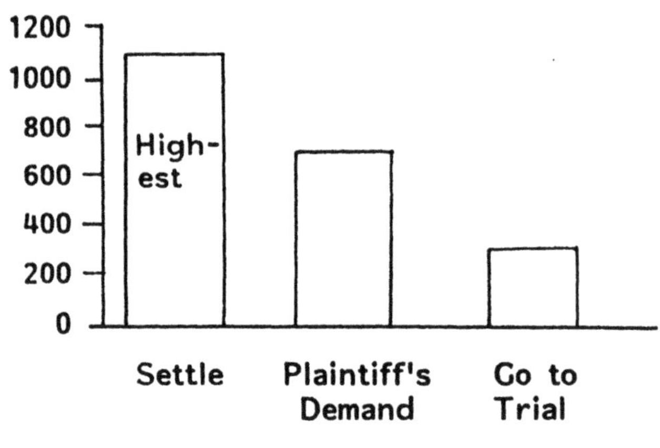

NOTES:

1. The expected value of settling from the plaintiff's perspective is $1,099,000, as described in the text (the first bar).
2. The middle bar shows that the plaintiff's first demand or best expectation was $700,000.
3. The expected value of going to trial from the plaintiff's perspective is only $290,000, as described in the text (the third bar).

Figure 4-2
Settle Versus Trial from the Defendant's Perspective

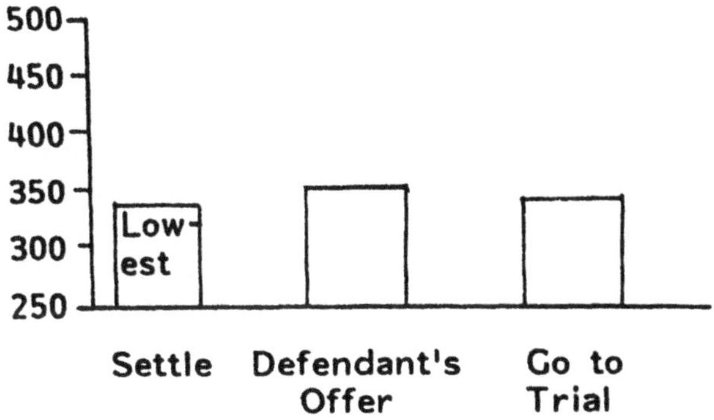

NOTES:

1. The value of settling from the defendant's perspective is only $326,000, which is $76,000 above the $250,000 baseline used in the above graph (the first bar).

2. The expected value of going to trial from the defendant's perspective is $330,000, which is $80,000 above the baseline (the third bar).

3. The second bar shows the defendant's first offer or best expectation. Note that the settlement is lower and thus better than the defendant's best expectation from the defendant's perspective.

4. The $326,000 settlement figure could be substantially lower and still bring the plaintiff to a settlement in view of the big gap in figure 4-1 between the settlement value and the trial value from the plaintiff's perspective.

problem is to find a number that is simultaneously bigger than $700,000 and smaller than $350,000, which are roughly the best expectations of the plaintiff and defendant, respectively.

Such a settlement can be arrived at by considering additional settlement criteria beyond the exchange of money. In almost every damages case, the defendant is an insurance company, a manufacturer, a transportation company, or some other company that can offer something of considerable value to the plaintiff, but having relatively low cost to the defendant. In this case, it was possible for the defendant to consider offering electronic equipment, insurance claims, and insurance annuities to the plaintiffs and their insurance companies. That combination of equipment, claims, and annuities had an estimated cost value of only $326,000 to the defendants as indicated by figure 4-2. That combination, however, had an estimated purchase value of $1,099,000 to the plaintiffs.

Such a solution could conceivably be developed without computer-aided mediation. CAM, however, greatly facilitates being able to deal with four or more criteria simultaneously from both the defendant's and the plaintiff's perspective. It also facilitates making calculations concerning the expected value of going to trial. From the plaintiff's perspective, the expected value of going to trial is only $290,000 as shown in figure 4-1, which is far less than the special settlement value of $1,099,000, or the traditional settlement value of something between $350,000 and $700,000. Likewise from the defendant's perspective, the expected value of going to trial is $330,000, which would cost the defendant more than the $326,000 settlement.

CAM is also helpful for arriving at a predicted damages figure and a predicted probability that liability will be established. Those predictions are based on various factual elements, diverse estimates, and previous experience. The predicted damages figure in this case was $756,250. The predicted victory probability in this case was .37. Thus the predicted or expected damages discounted by the probability of winning was approximately $300,000, which was roughly the cash settlement value of this case. That cash settlement can be considered as a fall-back settlement if the superoptimum settlement cannot be achieved.

Criminal Cases

Suppose in a criminal case the prosecutor's optimum position is a five-year sentence. That means the prosecutor considers five years to be the maximum realistic number of years that the defendant would be willing to go to prison. Five years may be less than the maximum that the statute allows. If five years is the prosecutor's optimum, then the prosecutor might be willing to settle for as little as two years. On the other hand, the defendant's optimum might be one year as the best possible settlement. That means the defendant might be willing to settle for as much as three years in prison.

An optimizing solution would thus be one that allows the prosecutor to have a settlement of more than five years and the defendant a settlement of less than one year. That seems impossible, but not necessarily so if the disputants can move on to a different settlement dimension, such as community service instead of prison. On that dimension, they might be able to reach an agreement in which the defendant agrees to serve ten years in a monastery. From the prosecutor's point of view, that may be better than five years in prison. From the defendant's point of view, that might be better than one year in prison. Thus ten years of monastic community service is an optimizing compromise where both sides feel they have come out ahead of their original optimum positions.

The win-plus solution in the criminal case might involve the defendant agreeing to commit himself to a long-term nonprison institutionalization, such as being part of a disease research program in a monastery or leper colony.

1. The prosecutor might find that solution to be worth more than ten years in prison if there is more than a ten-year commitment, especially since a ten-year prison sentence may mean release after five years or less with good-time off. The prosecutor might be especially happy since the state does not pay for monastery incarceration, and the maximum sentence specified in the statute is ten years.
2. The defendant might find that solution to be better than probation because there is no plea of guilty, and because the defendant's personality and aspirations may find pleasure in monastery life or even martyrdom to disease research.

There is actually nothing that novel about win-plus solutions in criminal cases where both sides come out ahead. It used to be somewhat commonplace in the case of delinquents to give them the option of joining the Marines, especially in wartime. The prosecutor feels that he or she is coming out ahead by not having to try the case and not burdening the taxpayer with incarcerating the defendant. The defendant feels that he is coming out ahead by avoiding jail or even probation, and even looking like a hero among his peer group as a new member of the U.S. Marines. Related solutions occur in the literature of French and English criminal prosecutions with regard to joining the French Foreign Legion or becoming a settler in Australia or some other distant part of the British empire.

The use of multicriteria dispute resolution in criminal cases raises important ethical or philosophical issues as to whether it is socially desirable to have such solutions. In both criminal and civil cases, it is desirable from a societal perspective to try to resolve matters without going to trial, especially if the resolution is the same as what would happen if the case did go to trial. That can be facilitated in a number of ways:

1. Flat sentencing whereby a convicted defendant receives a sentence of so many months or years in prison depending on the severity of the defendant's crime and prior record, and not at all dependent on whether there is a trial or a guilty plea.
2. Easily retrieved data showing the probability of conviction in various types of cases and what sentences are likely to be received. That kind of system better enables the plea bargaining to arrive at decisions like those that would occur upon trial.
3. Funds available to prosecutors so they can pursue difficult prosecutions without having to settle for an unduly lenient plea bargain. Also funds available to public defenders so that they can pursue difficult defenses without having to settle for an unduly harsh plea bargain.

Multicriteria dispute resolution can also result in out-of-court settlements, but the settlements are *not* likely to resemble closely the decisions that would be reached if the cases went to trial. That is not so bad if we place a high weight on avoiding expensive trials. That is bad, however, if we believe that sentences given as a result of trials have deterrent value partly for the immediate defendants, but mainly for other people who might otherwise commit similar crimes if the deterrence is not strong enough. In other words, we probably do not want defendants to go away from negotiations in criminal cases feeling that they have achieved something greater than their best expectations. Doing so could have an adverse effect on the higher goal of decreasing crime, even if it is in accordance with the lower goal of facilitating out-of-court settlements.

The same problem is not so present in civil cases. Both types of cases involve a societal concern for deterring undesirable behavior. In criminal cases, it is undesirable criminal behavior. In civil cases, it is undesirable behavior with regard to negligence, breach of contract, property damage, violation of family obligations, or other such responsibilities, but violating them is short of a criminal violation. Even civil settlements that are relatively satisfying to the defendant may have some deterrent value by virtue of legal expenses, the settlement payoff, and the adverse publicity. That is not so in the case of a win-plus solution for a criminal defendant who may have no legal expenses, jail time, or adverse publicity. A civil dispute may also be one in which it is socially desirable to enable the plaintiff and defendant to function together after the suit since they may be husband and wife, employer and employee, or people who otherwise need to interact with each other in future commercial transactions. Thus what may be a socially desirable win-plus settlement in a civil case may be a socially undesirable win-plus settlement in a criminal case.

Principles Derived from the ADR Committee

On February 20, 1987, the author presented a demonstration of the P/G% or Best Choice software before the Committee on Alternative Dispute Resolution (ADR) of the Chicago Bar Association. That presentation emphasized resolving a dispute over damages between a plaintiff and a defendant. The following points were generated as a result of the questions and comments raised by members of the committee:

1. In using P/G% to resolve disputes, it is desirable to have two microcomputers going simultaneously. One microcomputer can show the values and perceptions of the plaintiff, or one side. The other microcomputer can show the values and perceptions of the defendant, or the other side. The values consist of the criteria that each side is seeking to maximize or achieve and the relative weights of those criteria. The perceptions consist of the alternatives that are perceived as being available and how each alternative scores on each criterion.

2. The plaintiff's side should include the criteria from the perspectives of the plaintiff client and the plaintiff lawyer separately in order to reflect how their positions may differ. For example, if a contingency fee case is involved, the client customarily receives 67% of the damages, whereas the lawyer receives 33%. The lawyer's litigation costs and settlement costs are likely to be substantially more than the client's. If there is a settlement, the percentage to the client is generally 80%, whereas the lawyer receives 20%. For those reasons, the lawyer may be better off going to trial when the client is better off settling, or vice versa. There may thus be a need to develop a solution in which both the plaintiff client and the lawyer are better off settling, and so is the defendant.

3. The defendant's side should include the criteria from the perspective of the defendant client and the defendant lawyer to reflect how their positions may differ. For example, the defendant client (which may be an insurance company) may be better off going to trial when the defendant lawyer (who is on an annual salary) may be better off settling. There may thus be a need to develop a solution in which both the defendant client and lawyer are better off settling, and so is the plaintiff.

4. The criteria should consider both monetary and nonmonetary criteria. An important nonmonetary criterion is the extent to which the plaintiff lawyer and the defendant lawyer enjoy going to trial. For some lawyers, going to trial provides a fun benefit. For other lawyers, going to trial provides a negative experience to be avoided independent of the monetary considerations. One can have a criterion called trial enjoyment scored on a 1–5 scale—a 5 means highly positive feelings toward trial work in this case, a 4 means mildly positive, a 3 means neutral, a 2 means mildly negative, and a 1 means highly negative. The P/G% software is capable of adding monetary and nonmonetary benefits and costs in order to arrive at a meaningful overall evaluation of going to trial or settling.

5. To facilitate settlements in which both the plaintiff side and the defendant side come out ahead of their best expectations, try to find some criteria on which the defendant places a low value and the plaintiff places a high value, or vice versa. A good example is whatever product the defendant sells, such as insurance, automobiles, or municipal transportation. The value of giving up an automobile by General Motors as a defendant, for example, is relatively low. The value of receiving an automobile to the average plaintiff is relatively high. Thus one of the plaintiff's bargaining criteria might be labeled "Their Product," and the defendant's corresponding bargaining criterion might be labeled "Our Product."

6. To facilitate computer-aided mediation settlements, it is important to emphasize the need for using estimates as to damages likely to be awarded, the probability of victory, litigation costs, settlement costs, and other relevant criteria, rather than wasting time seeking precise figures or being paralyzed seeking precise figures. This is so because so often the bottom line of going to trial or settling is not influenced by even large margins of error. For example, if the plaintiff thinks the likely damages will be $500,000 with a 90% probability of victory, the plaintiff is correct in rejecting the $40,000 offer of the insurance company even though the true probability is 70% and the true damages if liability is established will be $100,000.

7. It is important for understanding computer mediation that it involves nothing more than trying to make explicit what good attorneys do implicitly when deciding whether to go to trial or settle out of court. The reasons for making the process more explicit are so a settlement can be arrived at more quickly, and so a settlement can be arrived at that is more likely to be better than each side's best expectations, rather than merely better than their worst expectations.

8. One should not shy away from computer-aided mediation on the grounds that it requires too much effort to learn the system or to acquire the needed information. As point 7 above indicates, good attorneys already know the system implicitly. It takes only a few minutes to learn what is involved in making the process more explicit. As point 6 above indicates, guesstimates and commonsense knowledge are highly acceptable in this context. If the initial data show the plaintiff would be better off going to trial, the computer can quickly inform all sides what it would take to bring a settlement up to first place among these two alternatives, or vice versa. One can then quickly determine whether those changes are feasible.

9. The plaintiff might try to rig his or her perceptions so as to generate a high threshold offer from the defendant. That may be difficult to do. The plaintiff cannot overly exaggerate the likely damages or the probability of victory in view of the availability of reasonably objective data from sources like the Jury Verdict Research Corporation. Likewise, the defendant might try to rig his or her perceptions so as to generate a low threshold offer from the plaintiff. For similar reasons, that is also difficult to do. One important aspect of computer-aided mediation (unlike traditional mediation) is that computer-aided mediation does not seek to find the midpoint btween what the plaintiff says is his or her minimum (for example, $100,000) and what the defendant says is his or her maximum (for example, $50,000). Rather, computer-aided mediation seeks to find a solution on multiple criteria that is both higher than the plaintiff's minimum (i.e., higher than $100,000) and simultaneously lower than the defendant's maximum (i.e., lower than $50,000). Giving the plaintiff an annuity from the defendant insurance company may easily be worth more than $100,000 to the plaintiff and less than $50,000 to the defendant.

10. One should not confuse computer-aided mediation with traditional decision analysis, which tends to be highly mathematical and highly contrary to an expert systems perspective that seeks to emulate how good decision-makers actually decide. Traditional operations research, management science, and statistical analysis tend to be much more complicated and less valid because they do not make adequate use of commonsense knowledge. Traditional decision analysis cannot so easily deal with multiple criteria, especially if some of the criteria are measured differently, like damages in terms of dollars and trial enjoyment on a 1–5 scale. Traditional decision analysis is also not so capable of dealing with multiple missing information, range estimates, or other rough scoring systems based on small samples and limited prior experience.

11. Many exotic forms of dispute resolution have been developed in recent years other than traditional adjudication such as binding, voluntary, or court-annexed arbitration, conciliation, and special forms of limited jury or bench trials. Regardless of the value of those alternatives, the most effective and efficient alternative to a traditional trial is likely to be an out-of-court settlement, especially one in which both sides achieve results better than their best expectations.

BROADER QUESTIONS AND ANSWERS

The purpose of this section is to raise and answer a set of broader questions about computer-aided mediation. These questions were originally raised by Robert Jones, editor of the *Dispute Resolution Forum,* as part of a special issue on the subject of "Programming the Process: An Examination of the Use of Computers in Dispute Resolution." The questions raised at the beginning of this chapter were more concerned with the techniques involved in computer-aided mediation. The questions raised here are more concerned with broader implications for the disputants, their representatives, and society. The answers were given by the author as part of a telephone interview.

What Does the Computer Offer to Those Working in Dispute Resolution?

The computer can aid in such forms of dispute resolution as negotiation, arbitration, adjudication, and mediation. A computer facilitates the dispute resolution process by working with many more variables simultaneously than can the individual mind. It can help with problems involving predicting, choosing, allocating, what-if analysis, packaging criteria, multidimensional goals, and missing information.

I am especially interested in computer-aided mediation where a third party seeks to bring two sides to settlement. There are two types of computer-aided mediation. One involves a settlement where both sides believe they come out ahead of their worst expectations and they settle because the alternatives to settlement are worse than the settlement. In the other type, the parties come out ahead of their very best expectations.

As a special master in a federal case in Illinois involving a major foreign electronics manufacturer and its foreign insurance company as defendants, and a domestic insurance company as the plaintiff, I suggested the use of computer-aided mediation. The plaintiff's initial settlement demand was for a minimum of $700,000. The defendants' initial settlement position was that they would not offer more than $350,000. With the use of computer-aided mediation we arrived at a solution where the plaintiff got more than $700,000 and the defendants paid less than $350,000. Both exceeded their very best expectations, as described in the section of this chapter on "Resolving Litigation Disputes." That is what I call a superoptimum solution, which is better than a win-win solution and which was possible using computer-aided mediation.

What Obstacles Exist to the Growth in the Use of Computers in Dispute Resolution?

Whatever obstacles exist to greater use of computers in dispute resolution are being rapidly overcome. My book, *Microcomputers as Decision Aids in Law*

Practice, was published in 1987. In it I listed problems in getting lawyers to adopt computers as decision aids. In a year since, many of these obstacles have been significantly reduced. For example, for the first time in journals for practicing lawyers, articles have appeared focusing on computer aids in litigation.

A 1986 survey of the nation's top 500 law firms disclosed that only 20 percent were using decision-aiding software. In 1987 the survey showed a jump up to 30 percent. This rapid increase indicates that the obstacles to the computer's use are diminishing.

Is There Any Basis for the Commonly Expressed Fear That Computers Could Replace the Human Element in Negotiations and Dispute Resolution?

Some lawyers see the use of computers in negotiations as strictly ivory tower stuff, overly simplistic, and removed from their own work. More lawyers view them as being more useless than a threat. Those who see the use of computers as threatening think they may be forced to learn all sorts of new things that will be disruptive to their usual way of doing things.

A March 28, 1988, *Time* cover story on computers said that in the future they would be both faster and smarter through the development of artificial intelligence. But the article's illustrations of smart computers were very rudimentary, incapable of any creative judgment within a dynamic process such as negotiation.

In the kind of computer uses for negotiation that we're talking about, the computer must be told what alternatives are available, what criteria exist for deciding among the alternatives, how each alternative scores in each criterion, and so on. Once instructed, the computer simply does the arithmetic to show where settlement packages leave the parties.

The computer allows for greater creativity. For example, the normal approach to the case I mentioned earlier would be to split the difference, with the defendants paying out $500,000. But the computer stimulated more creative thinking through a "what-if" analysis. A package was devised that gave both parties a settlement that was worth more than their best estimate. However, you have to come up with the "what if" questions for this to work.

What Will Be the New Areas of Computer Applications in Dispute Resolution?

The most exciting potential involves superoptimum solutions to disputes in which each side feels it comes out ahead of its best expectations. This is the opposite of the zero-sum approach and better than simply win-win solutions. There is a riddle that aptly captures the limitations of our current way of thinking about computers and decision-making. What has eight legs, a keyboard, and is good to sleep on? The answer is a spider, a typewriter, and a bed. By trying to think of one thing that has all three attributes, the mind gets trapped in the traditional rut of how riddles are supposed to be answered. With litigation, the traditional rut is that there are only two criteria: namely, one person gives money, the other receives. Moving to multicriteria decision-making, each side gives a lot of different things, perhaps not so valuable to them as they are to the other side. This is a whole new way of thinking that enables one to get all kinds of insights about how to resolve disputes.

The future of computer-aided mediation may not involve the widespread use of computer hardware or software in resolving disputes. Instead, the approach may be far more successful if it succeeds in changing the way in which lawyers think about dispute resolution. That new thinking would emphasize multiple criteria and creating alternatives whereby one side would give on some criteria that have relatively low values, and receive on other criteria that have relatively high values, with the opposite being true for the other side. Working with spreadsheet software facilitates that kind of thinking, but after the hardware and the software have been removed, the new attorneys may still react to disputes from the perspectives of multicriteria dispute resolution.

In that sense, computer-aided mediation will have best succeeded when it becomes so commonplace that lawyers will question the need for having computers to aid them in what they are now able to do implicitly without computers. In other words, the great value of a computer algorithm or routine may be that it makes explicit what good decision-makers do implicitly, and then spreads the ability among average decision-makers so that they also become good decision-makers in the implicit sense. This is analogous to Norman Thomas saying that the Socialist Party will have succeeded when nobody votes Socialist because the major political parties will have incorporated the socialist ideas, such that they are commonplace noncontroversies. Computer-aided mediation at the present time is controversial. Perhaps someday no one will vote in favor of it because the reasoning processes will have become incorporated into commonplace lawyer behavior.

OTHER EXAMPLES

A key example used in this chapter to illustrate computer-aided mediation in a legal policy context was the policy problem of mediating a dispute between the White House and Congress over how to provide legal services to the poor in civil cases. A key example used to illustrate computer-aided mediation in an adjudicative context was a products liability case between a U.S. insurance company and a foreign electronics manufacturer. Numerous other examples could be given by drawing upon the applications of microcomputers as decision aids in law practice from chapters 11, 12, and 13.

Thinking in terms of an adjudicative or legal policy context, those applications could lend themselves to examples regarding:

1. Mediating a dispute between the partners in a law firm on how to divide the profits (chapter 11).
2. Mediating a dispute between the beneficiaries of an estate on how to divide the remaining property (chapter 11).
3. Mediating a dispute between a husband and wife over problems of child custody, child support, or a property settlement (chapter 11).
4. Mediating a dispute between a plaintiff and a defendant over the payment of personal injury damages (chapter 11).
5. Mediating a dispute between an arrested person and the person who called the police in order to develop an appropriate reconciliation and restitution (chapter 12).
6. Mediating a dispute between blacks and whites, or two or more other ethnic groups in a community over civil rights problems (chapter 12).
7. Mediating a dispute between an administrative agency and an individual or business firm that the agency seeks to regulate, or to whom the agency gives grants (chapter 12).
8. Mediating a dispute between two or more countries over the violation of an arms control treaty or any kind of treaty, boundary, custom, or other matter (chapter 12).
9. Mediating a dispute between liberals and conservatives in a legislature over a disputed bill that relates to consumer protection, housing for the poor, no-fault divorce, alternative tort systems, crime reduction, judicial review, unemployment-inflation, arms control, right to counsel, juries in civil cases, or any other legal policy matter (see the legal policy sections of chapters 11, 12, and 13).

NOTES

1. For further details on computer-aided mediation, see Robert Jones (ed.), *Programming the Process: An Examination of the Use of Computers in Dispute Resolution* (Washington, D.C.: National Institute of Dispute Resolution, 1988); Don Nyhart (ed.), *Computer Models and Modeling for Negotiation Management* (Cambridge, Mass.: MIT Conference Proceedings, November 1987); Howard Raiffa, *The Art and Science of Negotiation* (Cambridge, Mass.: Harvard University Press, 1982); Christopher Moore, *The Mediation Process: Practical Strategies for Resolving Conflict* (San Francisco: Jossey-Bass, 1986); and S. Nagel, *Applying Microcomputers to Dispute Resolution* (Champaign, Ill.: Decision Aids, Inc., 1987).

2. For further details on multicriteria decision-making, see Allan Easton, *Complex Managerial Decisions Involving Multiple Objectives* (New York: John Wiley, 1973); Thomas Saaty, *Decision Making for Leaders: The Analytical Hierarchy Process for Decisions in a Complex World* (Belmont, Calif.: Wadsworth, 1982); Ching-Lai Hwang and Kwangsun Yoon, *Multiple Attribute Decision Making: Methods and Applciations* (Berlin: Springer-Verlag, 1981); and S. Nagel, *Evaluation Analysis with Micro-Computers* (Greenwich, Conn.: JAI Press, 1989).

SECTION B

Law Making

CHAPTER 5

Computer-Aided Legal Policy Evaluation

The essence of decision-aiding software is that it is designed to process a set of (1) goals to be achieved, (2) alternatives for achieving them, and (3) relations between goals and alternatives, in order to choose the best alternative, combination, or resource allocation in light of the goals, alternatives, and relations. The main benefits of decision-aiding software are in accurately and quickly handling five key methodological problems in decision-making:

1. Multiple dimensions on multiple goals. This is the apples and oranges program.
2. Multiple missing information.
3. Multiple alternatives that are too many to be able to determine the effects of each one.
4. Multiple and possibly conflicting constraints.
5. The need for simplicity in drawing and presenting conclusions in spite of all that multiplicity.[1]

ADDING APPLES AND ORANGES

Decision-making problems often involve multiple goals measured on a variety of different dimensions, such as miles, hours, dollars, 1–5 attitude scales, yes-no dichotomies, etc.

Some of the ways in which multiple dimensions are handled are:

1. Multiply the apples by two if you like each apple twice as much as each orange. Then everything will be expressed in orange units.
2. Ask whether the gain in apples from choosing one alternative is worth more or less than the gain in oranges from choosing a second alternative.

3. Convert the apple units into percentages by dividing the raw scores on the apple goal by the sum of the apples, and convert the orange units into percentages by dividing the raw scores on the oranges goal by the sum of the oranges.

These methods become clearer with the concrete illustrative example of choosing between two affirmative action programs for a medical school. One program produces a lot of minority students, but treats few patients. The other program produces few minority students, but treats a lot of patients. The example is shown in table 5-1.[2]

MISSING INFORMATION

We often do not know relation scores of each alternative on each goal, and we often do not know the relative weights of the goals. The key way in which missing information is handled is to allow the user to quickly and accurately determine the effects of inserting various values for the missing information. More specific techniques include:

1. What-if analysis, whereby the computer shows what would happen if we make changes in the goals, alternatives, and/or relations.
2. Threshold analysis, whereby the computer shows for each relation score and goal weight the value that would cause a tie between the second-place alternative and the first-place alternative.
3. Convergence analysis, whereby the computer shows for each goal weight at what magnitude the goal tends to dominate the other goals such that nothing is to be gained by increasing the weight further.
4. Best-worst analysis, whereby the computer shows what the conclusion would be using values that most favor a given alternative, and then values that least favor a given alternative. The two conclusions are then averaged.

These methods become clearer with the concrete illustrative example of deciding between nuclear energy and solar energy in light of their long-term value and cost, as is shown in table 5-2.[3]

ALLOCATING RESOURCES

Decision-aiding software can help in allocating resources, as contrasted to the generally easier problem of just finding a best alternative or combination. A good way of allocating resources is to convert into percentages the raw merit scores of the objects to which the resources are to be allocated. One can then apply the percentages to the grand total available to be allocated. A good way to convert the raw scores into percentages is by dividing them by their total within the same goal in order to get part/whole percentages. Those percentages can then be summed across the goals, using a weighted sum where the goals have different weights.

Table 5-1
Four Methods for Dealing with Multidimensional Tradeoffs

POLICY	RAW SCORE INCREMENTS: Students Trained (S)	RAW SCORE INCREMENTS: Patients Treated (P)	PART/WHOLE PERCENTAGING: Students Trained w=1	PART/WHOLE PERCENTAGING: Patients Treated w=2	PART/WHOLE PERCENTAGING: Unweighted Sum	PART/WHOLE PERCENTAGING: Weighted Sum
Policy A (X_1)	30	10	60%	36%	96%	132%
Policy B (X_2)	20	18	40%	64%	104%	168%
Total (Whole)	50	28	100%	100%	200%	300%
Difference (Increment)	+ 10S >>	- 8P ?				
Threshold			W60 + 36 = W40 + 64		W*= 1.40	

POLICY	PAIRED-COMPARISON MONETIZING: Students Trained $\$Y = (S)^{.92}$	PAIRED-COMPARISON MONETIZING: Patients Treated $\$Y = (P)^{.90}$	PAIRED-COMPARISON MONETIZING: SUM	WEIGHTED RAW SCORES: Students (Expressed in Terms of Patients) W=2	WEIGHTED RAW SCORES: Patients	WEIGHTED RAW SCORES: Sum
Policy A (X_1)	\$22.85	\$ 7.94	\$30.79	60	10	70
Policy B (X_2)	\$15.74	\$13.48	\$29.22	40	18	58
Total	\$38.59	\$21.42	\$60.01	100	28	128
Threshold				W30 + 10 = W20 + 18		W*= .80

NOTES:

1. Incremental analysis has the advantage of simplicity, especially where there are only a few policies and goals. It is also applicable to variables that are nonquantitative. It involves a minimum of transforming of the raw data. It reduces the value judgment to determining whether the incremental gain of one policy is preferred over the incremental gain of a second policy.

2. Percentaging analysis has the advantage of being applicable where there are many policies and goals. It reduces the value judgment to determining the relative weight of the goals.

3. Paired-comparison monetizing tends to consider all the values of the relevant decision-makers, although their values are not disaggregated into separate components. Working with monetized variables may also be more comfortable for many people. Paired-comparison monetizing reduces the value judgments to determining at what point a set of nonmonetary benefits is equal to a quantity of dollars.

4. Weighted raw scores have the advantage of being relatively easy to apply where all the goals have tangible units like students or patients, rather than intangible units like scores on a 1-9 attitude scale, where part/whole percentaging tends to be easier to handle.

Table 5-2
Threshold Values, Insensitivity Ranges, and Change Slopes

POLICIES \ GOALS	Long-Term Value (Y_1)	Low Cost (Y_2)	WEIGHTED SUM
Nuclear (X_a)	a_1 +1 4 (3 to ∞)	a_2 +1 3 (2 to ∞)	7
Solar (X_b)	b_1 -1 5 (-∞ to 6)	b_2 -1 1 (-∞ to 2)	6
Weights	W_1 -1 1 (-∞ to 2)	W_2 +2 1 (.5 to ∞)	

NOTES:

1. The symbol in the upper left-hand corner of each cell shows (1) the identifying symbol of each relation, with the letter indicating the goal; (2) the identifying symbol of each weight, with the subscript indicating the goal to which the weight refers.
2. The number in the middle of each cell shows (1) the value of the relation on a 1 to 5 scale; (2) the value of the weight, with the least important goal having a weight of 1.
3. The number in the upper right-hand corner of each cell shows by how much the gap changes between the two alternatives being compared if the input increases by one unit.
4. The number other than infinity in parentheses in each cell is the threshold value for each input. At that value, there will be a tie in the weighted sum of the two alternatives being compared.
5. The range in parentheses in each cell is the insensitivity range. That range shows how far down and up each input can go without affecting which alternative is the winner.

Table 5-3A shows how the P/G% software can be used in an allocation problem where the bottom line consists of allocation percentages. The alternative methods shown are trials and plea bargains. Additional alternatives could be added such as diversions or dismissals. The goals shown are to reduce delay and to increase respect for the legal system. Additional goals could be added such as reducing expense and increasing the probability of innocent defendants being acquitted.

Table 5-3
Allocating Cases to Methods of Resolving

A. THE RAW DATA

	Delay (Days)	Respect (0-10 Scale)
Trials	120	6
Pleas	30	2
	150	8

B. THE TRANSFORMED RAW DATA

	Speed (1/Days)	Respect (-5 to +5)
Trials	1/120 or .00833	+1
Pleas	1/30 or .03333	-3
	5/120 or .04166	-2

C. THE PART/WHOLE PERCENTAGES

	Speed P/W%	Respect P/W%	Aggregate P/W%	Allocation %
Trials	20%	100%	120%	60%
Pleas	80%	0%	80%	40%
	100%	100%	200%	100%

Table 5-3 (continued)

D. THE WEIGHTED P/W%'s

	Speed w = 1	Respect w = 2	Aggregate P/W%	Allocation %
Trials	20%	200%	220%	73%
Pleas	80%	0%	80%	27%
	100%	200%	300%	100%

NOTES:

1. The raw data are hypothetical, but realistic. The object is to decide on the optimum allocation of cases to trials versus pleas in light of the facts that (1) trials receive a score of 120 days on delay and pleas 30 days, and (2) trials receive a score of 6 on respect and pleas a score of 2.

2. Transforming the raw data involves (1) calculating the reciprocals for the raw score of the negative goals of delay; (2) recalculating the raw scores on respect using a scale that shows absolute zero. If N equals absolute zero, then subtract N from each of the original raw scores. For example, on a 0--10 scale the number 5 (or below) might be absolute zero.

3. Calculating the correct part/whole percentages involves (1) calculating the part/whole percentages on the inverted negative goal; (2) giving zero% to any alternative that has a negative raw score, then calculating the part/whole percentages for the other alternatives.

4. Calculating the allocation percentages involves (1) multiplying the part/whole percentages in each column by the relative weight of the goal to which the column pertains; (2) summing the weighted part/whole percentages across each alternative; (3) dividing those aggregate percentages by the sum of the weights. The results are the allocation percentages for each alternative or budget category.

The raw data show that in our hypothetical court system, the average trial takes 120 days, and the average plea bargain takes 30 days from arrest to disposition. The data also show that the trials alternative receives a respect score of 6 on a 0–10 scale in a rough survey of attorneys, and pleas receives a score of only 2. It would not be meaningful to add 120 days to a respect score of 6 to get an overall score for trials because (1) delay is measured in days, and respect is measured on a 0–10 scale, necessitating a common measure in order to be able to add these scores, (2) delay is a negative goal where high scores are undesirable, and (3) a score of 2 on respect may be a negative score such that each additional plea bargain decreases respect for the system.

To deal with those problems, we do the following:

1. The delay scores are converted into part/whole percentages by dividing each score by the sum of the delay column, but after inverting for the negative goal.

2. The inversion is done by working with the reciprocals of the delay scores. That means working with 1/120 and 1/30 rather than 120 and 30. Doing so preserves the fact that trials are four times as bad as pleas on the goal of delay, while making the pleas score higher than the trials score. We are then working with speed rather than delay as a goal. Speed should be given a weight of +1 if delay has previously been given a weight of −1.
3. The respect scores are also converted into part/whole percentages by dividing each score by the sum of the respect column, but after adjusting for the fact that pleas may have a negative score.
4. That means determining the value of a true zero on the 0–10 scale and subtracting that value from the 0–10 scores. Thus, if a 5 is the separation point between positive scores and negative scores, then a 6 is the equivalent of a +1, and a 2 is the equivalent of a −3. Those transformed numbers are shown in table 5-3B.

Table 5-3C converts the transformed data into part/whole percentages. Pleas is given 0% on respect because one would not want to allocate anything more than the minimum possible if pleas has a negative score and if more respect is the only criterion. We can now add across the percentages and obtain an aggregate percent of 120% for trials and 80% for pleas. We then divide by 2 to bring the sum of those percentages down to 100% because we cannot allocate more than 100%.

Table 5-3D takes into consideration that respect is considered to be twice as important as speed. That means multiplying the percentages in the respect column by 2. The new aggregate percentages are then 220% and 80%. We then divide by 3 or the sum of the weights to obtain the allocation percentages of 73% and 27%. Not all allocation problems involve multiple dimensions, negative goals, or negative scores. If, however, one can follow the allocation analysis of table 5-3, then one can deal with simpler allocation problems.[4]

ADJUSTING FOR CONSTRAINTS

Decision-aiding software can help in dealing with constraints that require minimums or maximums on the alternatives or the goals or other conditions that must be met, regardless of how high the scores are of an alternative on the goals.

The main ways in which constraints are handled are:

1. The constraints can be met *before* one allocates scarce resources or determines the relation scores. Doing so tends to result in giving an alternative more than it is entitled to where it only deserves the minimum. That result cannot occur if adjustments are made *after* allocating so as to bring alternatives up to their minimums.
2. The best way of resolving conflicting constraints is to expand the total benefits available or reduce the total costs to be imposed so that all the constraints can be satisfied simultaneously. If that is not possible, then resolve conflicting constraints by developing compromises that satisfy each constraint in proportion to its importance. Other less-desirable alternatives involve partially satisfying all constraints equally, or fully satisfying certain constraints in the order of their priority.

Adjusting for constraints is illustrated with the same problem as allocating a budget to police and courts in light of crime reduction and fair procedure (see table 5-4). The constraints specify minimum amounts to the police and the courts, but those minimums may add to more than the total budget available. A good way to adjust to satisfy the equity constraints with two, three, and four budget categories is as follows:

1. With two budget categories, suppose category A is below its minimum and category B is above its minimum. After allocating in proportion to their aggregate scores, then give category A its minimum. Give the rest of the total budget to category B.
2. With three budget categories, suppose A is below its minimum and B and C are above their minimums. Then give A its minimum. Divide the rest of the total budget between B and C in proportion to their aggregate scores.
3. With four or more budget categories, one can reason by analogy to the three-category situation. No matter how many budget categories are below their minimums in the initial optimizing, give them their minimums and then remove them from further allocating. The remainder of the total budget then gets divided proportionately among the other budget categories.[5]

SIMPLICITY OF ANALYSIS

Decision-aiding software that is based on multicriteria decision-making can greatly simplify the analysis of a variety of decision-aiding problems that have traditionally used more complicated and often less valid methods, such as arrow diagrams, payoff matrices, decision trees, optimum level curves, indifference curves, functional curves, and multiobjective programming. The essence of MCDM software is that it works with a table, matrix, or spreadsheet with alternatives on the rows, evaluative criteria on the columns, relation scores in the cells, and a summation column at the right showing the overall score or allocation percent of each alternative.

A good illustration of the simplicity of MCDM and P/G% software is the decision whether to take away or leave an abused child with the child's family. Table 5-5A shows the problem analyzed with a traditional payoff matrix, and table 5-5B shows the problem analyzed with a P/G% spreadsheet table. Both approaches show the alternatives on the rows. The payoff matrix shows contingent events and possibly their probabilities on the columns, whereas the P/G% approach shows goals and their relative weights on the columns. The payoff matrix shows relative payoffs in the cells, whereas the P/G% approach shows relation scores on a 1–5 scale in the cells between the alternatives and the goals. The payoff matrix shows benefits minus costs on the right side with each element discounted by the probability of its occurring, whereas the P/G% approach shows the weighted summation scores for each alternative at the right side.

Both approaches are applied to the same empirical situation in table 5-5. The payoff matrix tends to lead to a decision to take the child away because the probability of severe abuse is likely to be greater than the threshold probability. The P/G% approach leads to a closer decision because it emphasizes multiple criteria of avoiding abuse, preserving family love, and saving the taxpayer cost. One could argue that those three criteria are taken into consideration in the relative payoffs in the cells of the payoff matrix. However, by lumping all three criteria together, their separate existences and sensitivity values get overwhelmed by the criterion of avoiding abuse. The payoff matrix may thus lead to results that are less valid in terms of the decision-maker's goals than the P/G% approach.

The advantages of the P/G% approach over a payoff matrix include:

1. P/G% can explicitly consider any number of criteria such as the three shown above.
2. P/G% can explicitly consider any number of alternatives, such as take away to an institution, take away to a foster home, take away to a relative's home, leave with counseling, or leave without counseling.
3. Being able to consider multiple criteria and multiple alternatives makes the P/G approach more validly in conformity with reality, and not just a simplistic abstraction.
4. P/G% is also simpler with its 1–5 scales, weighted criteria, computerized threshold analysis, and logical way of analyzing a problem in terms of alternatives, criteria, and relations.[6]

SOME CONCLUSIONS

As mentioned at the beginning of this chapter, the main benefits of the decision-aiding software are its accuracy and speed in handling the five key methodological problems in evaluation analysis. To fully appreciate the relevance of the software, it is necessary actually to use it. We can, however, briefly describe how the software applies to each problem.

On the matter of *multiple dimensions* on multiple goals:

1. In comparing any two alternatives, one can show for each goal the incremental gain of the better alternative over the other alternative. This can be more easily done by putting the goals on the rows and the two alternatives on the columns since the software subtracts across the rows. One can then pick the alternative that has the more desired set of increments.
2. One can specify the importance of each goal relative to the least important goal. Those weights can consider both importance and the nature of the measurement units where raw scores are used.
3. The software is capable of working with the relations either as raw scores or part/whole percentages by exercising an option on the data management menu.

On the matter of *missing information:*

1. The software can do what-if analysis by allowing the user to change any of the inputs and quickly see how those changes affect the bottom-line conclusion.

Table 5-4
Data for Illustrating Equity Constraints and Adjustments to Satisfy Them

ALLOCATION CRITERIA / BUDGET CATEGORIES	RAW SCORES		TRANSFORMED SCORES			ALLOCATION RESULTS				
	Crime Reduction (1)	Fair Procedure (2)	Aggregate Scores (3)	Allocation Percentages 2-way (4a)	Allocation Percentages 3-way (4b)	Optimum Allocations 2-way (5a)	Optimum Allocations 3-way (5b)	Minimums (6)	Adjusted Allocations 2-way (7a)	Adjusted Allocations 3-way (7b)
POLICE	2.00	1.00	3.00	43%	39%	$214	$195	$240	$240 (Min.)	$240 (Min.)
COURTS	1.00	3.00	4.00 7.00	57%	51%	$286	$255	$ 80	$260 (100% of $260)	$218 (84% of $260)
CORRECTIONS	.50	.25	.75	N/A	10%	N/A	$ 50	$ 40	N/A	$ 42 (16% of $260)
Totals	—	—	7.75	100%	100%	$500	$500	$360	$500	$500

NOTES:

1. Optimizing can be done first, and then adjustments are made to satisfy the constraints if they have not been satisfied already. In other words, if we optimally allocate without considering the minimums, we obtain what is shown in column 5a (for two budget categories) and column 5b (for three budget categories). If we then consider the minimums, we obtain what is shown in columns 7a and 7b.

2. There is $500 available to be allocated this year. There was $450 available to be allocated last year. N/A = Not Applicable.

3. The minimums in column 6 are equal to 80% of last year's budget. Last year, the police received $300, the courts received $100, and corrections received $50.

4. The numbers in columns 1 and 2 are based on a rough survey of a small sample of some people who are knowledgeable about the criminal justice system.

5. The formulas for the numbers in the other columns are:

   (3) = (1) + (2) (4a) = (3)/7.00 (4b) = (3)/7.75 (5a) = (4a) ($500)
   (5b) = (4b) ($500) (6) = 80% of last year's allocation

6. The best way to make the adjusted allocations of 7a and 7b is to give any budget category its minimum (from column 6). If its optimum (from column 5a or 5b) falls below its minimum, then divide the residue among the other budget categories in proportion to their aggregate scores (from column 3).

Table 5-5
Comparing a Payoff Matrix with P/G% on Decision-Making Under Conditions of Risk (e.g., deciding whether to take away or leave an abused child)

A. THE PAYOFF MATRIX

	SEVERE SUBSEQUENT ABUSE: Would Not Occur	SEVERE SUBSEQUENT ABUSE: Would Occur	Benefits		Costs
TAKE AWAY	a -50	b +100	(P)(100)	-	(1-P)(50)
LEAVE	c +50	d -100			

B. THE P/G% APPROACH

	Avoid Abuse (w=2)	Preserve Family Love (w=1)	Save Taxpayer Cost (w=1)	Weighted Sum
TAKE AWAY	4	2	2	12
LEAVE	2	4	4	12

NOTES:

1. The cell entries in Table 5-5A are arrived at by asking the decision-makers the following questions:
   (1) Of the four possible occurrences, which ones are desirable (marked plus), and which ones are undesirable (marked minus)?
   (2) Of the undesirable occurrences, which one is the most undesirable (marked minus 100)?
   (3) How much more undesirable is the most undesirable occurrence in comparison to the less undesirable occurrence (marked minus 50 to show that cell d is twice as bad as cell a)?

2. With that information, one can determine the threshold probability as follows:
   (1) At the threshold, the discounted benefits equal the discounted costs (i.e., $100P$ = 50 minus $50P$).
   (2) The solution for P in that equation is $P^* = d/(a + d)$ or $P^* = 100/(50 + 100) = .33$.
   (3) That means that if the probability is greater than .33 that there will be severe subsequent abuse, then the child should be taken away.

3. The scoring of each alternative in Table 5-5B on each criterion is on a 1--5 scale, where 5 = highly conducive to the goal, 4 = mildly conducive, 3 = neither conductive nor adverse. 2 = mildly adverse to the goal, and 1 = highly adverse. Decimal scores can be given between these numbers where appropriate.

4. Avoiding abuse is considered to be twice as important as preserving whatever family love might exist or saving taxpayer cost.

Table 5–5 (continued)

5. By considering multiple criteria rather than emphasizing the probability of severe subsequent abuse, the decision is much closer and more dependent on the specific facts or scores on the first two criteria than on a general threshold probability.

6. If the criteria are given equal weight, then leaving the child wins by 10 points to 8 points. The threshold or tie-causing values of the weights are 2, 0, and 0. The threshold values of the relation scores are then 6, 4, 4, 0, 2, and 2, reading across the matrix. There will be a tie if any of those values are substituted for any weight or relation score when each goal is started with a weight of 1.

---

2. The main menu gives the user an option to do a threshold analysis or a convergence analysis to determine the critical values for relation scores or goal weights, above which one alternative would be better and below which another alternative would be better.
3. In specifying the criteria, one can divide each criterion into a best version and a worst version, such as the best possible cost on each alternative and the worst possible cost. The computer can then show the overall best score, the overall worst score, and the midpoint for for each alternative.
4. The software can also draw indifference curves or threshold curves showing the combination of scores on two or more variables that would lead to a tie between any two alternatives.

On the matter of *allocating resources:*

1. The user can specify the grand total available to be allocated. The program will multiply that grand total by the allocation percentages for each alternative or budget category.
2. The allocation percentages are calculated by obtaining an overall score for each alternative and then dividing each overall score by the sum of the scores in order to obtain part/whole allocation percentages.
3. The program can transform the raw scores by determining their reciprocals where negative goals are involved, or by subtracting the value of absolute zero from each raw score where negative scores are involved. Those transformations may, however, be easier to do with a calculator, and then just enter the results into the data matrix.

On the matter of *adjusting for constraints:*

1. The user can enter minimum constraints for each alternative, and the program can guarantee they will be met in whatever allocation is done. A better approach though would be to optimize ignoring the constraints, and then make adjustments for any alternative or criterion that violates its minimum or maximum.
2. The ease of doing what-if analysis facilitates resolving conflicting constraints and conflicting decision-makers by enabling both sides or a mediator to try different alternatives, criteria, weights, constraints, relations, and other inputs until a mutually satisfying solution is found.

On the matter of *simplicity:*

1. The essence of the software is the idea of putting alternatives on the rows of a spreadsheet matrix, criteria and weights on the columns, relations in the cells, and overall scores for the alternatives in the right-hand column.
2. That system is in conformity with a great deal of systematic decision-making, as indicated by the popularity of spreadsheet software, payoff matrices, decision trees, and other formats that can be reduced to a decision matrix.

This kind of evaluation analysis could be done with pencil and paper or even implicitly in one's mind. The analysis is, however, substantially facilitated by the availability of the software and microcomputers. The software encourages thinking more explicitly about evaluation problems without confining the user to quantitatively measured variables. It facilitates creativity by allowing changes to be so easily made. We may be at the advent of new ways of thinking about program evaluation, policy analysis, and decision-making to the benefit of the decision-makers and those who are affected by their decisions.[7]

OTHER EXAMPLES

This chapter has used a variety of examples from legal policy disputes or public-sector decision-making such as (1) comparing affirmative action programs, (2) comparing energy sources, (3) comparing ways of resolving criminal cases, (4) allocating scarce budget resources to the police and the courts, and (5) deciding whether to take an abused child away from its family. Examples 1, 2, and 5 involve choosing among discrete alternatives, whereas examples 3 and 4 involve allocating a continuum of resources. The energy example comes closest to developing prospective legislation. The other examples tend to be more in the nature of individual decision-making situations.

Chapters 11, 12, and 13 provide a variety of examples dealing with legal policy evaluation including:

1. Deciding among the marketplace, government subsidies, litigation, regulation, and government ownership as alternative and supplementary means for protecting consumers without depressing business productivity or unduly burdening the taxpayer (chapter 11).
2. Deciding among rent control, high-rise public housing, low-rise housing, rent subsidies, public housing condominiums, and mortgage subsidies as alternative and supplementary means for protecting consumers without depressing business productivity or unduly burdening the taxpayer (chapter 11).
3. Deciding among various divorce systems, including no divorces allowed, adultery divorces only, physical cruelty required, mental cruelty, or incompatibility without fault (chapter 11).
4. Deciding among various tort liability systems, including contributory negligence, comparative negligence, no-fault add-on, or pure no-fault (chapter 11).

5. Deciding among alternative and supplementary ways of reducing crime, such as decreasing legal technicalities, increasing the professionalism of criminal justice personnel, hardening crime targets, changing peer-group values, increasing sentence length, and increasing the lost legitimate opportunities as a result of committing crimes (chapter 12).
6. Deciding whether to have constitutional review ultimately in the hands of the chief executive, the parliament, the supreme court, or a combination (chapter 12).
7. Deciding on appropriate legislation for dealing with unemployment and inflation, including doing nothing, changing the workings of the federal reserve banking system, changing the workings of taxing and spending within the national budget, job creation, price-wage control, tax reductions accompanied by reductions in domestic spending, or quid-pro-quo incentives to business accompanied by reductions in defense spending (chapter 12).
8. Deciding among alternative forms of arms control legislation or treaties, including first-strike development, arms buildup, bilateral reduction, bilateral freeze, unilateral freeze, or unilateral reduction (chapter 12).
9. Deciding whether to provide right to counsel in all criminal cases, only felony cases, or only capital cases and at all stages, or exclude pretrial and posttrial (chapter 13).
10. Deciding on possible modifications to the civil jury system such as allowing less than 12 jurors, allowing less than unanimous decisions, and requiring the plaintiff to pay to have a civil jury (chapter 13).
11. Even the private practice applications lend themselves to legal policy problems such that one could talk about legislation for (1) dividing partnership profits, (2) allocating estates, (3) resolving disputes within divorces over property and children, (4) controlling what factors can be used to establish liability or damages in a civil case, (5) controlling what factors can be used to establish guilt or sentence length in a criminal case, (6) implementing Supreme Court decisions in the equal protection field, (7) defining proper procedure in administrative agency proceedings, (8) spelling out how the United States should participate in international disputes, (9) making plea bargaining the equivalent of a binding or nonbinding contract, and (10) establishing the circumstances (if any) under which statements made in negotiating damages can be subsequently used in trial (see the private practice sections of chapters 11, 12, and 13).

NOTES

1. For further details on optimizing in terms of goals, policies, relations, and conclusions, see S. Nagel, *Public Policy: Goals, Means, and Methods* (New York: St. Martin's, 1984), and Edward Quade, *Analysis for Public Decisions* (Amstrdam: North Holland, 1982). These two books could be referred to for any of the eight principles. The first book uses numerous legal examples. Other books that take an optimizing perspective toward law include Richard Posner, *Economic Analysis of Law* (Boston: Little, Brown, 1977), and Gordon Tullock, *The Logic of the Law* (New York: Basic Books, 1971).

2. On dealing with nonmonetary benefits and costs, see Mark Thompson, *Benefit-Cost Analysis for Program Evaluation* (Beverly Hills, Calif.: Sage, 1980), and Edward Gramlich, *Benefit-Cost Analysis of Government Programs* (Englewood Cliffs, N.J.: Prentice-Hall, 1981), although they may overemphasize monetizing nonmonetary

variables, rather than working with them in their original form or close to it. Also see S. Nagel, "Nonmonetary Variables in Benefit-Cost Evaluation," 7 *Evaluation Review* 37-64 (1983), and S. Nagel, "Economic Transformations of Nonmonetary Benefits in Program Evaluation," in James Catterall (ed.), *Economic Evaluation of Public Programs* (San Francisco: Jossey-Bass, 1985).

3. On dealing with missing information without having to gather additional information, see Mark Thompson, *Decision Analysis for Program Evaluation* (Cambridge, Mass.: Ballinger, 1982), and Clifford Harris, *The Break-Even Handbook* (Englewood Cliffs, N.J.: Prentice-Hall, 1978). Also see S. Nagel, "Dealing with Unknown Variables in Policy/Program Evaluation," 6 *Evaluation and Program Planning* 7-18 (1983), and S. Nagel, "New Varieties of Sensitivity Analysis," 9 *Evaluation Review* 772-779 (1985).

4. On diverse methods for dealing with the multiplicity of alternatives in allocation problems, see Philip Kotler, *Marketing Decision Making: A Model Building Approach* (New York: Holt, 1971) (calculus and statistical analysis); Claude McMillan, *Mathematical Programming: An Introduction to the Design and Application of Optimal Decision Machines* (New York: John Wiley, 1970) (reiterative guessing and operations research); and S. Nagel, *Policy Evaluation: Making Optimum Decisions* (New York: Praeger, 1982) (variations on part/whole percentaging in chapters 10-13). Also see S. Nagel, "Optimally Allocating Federal Money to Cities," 5 *Public Budgeting and Finance* 39-50 (1985).

5. On dealing with constraints in public policy analysis in general, see Nagel, *Public Policy,* especially the chapters on equity, effectiveness, human rights, discretion, economic structure, government structure, political feasibility, and ethical constraints. On quantitative constraints in allocation problems, see "Allocation Logic" in Nagel, *Policy Evaluation,* where the problem of allocating to police, courts, and corrections is also discussed.

6. On the matter of simplicity in drawing and presenting conclusions in evaluation analysis see S. Nagel, "Comparing Multi-Criteria Decision Making and P/G% with Traditional Optimizing," in Yoshikazu Sawaragi (ed.), *Multiple-Criteria Decision Making* (Berlin: Springer-Verlag, 1987) and "Simplifying Basic Methods" in Nagel, *Public Policy.* On the subject of taking away abused children, see "Neglect" in George Cooper et al., *Law and Poverty: Cases and Materials* (St. Paul: West, 1973).

7. On Policy/Goal Percentaging and the P/G% software, see Benjamn Radcliff, "Multi-Criteria Decision Making: A Survey of Software," 4 *Social Science Microcomputer Review* 38-55 (1986); S. Nagel, "P/G% Analysis: An Evaluating-Aiding Program," 9 *Evaluation Review* 209-214 (1985); and S. Nagel, "A Microcomputer Program for Dealing with Evaluation Problems," 9 *Evaluation and Program Planning* 159-168 (1987). On the applicability of P/G% to all five analytic problems, see S. Nagel, *Evaluation Analysis with Microcomputers* (Greenwich, Conn.: JAI Press, 1989).

CHAPTER 6

Computer-Aided Advocacy

This chapter will describe how microcomputers can aid in the appellate and trial advocacy work of public defenders and legal services lawyers.

Computer-aided advocacy refers to using a computer (especially a personal computer) to aid in determining what to advocate on appeal or in trial in order to increase the probability of victory for one's client. The idea of computer-aided advocacy (CAA) is a law variation on computer-aided manufacturing and computer-aided design, which are becoming increasingly important to the U.S. economy. Computer-aided advocacy is a substantially higher level of computer usage than litigation support, which usually refers to a system of information retrieval for handling litigation matters that involve many separate items. CAA should also be distinguished from document-drafting software, which incorporates decisions as to what to advocate into a well-typed brief by drawing upon a brief bank of related arguments.

The most appropriate software for computer-aided advocacy is probably software that enables one to process a set of (1) goals the decision-makers might have for reaching a decision, (2) the alternative positions they might take regarding the overall issue or subissues in the case, and (3) the relations between each position and each goal showing how conducive or adverse each position is to each goal. An example of such software is Policy/Goal Percentaging.[1]

THE *RODRIGUEZ* CASE: AID FOR LOW-INCOME SCHOOLS

The Inputs to a Spreadsheet Brief

Table 6-1 provides an example of a case brief using the P/G% software. The case is *San Antonio v. Rodriguez,* 411 U.S. Supreme Court 1 (1973). This landmark case in the field of legal services dealt with the extent to which a state is

Table 6-1
Appellate Advocacy in *San Antonio v. Rodriguez*

A. THE ALTERNATIVES AND THE CRITERIA

Alternative	Previous Outcome	Criterion	Meas.Unit	Weight
NO EQUALITY REQD.	YES	1 EDUCATED POP.	1-3	1.00
= $ PER STUDENT	NO	2 -DISCONTENT		1.00
MIN. $ PER STUDENT	NO	3 -DOWNGRADING		1.00
HIGH $ PER STUDENT	NO	4 ADMIN.EASE		1.00
OTHER	?	5 CONSIST.W/CASES		1.00
		6 -EXPENSE		1.00

B. THE SCORES OF THE ALTERNATIVES ON THE CRITERIA

	EDUCATED	-DISCON	-DOWNGR	ADMIN.EA	CONSIST.	EXPENSE
NO EQUALITY REQ	1.00	1.00	3.00	3.00	2.00	3.00
= $ PER STUDENT	2.00	2.00	1.00	1.00	2.00	2.00
MIN.$ PER STUDE	2.00	2.00	2.00	1.00	2.00	1.50
HIGH $ PER STUD	3.00	3.00	2.00	1.00	1.00	1.00

C. THE TOTAL SCORES OF THE ALTERNATIVES

Alternative	Combined Rawscores	Previous Outcome
NO EQUALITY REQD.	13.00	YES
= $ PER STUDENT	10.00	NO
MIN.$ PER STUDENT	10.50	NO
HIGH $ PER STUDENT	11.00	NO

D. WHAT IT WOULD TAKE TO BRING THE SECOND PLACE ALTERNATIVE UP TO FIRST PLACE

	NO EQUALIT	MIN.$ PER	Weight
EDUCATED POP.	−1.50	4.50	3.500
- DISCONTENT	−1.50	4.50	3.500
- DOWNGRADING	0.50	4.50	−1.500
ADMIN.EASE	0.50	3.50	−0.250
CONSIST.W/CASES	−0.50	4.50	??
- EXPENSE	0.50	4.00	−0.667

constitutionally required to help equalize expenditures per student across school districts within the state. This type of brief could be prepared after the case has been decided in order to plan future advocacy strategy. The brief could also be prepared while the case is still in process in order to plan better what ideas to emphasize.

Table 6-1A of the brief shows that the Supreme Court was faced with (or could be faced with) the four basic alternatives of (1) no equality required, (2) equal expenditures per student, (3) a minimum amount of expenditures per student but otherwise allowing for inequality, or (4) a requirement of equality but at a high level. The first part of the brief also shows that the court answered yes to the first alternative (or could answer yes), but no to the others.

The right side of table 6-1A shows there are about six relevant criteria, including (1) having an educated population, (2) decreasing discontent due to educational disparities, (3) avoiding the downgrading of affluent schools, (4) administrative ease, (5) consistency with prior cases, and (6) avoiding heavy taxpayer expense. All six goals seem quite reasonable for the Supreme Court to have, although not with equal importance.

Table 6-1B of the brief shows how each alternative scores on each criterion using a simple 1–3 scale, where 3 = conducive to the goal, 1 = neither conducive nor adverse, and 1 = adverse to the goal. Table 6-1C of the brief shows the combined raw scores for each alternative using the 1–3 scoring. The alternative with the highest combined raw score is "no equality required," which is the alternative that the Supreme Court adopted.

Converting a Loser into a Winner

Table 6-1D of the brief is the threshold analysis. It shows what it would take to bring the second-place alternative up to first place. There was a gap of 2.50 points between first and second place on the combined raw scores. That gap would be eliminated if the "no equality" alternative were to drop by 2.50 points on any of the six criteria. That would be too big a drop on any one criterion since these criteria cannot go below 1.00. The gap would also be eliminated if the second-place alternative of having a "minimum number of dollars per student" were to increase by 2.50 points on any of the six criteria. That would be too big an increase on any one criterion since these criteria cannot go above 3.00. The gap could also be eliminated if the Supreme Court were to place substantially more weight on having an educated population or on decreasing discontent due to educational inequalities. Those are two areas that the advocates of a minimum-dollars position should emphasize. The gap would be eliminated if the other criteria were given negative weights, which is unlikely. Changing the weight would not help with regard to consistency with prior cases, since both alternatives score the same on that criterion.

In computer-aided advocacy, the most helpful computer output is information like that shown at the end of table 6-1 with regard to what it would take to bring a second-place or other alternative up to first place. The most useful part of that threshold analysis is generally how the relative weights of the criteria or goals would have to change in order to make the second-place alternative into a winner. That is so because the relative importance of the criteria is more subjective and more subject to change through convincing advocacy than the relations between the alternatives and the criteria.

One might note that high dollars per student came in second in the initial analysis shown in table 6-1C. High dollars per student, however, does not do so well when compared with no equality required because high dollars per student does so poorly on avoiding extra expense. In other words, the third-place alternative does better on the threshold or sensitivity analysis than the second-place alternative. The third-place alternative has the economic feasibility that the second-place alternative lacks. It also has the political feasibility that may be lacking in the alternative of equal dollars per student. That alternative would probably mean bringing down the influential school districts that spend high dollars per student. For a third-place alternative to do better than a second-place alternative in capturing first place is like a third-place baseball team that is physically fit doing better in capturing first place (at the end of the season) than the second-place team that has a number of injured players.

What incremental benefits does this kind of briefing have over more traditional briefing? The benefits include:

1. Thinking more explicitly about the alternatives that were or are available to the court, rather than working with just what the court defined as the issue or the adopt-reject decision.
2. Thinking more explicitly about the goals that might be achieved by whatever decision is reached.
3. Recognizing that consistency with prior cases as a goal is generally not enough to explain court decisions, especially decisions on new issues.
4. Seeing more clearly from an appellate advocacy perspective the position that might be most meaningful to encourage the court to adopt.[2]

THE *DANDRIDGE* CASE: AID FOR LARGE BUT POOR FAMILIES

Background on the *Dandridge* Case

In addition to losing the *Rodriguez* case, the Legal Services Program in 1970 also lost the landmark *Dandridge v. Williams* case, 397 U.S. 471 (1970). Both cases together represented a turning point in the decisions of the Supreme Court toward poverty law cases. The court had previously decided a number of important decisions in favor of the Legal Services Program such as (1) *King v. Smith,* 392 U.S. 309 (1968), which held that merely being found with a man in the house was not enough to deprive a family of welfare benefits; (2) *Shapiro v. Thompson,* 394 U.S. 618 (1969), which held that one could establish residency for welfare and related purposes without having to live in a place for an extended period of time such as a year; and (3) *Goldberg v. Kelly,* 397 U.S. 254 (1970), which held that welfare recipients were entitled to at least minimum due process in a termination case, including the right to have notice, present witnesses, cross-examine accusers, and have a judge who was not the complaining welfare worker.

The turnaround in the Supreme Court's decisions of 1973 is often attributed to changes in the court personnel, especially Chief Justice Burger replacing Chief Justice Warren. That, however, may be questionable since in 1972 Chief Justice Burger wrote the opinion in the *Argersinger* case, 407 U.S. 25 (1972), which held that indigent defendants were entitled to court-appointed counsel in any criminal case no matter how minor so long as there was a possibility of serving as much as one day in jail. An alternative explanation is that the Legal Services Program brought first the cases that were easy to win in the late 1960s (like *King, Shapiro,* and *Goldberg*), as contrasted to *Rodriguez* and *Dandridge.* Another at least partial explanation might be that the Legal Services Program became overly confident and a bit sloppy by late 1970 and lost the *Rodriguez* and *Dandridge* cases partly through bad appellate advocacy.

The *Rodriguez* case has already been discussed with regard to how advocating the alternative of a minimum number of dollars per student may have been a winning position at the Supreme Court, as contrasted to advocating that students in poor schools should be brought up to the level of the most-well-funded students in the state. The *Dandridge* case involved a related failure to present an acceptable alternative and a resulting total loss for the position of the Legal Services Program.

Inputs to the *Dandridge* Case

Table 6-2 in abbreviated form shows the three alternative positons that could have been argued at the Supreme Court. The Legal Services Program argued that if the family allowance for three children is $300 a month, then for four children it should be $400 a month, and $500 for five children, and so on with $100 for each successive child. The State of Maryland argued there should be a maximum grant of approximately $300 per family, regardless of how many children there are, even though the maximum is reached with only about three children. The Legal Services Program (LSP) justified its position by claiming that this was a blatant denial of equal protection because the third child in the family would get an extra $100 and the fourth child would get nothing, which does sound rather arbitrary. The State of Maryland, however, justified its position by claiming that with three children, they average $100 apiece. With four children, they average $75 apiece. That means the fourth child is getting about $75, rather than nothing. The state of Maryland further claimed that children are cheaper by the dozen, and that it makes sense that with each successive child the amount of additional family allowance should go down.

The position that was never argued is that the increment should go down with each successive child, given economies of larger-scale operation, but not down to zero. The LSP position was that it should not go down at all. The Maryland position was that it should in effect go down to nothing since a family of four children gets nothing more than a family of three. A logical alternative position would be that if a family of three children gets $300, then a family of four children should not get $400, but likewise they should not get merely $300. Instead they should get about $350. That alternative recognizes that if three children average $100 apiece in a three-child family, then four children should average less than $100 apiece in a four-child family. The figure of $350 means they will be averaging $87.50 apiece, which is between the $100 asked for by LSP and the $75 asked for by the state.

Table 6-2
Appellate Advocacy in *Dandridge v. Maryland*

A. THE ALTERNATIVE POSITIONS AND THE CRITERIA FOR EVALUATING THEM

Alternative	Previous Outcome
1 MAXIMUM GRANT	APPROVED
2 PROPORTION.GRANT	REJECTED
3 DIM.RETURNS GRANT	-PRESENT

Criterion	Meas.Unit	Weight
1 -TAXPAYER BURDEN	1-5 SCALE	1.00
2 MIN.FOOD ETC.		1.00
3 CONSISTENCY CASES		1.00
4 ECONOMIES/SCALE		1.00
5 -ADMIN.BURDEN		1.00

B. THE 1-5 SCORING OF THE ALTERNATIVES ON THE CRITERIA

	-TAXPAYE	MIN.FOOD	CONSISTE	ECONOMIE	-ADMIN.B
MAXIMUM GRANT	5.00	1.00	4.00	1.00	3.00
PROPORTION.GRAN	1.00	5.00	2.00	1.00	3.00
DIM.RETURNS GRA	3.00	3.00	3.00	5.00	2.00

C. THE OVERALL SCORES OF EACH ALTERNATIVE

Alternative	Combined Rawscores	Previous Outcome
1MAXIMUM GRANT	14.00	APPROVED
2PROPORTION.GRANT	12.00	REJECTED
3DIM.RETURNS GRANT	16.00	-PRESENT

D. BRINGING THE MAXIMUM GRANT POSITION UP TO THE LEVEL OF THE DIMINISHING RETURNS POSITION

	MAXIMUM GR	DIM.RETURN	Weight
-TAXPAYER BURDEN	7.00	1.00	2.000
MIN.FOOD ETC.	3.00	1.00	0.000
CONSISTENCY CASES	6.00	1.00	3.000
ECONOMIES/SCALE	3.00	3.00	0.500
-ADMIN.BURDEN	5.00	0.00	3.000

The second part of table 6-2A shows some of the criteria that were explicitly or implicitly mentioned by the Supreme Court in deciding between the two alternatives of the proportionate grant system advocated by LSP and the maximum grant position advocated by Maryland. The criteria are (1) minimize the taxpayer burden; (2) provide at least a minimum amount of food, shelter, and clothing to dependent children; (3) preserve consistency with past cases; (4) recognize economies of scale; and (5) minimize the burden on public administrators.

Table 6-2B shows how each of the three alternatives score on each of the five criteria using a 1–5 scale. Under such a scale, a 5 means highly conducive to the goal or criterion, a 4 means mildly conducive, a 3 means neither conducive nor adverse, a 2 means mildly adverse, and a 1 means highly adverse. On the matter of minimizing taxpayer burden, the maximum grant position is clearly the best and the proportionate grant is the worst. On providing minimum food, shelter, and clothing to dependent children, the situation is reversed with the proportionate grant the best, and the maximum grant the worst.

On consistency with prior cases, the differences are not so great among the three alternatives, but the maximum grant position is probably more consistent than the proportionate grant. The Supreme Court tends to consider the equal protection clause satisfied by minimally constitutional positions, rather than requiring optimum positions. On the matter of economies of scale, diminishing returns does well, whereas the other two alternatives ignore diminishing returns. On the matter of minimizing the administrative burden, both the maximum grant and the proportionate grant score equally well at about neutral. Figuring the diminishing returns amount may require more research and analysis, although not necessarily if one simply splits the difference between the maximum grant and proportionate grant positions, as was done above.

Results of the *Dandridge* Case

Table 6-2B shows how each of the three alternatives score on each of the five rows of table 6-2B. Table 6-2C shows that when it comes to a contest between maximum grant and proportionate grant, maximum grant is likely to be the winner, which it was in the *Dandridge* case. More interesting, however, is that the alternative of a diminishing returns grant (which was not presented in the *Dandridge* case) gets more points than either of the two alternatives that were presented.

Not only is the diminishing returns grant the winner in a three-way contest, but it is also a big winner over the maximum grant position, which the Supreme Court approved in the two-way contest. The size of the win of the diminishing returns grant is not measured just by the number of points it receives more than the maximum grant position. It is also measured by observing what it would take to bring the maximum grant position up to the level of the diminishing returns position, as is shown in Table 6-2D. That table shows that for the maximum grant position to be the overall winner, one would have to do such things as consider providing minimum food to dependent children to be worth no weight whatsoever, or to consider economies of scale also to be worth virtually no weight. Table 6-2D also shows that the maximum grant position could be a winner if unreasonably high scores were given to it on the five criteria, such as giving it a score of 7 on minimizing the taxpayer burden when it already received a score of 5 on a 1–5 scale. One could also give unreasonably low scores to diminishing returns on the five criteria to make maximum grant the winner, such as perceiving that diminishing returns is highly adverse to providing dependent children with minimum food. One could also make the maximum grant position the winner if unreasonably high weights were given to minimizing the taxpayer burden, relative to providing minimum food needs and economies of scale.

Thus this analysis tends to show that the Legal Services Program quite possibly could have turned the *Dandridge* case from a total failure into a substantial success if they had thought out more carefully the alternatives available to advocate, and how those alternatives would be likely to score on the criteria that the Supreme Court might be likely to consider. Losing the *Dandridge* case not only meant establishing a bad precedent in calculating benefit levels for all public aid programs, it also tended to demoralize appellate advocacy at LSP. It may thus have had an unreasonably adverse effect on the willingness to bring future test cases before the Supreme Court on the possibly mistaken theory that the Court was not receptive to reason.[3]

THE *McCLESKEY* CASE: RACIALLY DISCRIMINATORY CAPITAL PUNISHMENT

The Alternatives, Criteria, and Relations

Table 6-3 shows an appellate advocacy analysis for the 1987 Supreme Court case of *McClesky v. Georgia,* 107 S. Ct. 1756 (1987). Table 6-3A shows the alternative positions in the case. The position approved by the Supreme Court was to allow capital punishment even though a racially discriminatory pattern might be shown. The position of the American Civil Liberties Union, the National Association for the Advancement of Colored People, and other groups opposed to capital punishment was that the presence of racial discriminaton should be a justification for abolishing capital punishment. The middle position, which was not advocated, is to disallow capital punishment for those states where a discriminatory pattern is shown beyond a certain acceptable threshold.

The discriminatory threshold could be considered as being exceeded in a state if the percentage of blacks (convicted of capital crimes who are sentenced to die) is more than 20 percentage points higher than the percentage of whites (convicted of capital crimes who are sentenced to die). For example, if a state has sentenced 50% of the convicted blacks to die and less than 30% of the convicted whites, then that threshold would be violated. The percentage threshold could be any percentage difference that the Supreme Court considers

Table 6-3
Appellate Advocacy in *McCleskey v. Georgia*

A. THE ALTERNATIVE POSITIONS AND THE CRITERIA FOR EVALUATING THEM

Alternative	Previous Outcome
1 ALLOW DISCRIM.CP	APPROVED
2 DISALOW DISCRIM.CP	-PRESENT
3 DISALLOW CP	REJECTED

Criterion	Meas.Unit	Weight
1 -HOMICIDE	1-5 SCALE	1.00
2 SEPARATE INNOCENT		1.00
3 -DELAY & COST		1.00
4 EQUALITY RACIAL		1.00
5 PUBLIC OPINION		1.00
6 PREDICTABILITY		1.00
7 -OVER PRECEDENT		1.00

B. THE 1-5 SCORING OF THE ALTERNATIVES ON THE CRITERIA

	-HOMICID	SEPARATE	-DELAY &	EQUALITY	PUBLIC O	PREDICTA	--OVER PRE
ALLOW DISCRIM.C	3.50	2.00	2.00	1.00	2.00	2.00	2.50
DISALOW DISCRIM	3.00	3.00	3.00	5.00	4.00	4.00	4.00
DISALLOW CP	2.50	4.00	4.00	4.00	2.00	3.00	2.00

C. THE OVERALL SCORES OF EACH ALTERNATIVE

Alternative	Combined Rawscores	Previous Outcome
1ALLOW DISCRIM.CP	15.00	APPROVED
2DISALOW DISCRIM.CP	26.00	-PRESENT
3DISALLOW CP	21.50	REJECTED

D. BRINGING THE ALLOWING OF DISCRIMINATORY CAPITAL PUNISHMENT UP TO THE LEVEL OF DISALLOWING ALL CAPITAL PUNISHMENT

	ALLOW DISC	DISALLOW C	Weight
-HOMICIDE	10.00	-4.00	7.500
SEPARATE INNOCENT	8.50	-2.50	-2.250
-DELAY & COST	8.50	-2.50	-2.250
EQUALITY RACIAL	7.50	-2.50	-1.167
PUBLIC OPINION	8.50	-4.50	??
PREDICTABILITY	8.50	-3.50	-5.500
-OVER PRECEDENT	9.00	-4.50	14.000

E. BRINGING THE ALLOWING OF DISCRIMINATORY CAPITAL PUNISHMENT UP TO THE LEVEL OF DISALLOWING DISCRIMINATORY CAPITAL PUNISHMENT

	DISALOW DI	ALLOW DISC	Weight
-HOMICIDE	-8.00	14.50	23.000
SEPARATE INNOCENT	-8.00	13.00	-10.000
-DELAY & COST	-8.00	13.00	-10.000
EQUALITY RACIAL	-6.00	12.00	-1.750
PUBLIC OPINION	-7.00	13.00	-4.500
PREDICTABILITY	-7.00	13.00	-4.500
-OVER PRECEDENT	-7.00	13.50	-6.333

to be too great. Perhaps 10 percentage points is too great. Perhaps 30 percentage points might be considered the threshold. The important idea is that there should be some critical difference between the percentage of blacks sentenced to die and the percentage of whites in a given state such that the Court says that difference has gone too far. Actually the key percentages to compare are not the percent of blacks sentenced to die versus the percent of whites sentenced to die, but rather the percent of defendants with white victims versus the percent of defendants with black victims. *McCleskey* found a substantially stronger discriminatory pattern based on the race of the victims than on the race of the defendants.

If the Court were to take such a position, then it would be up to the individual state that was found to have violated the threshold to decide how it would remedy that disparity. In the meantime, capital punishment would be suspended in that state. The remedy could consist of commuting the death sentences of some black defendants to life imprisonment to bring down the black percentage. In theory, the remedy could also consist of raising the white percentage. That could not be done with white defendants who had already been sentenced to life imprisonment, since resentencing would be a violation of double jeopardy. That, however, could be done with new white defendants. Doing so, though, would mean equalizing the disparity by having more capital punishment, not less, and that would probably be considered undesirable to the groups attacking capital punishment and possibly also undesirable to the sentencing authorities in the states involved.

Table 6-3A also shows the criteria that the Court may have had in mind in deciding among the alternatives presented: (1) reducing homicides, (2) separating the innocent from the guilty, (3) reducing delay and court costs, (4) promoting racial equality, (5) satisfying public opinion, (6) encouraging predictability, and (7) avoiding overly broad precedents. To begin with, we operate under the assumption that those goals have approximately equal weight although that assumption is subject to change when we see the threshold analysis that shows the effects of different weights on the relative desirability of the competing alternatives.

Table 6-3B shows how each alternative is likely to score on each criterion. For example, allowing capital punishment even with discrimination may be thought of as helping to reduce homicides although not greatly, whereas completely disallowing capital punishment would have the opposite effect. On the other hand, allowing capital punishment does tend to interfere with separating the innocent from the guilty. This is so because innocent defendants are more likely to be convicted in capital crimes where there is no victim to testify, and such a conviction would be irretrievable if implemented. Disallowing capital punishment helps reduce delay and expense of the lengthy appeal process, which capital punishment encourages. On the matter of equality, the conditional disallowance would promote more equality than total disallowance. It would also score relatively high on promoting predictability, especially predictability based on the law and the facts, regardless of the race of the defendant or the victim. Limiting the decision to states with unduly discriminatory patterns would also be in conformity with not having an overly broad precedent. The scoring indicates that public opinion would probably be opposed to both allowing discriminatory capital punishment and totally disallowing capital punishment, but might favor the conditional disallowance alternative. Even if that criterion is wrongly perceived or scored, reasonable changes in the scoring would not affect the overall scores.

The Overall Scores and the Sensitivity Analysis

As for the overall scores, the conditional disallowance alternative seems to be a clear winner. One might then ask why did it not win? The answer is largely that it was not presented. The overall scores also show that total disallowance scores higher than continuing capital punishment with racially discriminatory patterns. One might then ask why that low-scoring alternative came out the winner. The answer might be that the Court did not give equal weight to all the criteria.

Table 6-3D shows that the alternative of allowing discriminatory capital punishment will win over total disallowance if the Court gives extra weight to decreasing homicide and avoiding overly broad precedents. That may have been exactly what happened in the judges' minds in *McCleskey*. They may have been thinking that the total disallowance alternative would be unacceptable by virtue of the assumed adverse effect on decreasing homicide, and especially by virtue of the broadness of the precedent that would be established. If capital punishment were declared unconstitutional because it is administered in a racially discriminatory way, then such a precedent could possibly be used to obtain a declaration of unconstitutionality regarding all sentencing and many other forms of governmental behavior.

Table 6-3E tends to reinforce the idea that if the conditional disallowance position had been advocated, then it would have been a strong winner. Table 6-3E shows that in order to allow discriminatory capital punishment over the conditional disallowance, the Court would have to give an extremely high weight to decreasing homicide. Furthermore, the Court would have to give negative weight to such goals as separating out the innocent, reducing delay-cost, or the other goals. Those negative weights seem unlikely. Especially unlikely is the idea that the Court would perceive that disallowing discriminatory capital punishment would rate such low negative scores on the criteria, or that allowing discriminatory capital punishment would rate such high positive scores on other criteria. Those negative scores are below 1 on the 1–5 scale, and those positive scores are above 5 on the 1–5 scale.[4]

GENERAL IDEAS AND CONCLUSIONS

Comparing the Cases

There are a number of ideas that cut across these three case studies. One might first clarify some important similarities and differences between the cases. In each case, three alternative positions are discussed. One position is a highly liberal position that the Supreme Court (at least as of that point in time) was unlikely to adopt, including (1) upgrading poor schools to the quality of the richest schools, (2) providing for welfare payments at a constant amount per child regardless of the number of children, and (3) totally abolishing capital punishment because it often involves racial discrimination. A second position was a highly conservative position that the Supreme Court did adopt in all three cases, including (1) saying that the states have no obligation at all to upgrade poor schools, (2) saying the states have no obligation to provide any addiitonal money at all for an additional child beyond a certain low number of children, and (3) allowing capital punishment regardless how it might be associated with racial discrimination. The third position was left out in the advocacy in each case although it could have been a winner, including (1) saying that poor schools should be upgraded to at least a minimum level of decency, (2) saying that incremental children should receive some incremental food, shelter, and other allowance, although permissibly at a diminishing rate of increase, and (3) saying that capital punishment should be suspended in those states where the racial disparity is beyond an acceptable threshold until it is brought down to that threshold.

In *Rodriguez,* the middling position might have been a winner if it had been advocated and if the Supreme Court could have been more convinced of the importance of having an educated population and reducing the discontent that comes from having less than the average educational opportunities for one's children. In *Dandridge,* the middling position might have been a winner if it had been advocated without even having to change the Supreme Court's values, since it does seem to be an objectively more tenable position than the conservative one, although the conservative position may be more tenable than the liberal position. In *McCleskey,* the middling position might have been a winner if it had been advocated since it also seems to be objectively more tenable than either the conservative or the liberal position.

Half a Loaf As No Better Than None

On a higher level of generality, we should address ourselves to the point that pursuing the middling position is rather unambitious. Worse than unambitious, one might be able to argue in some situations that the middling position is almost worthless where one is dealing with an S-shaped takeoff curve. Under those circumstances, there is no real achievement until one gets above the takeoff point. For example, a lawyer working one, two, or three hours in developing an appellate brief may be just as much a loser as a lawyer working four or five hours because the nature of the case requires between five and ten hours' worth of work in order to be handled successfully. Thus anything at five hours or below is the equivalent of half-a-time loaf, and is equally worthless.

Possibly worse is that one might win the case by putting in a small amount of time, but win at a very low level of victory. Just winning, however, might cause a satiated feeling of accomplishment, such that one does not come back again to pursue higher and more appropriate goals, which one would have done if one had lost completely. In other words, one can argue that half a loaf is worse than none. One can especially argue that the idea (of half a loaf being better than none) is nonsense if carried to its logical extreme. At that extreme, a half a bread crumb is also considered better than none.

Benefits of Incremental Optimizing

On the other side of this issue are generally a number of arguments that are much stronger, although one does need to take into consideration the specific facts. One of the main arguments in favor of pursuing half a loaf is that if it is done in terms of successive halves, then one very soon has the whole loaf. For example, if one achieves half of whatever total achievement is in one day, then on a second day one could be at the 75% level by cutting the remaining 50% in half. On the third day, one could be at the 87.5% level by cutting the remaining 25% in half. On the fourth day, one can be over the 90% level which should generally be enough for all but the most greedy. In other words, *just* settling for a half a loaf may conceivably be worse than none. There is, however, no reason why in appellate advocacy one cannot pursue the middling position today, and then come back tomorrow to court to pursue the 75% position, and then next week the 87.5% position. In fact, that is the way the constitutional revolution has worked in the U.S. Supreme Court process. The key desegregation case of *Brown v. Board of Education* was not built in a day. Nor was right to counsel for indigent parties established with a single case. It took a series of cases starting with right to counsel in capital cases, felony cases, appellate cases, police interrogation, misdemeanor cases, and the next step will probably be civil cases.

The incremental process may sound slow-going for a middling position, and then for the middling position between the previous middling position and the top. In reality, it may work faster than going for the top all at once. There is nothing inherently slow about incrementalism. The half-life of some newly found radioactive elements is less than a second. That means those elements in effect chop themselves in half in successive choppings until they have reached the point where they cease to exist, and not even one second has gone by. Incremental court caes do not work that fast. It is quite possible, however, that if the foundation was not laid for *Brown v. Board of Education* by way of chipping off the more blatant forms of education discrimination and segregation, then we might still be trying to convince the Supreme Court to declare segregated schools unconstitutional without any prior intermediate precedents.

Even if one could succeed in going for the big win all at once, the incremental approach might be more desirable because it allows the opposition, the neutrals, and even the supporters to digest the gains in such a way as to faciliate implementation with a minimum of problems. There is learning experience at each step in the process that enables the next step to be handled better than it otherwise would have been if the next step had been the first step. Civil liberties change has proceeded in the United States through a set of eras that could not have been easily compressed. For example, the Woodrow Wilson era was the first modification from unrestrained capitalistic activity. It established the Federal Trade Commission and the Pure Food and Drug Administration, which were early forms of middle-class consumer protection. In the New Deal era of the 1930s, the rights of workers to form unions without being subject to being fired for doing so was established. In the 1960s, the rights of blacks and women were established, which could not have been so easily done without the precedents of workers' rights and consumers' rights. Indeed, the women's rights movement built to a great extent on the black civil rights movement.

A key point is that an incremental approach does not mean one has low goals. It can mean that one has very high goals but that one seeks to achieve them through a series of steps, partly to avoid the risk of going for the top all at once and winding up with nothing. Worse than that, such a defeat can be demoralizing so that one does not easily spring back to try again. If one loses when seeking a middling position, one does not lose so much and is likely to be less demoralized. This does not run contrary to the idea that it is better to set one's goals high and get only halfway there than to set one's goals low and get three-fourths of the way there. Pursuing the middling position in appellate advocacy is unambitious if that is all one wants. It is like climbing a ladder. Obviously it makes more sense to go up one rung at a time than it does to try to jump for the top rung.

Computer-Aided Advocacy and Multiple Alternatives

One point that might be especially made in the context of this chapter is that even if middling positions make sense, what value does computer-aided advocacy have? Why could one not come to the conclusion that the middling position made more sense than the extreme liberal position as an intermediate step in *Rodriguez, Dandridge,* and *McCleskey* without decision-aiding software? The answer is that anything a computer could do can probably also be done by an individual without a computer if the person wants to work long enough and hard enough at it, such as finding the 128th root of an 80-digit number. Why, though, should anybody handicap or deprive themselves of what could be a useful tool for broadening one's perspectives and for simulating the behavior of the appellate court where one is going to argue their case? Decision-aiding software that is based on a spreadsheet format and multicriteria decision-making like the software described in this chapter do encourage thinking in terms of both multiple criteria and multiple alternatives. Otherwise there is a tendency to think in terms of two alternatives—namely, the plaintiff's position and the defendant's position, or the liberal position and the conservative position—rather than three or more alternatives. Likewise there is a tendency to think in terms of one criterion in appellate advocacy, namely, consistency with the prior cases. That one criterion is not so likely to enable one advocate to win over another since both positions are likely to be reasonably consistent with the prior cases. If one position was so obviously consistent or inconsistent, the Supreme Court probably would not even grant certiorari to hear the case.

Another related point is that the demonstration of the software looks impressive only because the cases have already been decided, and that all we are seeing is hindsight in action. The answer to this is that everything shown in tables 6-1, 6-2, and 6-3 could have been done before the cases were decided. There is no information in those tables that required the cases to be decided in order to have the information. There is no question that one can do better in analyzing cases after they have been decided than before. That, however, is not the same thing as saying that one cannot do a systematic, meaningful analysis before the cases are decided. The more that is at stake, the more justification there is for going to the trouble of trying to think out what all the alternative positions might be that one could argue, and what all the criteria might be that the Court might take into consideration. Doing that should enable the appellate advocate to arrive at a better position of what alternatives to argue, what criteria to emphasize, and what perceptions of the relations between the alternatives and the criteria to try to get the Court to accept.

In spite of all that has been said above about the importance of systematic appellate advocacy, it might be noted that appellate advocacy has considerable limitations even in (and maybe especially in) the kinds of civil liberties case that were used for illustrative examples. The big limitation is that there is not much more that the Supreme Court can do with regard to broadening the interpretation of the equal protection clause of the Constitution or other civil liberties. The most blatant forms of discrimination have been declared unconstitutional or statutorily illegal regarding race, gender, class, and geography, and regarding rights that relate to voting, criminal justice, education, employment, housing, and being a consumer. The new frontiers in these areas may be mainly with regard to congressional and presidential action concerning subsidies, tax breaks, and other incentives designed to make the economy more prosperous so that blacks, women, poor people, rural people, and others will have more and better employment opportunities. They can then take better advantage of the removal of discriminatory barriers. That, however, may simply mean that in the spreadsheet analysis, one should also include alternatives relating to congressional action, not just Supreme Court action.

The spreadsheet format emphasizes multiple alternatives (rather than dichotomies) and multiple criteria (rather than single objective functions or goals). That kind of perspective can be helpful in deciding not only what position to argue in a given Supreme Court case or whether to go to Court or the legislature, but also for deciding among alternatives like (1) going through the federal courts versus the state courts; (2) deciding among alternative test cases; (3) deciding whether or not to appeal; (4) deciding whether to pursue a constitutional abuse that affects a lot of people in a small way, like pretrial detention, or that affects a few people in a big way, like capital punishment; and (5) pursuing alternative forms of dispute resolution that are becoming increasingly popular, such as mediation including computer-aided mediation. Thus the spreadsheet format of decision-aiding software has many possibilities for the appellate advocate beyond traditional appellate advocacy. It is hoped that this chapter will help bring out some of those possibilities toward making appellate advocacy more effective, efficient, and equitable.

OTHER EXAMPLES

In discussing computer-aided advocacy, this chapter has mainly used examples from the field of constitutional law. The reason for doing so is because that is the field in which the case studies are most likely to be known among lawyers in general, and even among members of the general public. That is especially true of constitutional law cases that relate to civil liberties matters like alleged discrimination along racial lines or economic class, as in these three cases.

The methods discussed, however, can be applied to any field of law. For example, the methods are applicable to all the legal policy or law-making problems discussed in chapters 11, 12, and 13, including:

1. Advocating a system of quid-pro-quo government subsidies and other incentives as a generally better way of providing consumer protection than regulation with threats of jail and fines that are highly difficult to enforce (chapter 11).
2. Advocating a system of rent supplements to enable poor people to obtain rental housing in the private market, rather than provide government-owned public housing (chapter 11).
3. Advocating a divorce system based on granting divorces where incompatibility is shown regardless who is at fault, but developing improved mediation capabilities for bringing about reconciliations (chapter 11).
4. Advocating a tort law system that allows the plaintiff to collect by showing an injury occurred on the job, as a result of a manufacturer's product, or in an automobile accident regardless who was at fault, but agreeing in advance to limit the amount that can be collected, with the alternative of suing without such a limit but with the defendant having fault defenses available (chapter 11).
5. Advocating that the best way to decrease crime is to provide meaningful alternative opportunities for would-be criminals that they risk losing by committing crimes (chapter 12).
6. Advocating that the best way to provide constitutional review is through the courts, rather than the executive or legislative branch of government, if one wants sensitivity to minority rights while providing for at least a minimum of popular responsiveness (chapter 12).
7. Advocating that the best way to deal with unemployment and inflation is through legislation designed to provide subsidies, tax breaks, and low-interest loans for (a) hiring the unemployed, (b) obtaining retraining, (c) not raising prices or wages, and (d) other forms of socially desired behavior to be paid from decreased defense spending without decreasing defense capability (chapter 12).

8. Advocating that the best form of arms control treaty is one that provides for bilateral reduction brought about by appropriate stimuli, rather than a weapons freeze or a continued arms buildup (chapter 12).
9. Advocating right to counsel for the poor in capital, felony, and misdemeanor cases at trial, pretrial, and posttrial mainly through a public defender system of salaried government lawyers (chapter 13).
10. Advocating the retention of the civil jury in its full form of 12 persons deciding unanimously, with the costs covered by the legal system rather than the individual plaintiff (chapter 13).
11. Advocating the opposite of all ten positions advocated above. There is no reason why computer-aided advocacy should be inherently liberal, conservative, vegetarian, or associated with any specific ism. Like microcomputers as decision aids in general, computer-aided advocacy is available to all sides, especially given the low cost of what is involved. The effect is not to neutralize the opposing sides, but instead to raise the level of advocacy to a higher plane in the sense of simultaneously considering more alternatives, more criteria, and more relations, thereby facilitating mutually beneficial solutions.
12. All the private practice applications can also lend themselves to computer-aided advocacy in the sense that one could talk in terms of being an advocate for (a) a partner who feels he or she should receive more of the profits, (b) a beneficiary of an estate who feels he or she should be getting more of the estate, (c) a spouse in a divorce dispute who feels he or she should be getting more from the property settlement, (d) a plaintiff in a civil case who feels cheated by the circumstances that led to the litigation, (e) a prosecutor in a criminal case who feels the defendant is guilty and should receive a long sentence, (f) a civil rights complainant who feels he or she has been denied a job, a promotion, an apartment, or some other benefit because of racial considerations, (g) a welfare recipient who feels he or she has been wrongly denied eligibility or terminated, or (h) the United States as a party to an international dispute (see the private practice sections of chapters 11 and 12).
13. One could likewise be an advocate for the other side of those eight types of disputes representing, for example, the other partners, the other beneficiaries, the other spouse, the civil defendant, the arrested person, the allegedly discriminatory employer, the welfare agency, or the opponent of the United States, which might be a U.S. business firm.[5]

NOTES

1. For further details on computer-aided legal decisions (CALD), see David Johnson and Paul Mode, *Improving Law Firm Productivity by Encouraging Lawyers' Use of Personal Computers* (New York: Harcourt Brace Jovanovich, 1985); John Burns and Jim Hodde, "Decision Analysis: Using Computers to Make Better Choices," 6 *Attorney's Computer Report* 1-4 (February 1988); S. Nagel, "Computer-Aided Law Decisions," 21 *Akron Law Review* 73-96 (1987); and S. Nagel, *Microcomputers as Decision Aids in Law Practice* (Westport, Conn.: Greenwood-Quorum, 1987). On computer-aided decision-making in general or decision-aiding software, see Patrick Humphreys and Ayleen Wisudha, *Methods and Tools for Structuring and Analyzing Decision Problems* (London: London

School of Economics and Political Science, 1987), and Gautam Mitra (ed.), *Computer Assisted Decision Making: Expert Systems, Decision Analysis, Mathematical Programming* (Amsterdam: North Holland, 1986). On decision-making from the perspective of multiple criteria and multiple alternatives, see Ching-Lai Hwang and Kwangsun Yoon, *Multiple Attribute Decision Making: Methods and Applications* (Berlin: Springer-Verlag, 1981), and Milan Zeleny, *Multiple Criteria Decision Making* (New York: McGraw-Hill, 1982).

2. For further details concerning the *Rodriguez* case and aid to low-income schools, see John Coons, W. Clune, and S. Sugarman, *Private Wealth and Public Education* (Cambridge, Mass.: Harvard University Press, 1970); J. Guthrie (ed.), *School Finance Policies and Practices in the 1980s: A Decade of Conflict* (Cambridge, Mass.: Ballinger, 1980); C. Campbell, *The Reform of Educational Finance: A Selected Annotated Bibliography* (New York: New York State Library, 1981); and S. Carroll and R. Park, *The Search for Equity in School Finance* (Cambridge, Mass.: Ballinger, 1983).

3. For further details concerning the *Dandridge* case and aid to large but poor families, see Arthur LaFrance et al., *Law of the Poor* (St. Paul: West, 1973); Arthur Berney et al. (eds.), *Legal Problems of the Poor: Cases and Materials* (Boston: Little, Brown, 1975); and Eli Jarmel (ed.), *Problems in the Legal Representation of the Poor: Cases and Materials* (New York: Matthew Bender, 1972).

4. For further details concerning the *McCleskey* case and racially discriminatory capital punishment, see Kenneth Haas and James Inciardi (eds.), *Challenging Capital Punishment: Legal and Social Science Approaches* (Newbury Park, Calif.: Sage, 1988); W. White, *The Death Penalty in the Eighties: An Examination of the Modern System of Capital Punishment* (Ann Arbor: University of Michigan Press, 1987); David Baldus et al., "Comparative Review of Death Sentences: An Empirical Study of the Georgia Experiences," 74 *Journal of Criminal Law and Criminology* 661 (1983); and Robert Burt, "Disorder in the Court: The Death Penalty and the Constitution," 85 *Michigan Law Review* 1741 (1987).

5. For further details concerning advocacy in general, especially appellate advocacy, see UCLA Moot Court Honors Program, *Handbook of Appellate Advocacy* (St. Paul: West, 1986); Alan Hornstein, *Appellate Advocacy in a Nutshell* (St. Paul: West, 1984); Harvard Board of Student Advisers, *Introduction to Advocacy* (Mineola, N.Y.: Foundation, 1981); Paul Bergman, *Trial Advocacy in a Nutshell* (St. Paul: West, 1979); and J. Patterson and David Zarefsky, *Contemporary Debate* (Boston: Houghton Mifflin, 1983).

SECTION C

Law Prediction

CHAPTER 7

Generalizing from Cases

The purpose of this brief chapter is to describe how microcomputers can be helpful in analyzing the characteristics of a set of cases in order to generate a decision rule as to how related future cases are likely to be decided.

APPELLATE CASES

A simple form of computer-aided case prediction involves the following steps:

1. Obtain a set of past cases that deal with whatever subject or issues one is interested in.
2. Count how many of the cases resulted in victory for the plaintiff or a given position, and how many resulted in victory for the defendant or the other position. The plaintiff victories divided by the total cases is the probability of plaintiff victory.
3. Just working with the plaintiff victory cases, determine the average amount of damages awarded or the average sentence received by the defendant.
4. By multiplying the probability from Step 2 by the average from Step 3, one can determine the expected value for the type of case involved.

That kind of prediction may, however, often be insufficient. For example, the prior set of cases may have yielded a probability of .70 and average damages of $100,000. One may be reluctant to predict that the next case is likely to be worth $70,000 because one knows that it has some characteristics that give it a higher or lower probability or a larger or smaller predicted damages. One may, therefore, prefer a method that takes the relevant characteristics of the cases into consideration, rather than just what general typology the cases fit into.

The essence of multicriteria decision prediction is the idea of working with two or more predictive criteria, rather than just looking at overall probabilities and averages for a given type of case. More specifically, MCDP involves the processing of a set of (1) alternative cases, case types, or other occurrences, (2) various predictive or explanatory criteria, and (3) relations between the alternatives and the criteria in order to develop a decision rule that will accurately predict or explain 100% of the past decisions so as to facilitate predicting future decisions.

There are two especially effective ways of developing a predictive decision rule with no inconsistencies. One involves changing the weights of the predictive criteria, and the other involves changing the measurement of the relations between the cases and the predictive criteria. The first method can be illustrated with legislative redistricting cases and the second with welfare proceedings.[1]

Changing the Weights of the Predictive Criteria

Table 7-1 provides an example of synthesizing a set of appellate cases using the P/G% software. There are nine appellate cases dealing with legislative redistricting from *Colegrove v. Green* in 1948 to *Baker v. Carr* in 1962. Each case is scored yes with a 2 and no with a 1 on each of the four predictive criteria. The criteria include (1) whether equality is explicitly required by the relevant federal or state constitution, (2) whether a state or federal legislature is involved, (3) whether the degree of equality violation is big or little, and (4) whether a federal or state court is involved. The yes answer is the one that favors a decision for the side that is attacking the existing redistricting system.

The next-to-last column shows how each case was decided in terms of whether the winner was the defender or the attacker of the existing redistricting system. The third-to-last column shows the sum of the raw scores. It leads to a decision rule that says: "If there is a total raw score of 7 or above, then the attacker wins; and if there is a total raw score of 6 or below, then the defender wins." That decision rule, however, has one inconsistency. It is the *Grills* case, in which there were only 6 points, but the attacker still won.

To eliminate such inconsistencies, one can do a variety of legitimate things, as indicated in the notes below the table. The most meaningful approach is generally to give the predictive criteria different weights to indicate their relative importance. In this context, the most important criteria are the first criterion (which deals with the nature of the law) and the third criterion (which deals with the key facts). Of the two, the equality requirement is the most important since the degree of equality violation would mean little if there is no equality requirement. Giving the equality requirement a weight of 2 doubles all the numbers in the first column. Doing so changes the summation scores. The new weighted summation scores now lead to a decision rule that says: "If there is a total raw score of 8 or above, then the attacker wins; and if there is a total raw score of 7 or below, then the defender wins." That new decision rule results in no inconsistencies. The set of cases has thus been synthesized into a meaningful decision rule.

Table 7-1
Data for Predicting Redistricting Cases

Cases \ Criteria	Equality Requirement W = 1 (or 2)	State Legislature W = 1	Equality Violation W = 1	Federal Court W = 1	SUM (Weighted)	OUTCOME Winner	OUTCOME Award
Colegrove	1 (2)	1	1	2	5 (6)	D	$0
Grills	2 (4)	2	1	1	6 (8)	A	2
Maryland	1 (2)	2	2	1	6 (7)	D	0
Scholle	1 (2)	2	2	1	6 (7)	D	0
WMCA	1 (2)	2	1	2	6 (7)	D	0
Asbury	2 (4)	2	2	1	7 (9)	A	6
Dyer	2 (4)	1	2	2	7 (9)	A	8
Baker	2 (4)	2	2	2	8 (10)	A	9
Magraw	2 (4)	2	2	2	8 (10)	A	10

NOTES:

1. A 1 in columns 1 to 4 means No. A 2 means Yes. An "A" in the outcome column means that the attacker wins. A "D" means that the defender wins.

2. The decision rule that the above data initially generate is the following:
   (1) If a redistricting case during the time period covered has a summation score of 7 or above, the attacker wins.
   (2) With a summation score of 6 or below, the defender wins.

3. That decision rule generates one inconsistent case. The inconsistency can be eliminated by (1) changing the decision rule to say that a summation score of 6 leads to an unclear outcome; (2) giving the first variable a weight of 2, which would be consistent with the importance of requiring equality; (3) adding a fifth variable called "Deciding after the Maryland Case;" (4) eliminating the Grills case, but that does not seem justifiable; (5) changing the measurement on the first variable from no-yes to a 1--3 scale and giving Grills a score of 3; (6) finding that Grills really deserves a relation score of 2 on the third of the four variables.

4. Each predicted criterion is initially given an equal weight of 1. If the equality requirement is given a weight of 2 in view of its substantive importance, then the Grills case would no longer be an inconsistently low-scoring case in which the attacker won. The new predictive decision rule would be the following:
   (1) If a redistricting case has a weighted summation score of 8 or above, the attacker wins.
   (2) If the weighted summation score is 7 or below, the attacker loses.

5. The dollar amounts in the last column represent hypothetical data showing how many thousands of dollars the successful attacker received in the form of damages. That information is useful for illustrating how the methodology can predict a continuum outcome as contrasted to a dichotomous outcome of winning versus losing.

The data shown in table 7-1 can not only be used to illustrate how to develop a decision rule for predicting who will win in a set of cases. That same data can be used to develop a decision rule for predicting what the damages or other judgment will be. The last column is called "Award." It contains hypothetical data for the nine cases. Using a two-variable regression analysis program, one can easily develop a predictive equation of the form, Award = A + B(Sum). That equation says that the predicted award will be equal to a base amount (when the summation score is zero) plus the summation score times a computer-generated multiplier. The computer generates a numerical value for both A and B in order to maximize the accuracy of one's ability to predict awards from summation scores given the data available. That kind of software is included with the P/G% program.

Changing the Measurement of the Relations

Table 7-2 provides an example of how the P/G% software can be used to synthesize a set of cases. This example differs from the previous one in the following ways:

1. The alternatives are not specific cases, but rather case types or sets of facts that may or may not have actually occurred.
2. Inconsistencies are eliminated by changing the measurement of the relations between the case types and the predictive criteria, rather than changing the relative weights of the predictive criteria.
3. The example is substantively different in dealing with welfare caes, rather than with redistricting cases.

There are 12 alternative case types in these welfare cases. One dimension for the case types relates to whether the welfare recipient was denied eligibility, subjected to reduced benefits, terminated, or criminally prosecuted. A second dimension relates to whether the welfare recipient was denied a free attorney, a hearing with direct and cross examination, or reasons for the administrative treatment. The first dimension relates to substance, and the second to procedure. The first dimension has four categories and the second has three. There are thus 12 alternative case types.

There are two predictive criteria. One criterion relates to what the case involves in terms of procedure. A simple way of scoring each case type on each criterion is a rank order. We can obtain widespread agreement that the worst substantive treatment is criminal prosecution and the least severe is eligibility denial. Next to the worst is termination, and next to the least severe is benefits reduction. That means a 1–4 scale. Likewise, we can obtain widespread agreement that the worst procedural treatment is to be denied reasons. The least severe procedural treatment is to be denied a free attorney. In between is being denied a hearing. That means a 1–3 scale.

Table 7-2
Changing the Measurement of the Relations Predicting Welfare Cases

A. THE ORIGINAL 1-3 MEASUREMENT ON THE PROCEDURAL CRITERION

Alternative	SUBSTANC	PROCEDUR	Combined Rawscores	Previous Outcome
1-ELIGIBLE, -LAWYER	1.00	1.00	2.00	L
2-BENEFITS, -LAWYER	2.00	1.00	3.00	L
3-ELIGIBLE, -HEARING	1.00	2.00	3.00	L
4-TERMINATE,-LAWYER	3.00	1.00	4.00	L
5-BENEFITS, -HEARING	2.00	2.00	4.00	?
6-ELIGIBLE, -REASONS	1.00	3.00	4.00	W
7-CRIM.PROS, -LAWYER	4.00	1.00	5.00	W
8-TERMINATE,-HEARING	3.00	2.00	5.00	W
9-BENEFITS, -REASONS	2.00	3.00	5.00	W
10-CRIM.PROS, -HEARING	4.00	2.00	6.00	W
11-TERMINATE,-REASONS	3.00	3.00	6.00	W
12-CRIM.PROS, -REASONS	4.00	3.00	7.00	W

B. THE NEW .99-3.01 MEASUREMENT ON THE PROCEDURAL CRITERION

Alternative	SUBSTANC	PROCEDUR	Combined Rawscores	Previous Outcome
1-ELIGIBLE, -LAWYER	1.00	0.99	1.99	L
2-BENEFITS, -LAWYER	2.00	0.99	2.99	L
3-ELIGIBLE, -HEARING	1.00	2.00	3.00	L
4-TERMINATE,-LAWYER	3.00	0.99	3.99	L
5-BENEFITS, -HEARING	2.00	2.00	4.00	?
6-ELIGIBLE, -REASONS	1.00	3.01	4.01	W
7-CRIM.PROS, -LAWYER	4.00	0.99	4.99	W
8-TERMINATE,-HEARING	3.00	2.00	5.00	W
9-BENEFITS, -REASONS	2.00	3.01	5.01	W
10-CRIM.PROS, -HEARING	4.00	2.00	6.00	W
11-TERMINATE,-REASONS	3.00	3.01	6.01	W
12-CRIM.PROS, -REASONS	4.00	3.01	7.01	W

NOTES:

1. A "W" in the outcome column means that the welfare recipient wins. An "L" means the welfare recipient loses. The Goldberg case is case type 8, and the Argersinger case is case type 7.

2. The decision rule that the above data generate is the following:
   (1) If a welfare case involves a summation score of 4.01 or above, the welfare recipient wins.
   (2) With a summation score of 3.99 or below, the welfare recipient loses.
   (3) With a score of 4.00, the outcome is unclear.

3. The leading case is Goldberg v. Kelly. It involved a summation score of 5.00, and the welfare recipient won. Therefore, one would expect the welfare recipient to win even more with scores higher than 5.00. That covers case types 9, 10, 11, and 12. The outcome of case 7 is known from the Argersinger case. The outcomes of case types 1, 2, 3, 4, and 6 are known from things said in the Goldberg case, not from a fortiori deduction.

4. With the 1-3 measurement, there are three inconsistent cases, all of which received an overall score of 4.00. One case was a loser; one was a winner; and the outcome of the third is unknown. With the .99-3.01 measurement, there are no inconsistencies. The losing case gets a score of 3.99; the winning case gets a score of 4.01; and the questionable case gets a score of 4.00.

5. The justification for changing the scale from 1-3 to .99-3.01 is secondarily to remove the inconsistencies. The primary justification is because the changes make substantive sense. Giving no reasons is practically the ultimate in deprivation of procedural due process. It should therefore score higher than 3 on a 1-3 scale. Not having an attorney in a civil matter is relatively minor compared to not having reasons or a hearing. It should therefore score lower than a 1 on a 1-3 scale.

If we use a simple rank-order scoring and then sum the two ranks across each case type, we find a set of inconsistencies. There are three cases that score 4.00. They include termination without a lawyer, in which the welfare recipient is likely to lose unless there are other considerations. The three cases also include denial of eligibility without giving reasons, in which the welfare recipient is likely to win unless there are other considerations. The third case involves a benefits reduction without a hearing, which as of the time of this analysis was a questionable situation as to how the courts were likely to decide. If three cases receive the same score and are decided in three different ways, then two out of the three cases are being inconsistently handled in the synthesis. The summation column and the previous outcome column do not generate a decision rule that predicts or explains the cases.

If, however, we change the simplistic 1–3 scoring on the procedural dimension to a scale that considers the subject matter more validly, then the inconsistencies and mispredictions can be eliminated. Doing so involves taking into consideration that giving no reasons is such an abuse of procedural due process that it deserves a score higher than 3 on a 1–3 scale where no lawyer receives a 1, and no hearing receives a 2. Likewise, not being given a free lawyer in a civil case deserves a score lower than a 1 where no hearing receives a 2, and no reasons receives a 3.

If one works with a .99 to 3.01 scale, rather than a 1–3 scale, one can get perfect prediction in this context. That means alternative 5 receives a summation score of 3.99 and loses. Alternative 7 receives a summation score of 4.01 and wins. Alternative 6 still receives a score of 4.00, which is fitting given its questionable outcome. Thus we have a good illustration of how changing the measurement can convert a 10 out of 12 prediction into 100% accuracy.[1]

TRIAL CASES

Table 7-3 contains data for predicting criminal cases. These data are hypothetical, but for methodological purposes such data should be just as usable as real data. Table 7-3A shows how the five cases were decided. It also shows the four predictive criteria used to separate the conviction cases from the acquittal cases. The predictive criteria are given equal weight to begin with.

Convict or Acquit

Table 7-3B shows how the cases score on the predictive criteria. The scoring is on a 1–2 scale, with 2 meaning relatively high and 1 meaning relatively low. The predictive criteria relate to:

1. Whether the charge was a misdemeanor or a felony.
2. Whether the geographical area of the courthouse involved people with a low or high gross national product per capita.

Table 7-3
Data for Predicting Conviction or Acquittal

A. THE CASES AND THE PREDICTIVE CRITERIA

Alternative	Previous Outcome	Criterion	Meas.Unit	Weight
1 JONES (C)	CONVICT	1 MISD.V.FELONY	2/YES-1/NO	1.00
2 SMITH (C)	CONVICT	2 LOW GNP V.HIGH		1.00
3 BROWN (A)	ACQUIT	3 REP.JUDGE V.DEM.		1.00
4 GREEN (A)	ACQUIT	4 BLACK DEF.V.WHITE		1.00
5 MILLER (A)	ACQUIT			

B. HOW THE CASES SCORE ON THE PREDICTIVE CRITERIA

	MISD.V.F	LOW GNP	REP.JUDG	BLACK DE
JONES (C)	2.00	2.00	2.00	1.00
SMITH (C)	2.00	2.00	1.00	1.00
BROWN (A)	1.00	1.00	1.00	1.00
GREEN (A)	2.00	1.00	1.00	2.00
MILLER (A)	1.00	1.00	1.00	2.00

C. THE OVERALL SCORES OF THE CASES BEFORE AND AFTER ADJUSTING THE WEIGHTS

Alternative	Combined Rawscores	Previous Outcome	Alternative	Combined Rawscores	Previous Outcome
1JONES (C)	7.00	CONVICT	1JONES (C)	9.00	CONVICT
2SMITH (C)	6.00	CONVICT	2SMITH (C)	8.00	CONVICT
3BROWN (A)	4.00	ACQUIT	3BROWN (A)	5.00	ACQUIT
4GREEN (A)	6.00	ACQUIT	4GREEN (A)	7.00	ACQUIT
5MILLER (A)	5.00	ACQUIT	5MILLER (A)	6.00	ACQUIT

D. REVERSING THE WEAKEST ACQUITAL OR CONVICTION

	GREEN (A)	SMITH (C)	Weight
MISD.V.FELONY	3.00	1.00	??
LOW GNP V.HIGH	1.50	1.50	1.000
REP.JUDGE V.DEM.	2.00	0.00	??
BLACK DEF.V.WHITE	3.00	0.00	2.000

NOTES:

1. The case names, predictive criteria, and the scores of the cases on the criteria are hypothetical. That hypothetical data first appeared in S. Nagel, "Using Simple Calculations to Predict Judicial Decisions", 4 American Behavioral Scientist 24-28 (1960) and 7 Practical Lawyer 68-74 (1961).

2. If the predictive criteria are given equal weight, then inconsistent predictions occur. There are two cases with total scores of 6, but one resulted in a conviction and one an acquittal. If, however, area income is given extra weight as a predictive criterion, then the inconsistencies are eliminated.

3. The decision rule generated by this data is that if there are 8 or more points, there will be a conviction, but if there are 7 or less points, there will be an acquittal.

3. Whether a Republican or Democratic judge heard the case.
4. Whether the defendant was black or white.

Table 7-3C shows the summation scores per case when the weights were all set at 1.00. The Smith case and the Green case then both received 6 points. Smith was, however, convicted, and Green was acquitted, meaning they are an inconsistent pair. If, however, the income variable is given a little extra weight, then the inconsistencies are eliminated. The new decision rule becomes that if there are 8 or more points, there will be a conviction. If there are 7 or less points, there will be an acquittal.

Extra weight should be given to a predictive criterion whose scores have an especially close relation with case outcome. Area income has a perfect relation. Wherever income was relatively high, there was an acquittal. Wherever income was relatively low, there was a conviction.

Possible explanations for the relations between the predictive criteria and the case outcomes are:

1. Misdemeanors may be more likely to result in convictions than felonies, because felony defendants fight harder, and more due process is provided in felony trials.
2. Poorer jurisdictions may have higher conviction rates, because they cannot afford to provide as good right to counsel as wealthier jurisdictions do.
3. Republican judges may have higher conviction rates, because they tend to believe more in individual (rather than social) responsibility in comparison to Democratic judges, and they are more likely to place a higher value on avoiding acquittal errors.
4. Black defendants may be more likely to be convicted than white defendants, because they are more likely to be poor and have less expensive counsel. They may also have less sympathetic judges and juries, especially if white victims are involved.

Table 7-3D shows that one way the Green case might get as high a score toward conviction as the Smith case would be if Green were tried by a Republican judge. One way that the Smith case might get as low a score toward acquittal as the Green case would be if Smith were charged with a felony rather than misdemeanor. The cases would be tied if the income of the area were given a weight of 1, rather than a weight of 2.

Length of Sentence

Table 7-4 contains the data for predicting length of sentence from a small sample of only three cases for illustrative purposes. Two of the three are the Jones and Smith cases from table 7-3. Both resulted in a conviction. Jones had an adjusted summation score of 9, and Smith had a score of 8. A third case was added with a summation score of 10. That means the third case had a yes answer on all four predictive criteria. As part of the hypothetical data, Smith received a 10-year prison sentence, Jones received 10.5 years, and the third case received 10.75 years. Those data are given in table 7-4A.

Table 7-4
Data for Predicting Length of Sentence

A. THREE CONVICTION CASES, THEIR SUMMATION SCORES AND THEIR SENTENCES

I	X	Y
Point 1	8	10.00
Point 2	9	10.50
Point 3	10	10.75

B. THE PREDICTION EQUATION COEFFICIENTS

LINEAR REGRESSION

$$Y = 7.04 + .38(X)$$

Coefficient of Determiniation (R^2) = .96
Coefficient of Correlation (R) = .98

GEOMETRIC REGRESSION

$$Y = 5.09(X)^{.33}$$

Coefficient of Determination (R^2) = .97
Coefficient of Correlation (R) = .99

C. APPLYING THE EQUATION TO POSSIBLE SUMMATION SCORES

X	Y1	Yg
5	8.92	8.61
6	9.20	9.14
7	9.67	9.61
8	10.04	10.03
9	10.42	10.43
10	10.79	10.79

NOTES:

1. The data are hypothetical. Points 1 and 2 are the Smith and Jones cases from Table 7-3. Point 3 is a new case called the Atkins case. The X variable is their summation scores, and the Y variable is their sentences expressed in years.

2. The above output was generated by working with a public domain program called REGRESS, which is part of the Math/Stat package of PC-SIG group of 1556 Halford Avenue, Santa Clara, CA 95051. The program is now available as part of the P/G% Disk #1.

3. Table 7-4B shows the prediction equations. They are Y = 7.04 + .375(X), and $Y = 5.09(X)^{.33}$. The linear equation means that with a summation score of 0, the predicted sentence is 7 years. As the summation score goes up one unit, the predicted sentence goes up 3/8 of a year. The nonlinear equation means that with a summation score of 1, the predicted sentence is 5 years. As the summation score goes up 100%, the predicted sentence goes up 33%.

In order to convert those data into a decision rule, they are inputted into a simple linear and nonlinear regression analysis program called Regress. The program is an example of public domain software. It is now available as part of the P/G% package. A future version of P/G% will enable the regression analysis to be automatic if requested. One will thereby avoid having to type the P/G% output in order to provide the regression input.

The decision rule (as determined by the linear regression analysis) is expressed in the equation, $Y = 7.04 + .375(X)$. That means when the summation score is 0, the predicted sentence is 7 years. As the summation score goes up one unit, the predicted sentence goes up 3/8 of a year. The decision rule (as determined by the diminishing returns analysis) is expressed in the equation, $Y = 5.09(X)^{.33}$. That means when the summation score is 1, the predicted sentence is 5 years. As the summation score goes up 100% or doubles, the predicted sentence goes up 33% or up by 1/3.

Table 7-4C applies the two equations to various values of X. That aspect of the program is useful for making fast predictions in light of either equation. Those predictions can include summation scores that do not correspond to any of the actual cases. The predictions are designed to minimize the sum of the squared deviations between the predicted sentences and the actual sentences for the three cases in the data set, while preserving a straight-line relation in the linear regression and a smooth curve in the nonlinear regression.

In addition to providing the information for the predictive equations, table 7-4B also shows there is almost a perfect fit between the linear regression line and the three points, and likewise between the nonlinear regression line and the three points. The nonlinear fit is slightly higher, as indicated by the R^2 value. There is not much room for improvement in the goodness of fit here. In other situations, the goodness of fit can be improved by changing the weights of the predictive criteria, adding predictive criteria, changing the measurement units, or doing other things that make substantive sense and bring the changes in the X scores even more in line with changes in the Y scores. This is much easier to do when all the predictive criteria have been combined into a summation score, rather than left separate.

Sensitivity analysis in predicting sentence length or some other continuum outcome is different from predicting conviction-acquittal or some other dichotomous outcome. If one wants to know how much a prediction concerning sentence length is likely to change as a result of changes in the characteristics of the defendant or the case, then go through the following three steps:

1. Apply the predictive equation $Y = a + bX$ or $Y = aX^b$ to the case using its original characteristics.
2. Apply the predictive equation $Y = a + bX$ or $Y = aX^b$ to the case using its new characteristics.
3. Determine the difference between Y_1 and Y_2. That difference shows how much the prediction is likely to change as a result of those changes in the characteristics.[2]

One might note that the Y variable we are trying to predict is sentence length, damages, winning or losing (expressed as a 1 or a 0), or some other decisional outcome. The X variable that we are trying to predict from is the summation score of the case at hand. This is different from traditional prediction from cases, which is called multivariate regression analysis. It involves predicting from the scores of the case at hand on each of the individual criteria, rather than from a summation score. Such a method tends to be more complicated and less valid. The greater complexity is due to trying to predict from so many variables at the same time without first aggregating them. The lowered validity is due mainly to the fact that the separate variables tend to interact with each other in ways that hide or accentuate spurious causation, reciprocal causation, and other confounding interactions. The P/G% prediction system decreases those occurrences by encouraging the user of the method to adjust the weights in light of his or her knowledge of the subject matter.[3]

NOTES

1. For further details on this analysis, see S. Nagel, "Using Microcomputers and P/G% to Predict Court Cases," 18 *Akron Law Review* 541-574 (1985), and S. Nagel, *Causation, Prediction, and Legal Analysis* (Westport, Conn.: Greenwood-Quorum, 1986). On the P/G% software applied to case prediction and other law practice matters, see S. Nagel, *Microcomputers as Decision Aids in Law Practice* (Westport, Conn.: Greenwood-Quorum, 1987), and S. Nagel, "Case Prediction by Staircase Tables and Percentaging," 25 *Jurimetrics Journal* 169-196 (1985). Also see Karl Llewellyn, *The Common Law Tradition: Deciding Appeals* (Boston: Little, Brown, 1960). Relevant software for inductively synthesizing appellate cases could include statistical analysis software, such as "SPSS-PC," 444 N. Michigan Avenue, Chicago IL 60611.

2. On predicting decisions from the characteristics of a situation, see Harold Spaeth, *Supreme Court Policy Making: Explanation and Prediction* (San Francisco: Freeman, 1979); Glendon Schubert (ed.), *Judicial Behavior: A Reader in Theory and Research* (Chicago: Rand McNally, 1964); Harry Jones, John Kernochan, and Arthur Murphy (eds.), *Legal Method: Cases and Text Materials* (Mineola, N.Y.: Foundation Press, 1980); and S. Negal, "Microcomputers and Improving Social Science Prediction," 10 *Evaluation Review* 635-660 (1986). Notice that if one merely predicts the average outcome for the data in table 7-4, then one would always predict an acquittal, and one would be wrong two out of five times. Predicting from the characteristics of the cases leads to being wrong zero out of five times for the sample of five cases. Likewise, predicting the average outcome would lead to predicting that all convicted defendants would receive a sentence of 10.42 years since that is the average of the three conviction cases. Doing so would lead to bigger differences between the actual years and the predicted years in the three cases than predicting from the summation scores of the cases, which take their characteristics into consideration.

3. The P/G% prediction from cases produces approximately the same results as multivariate regression analysis if there is little overlap among the predictive criteria or if one assigns multiplier weights to take the overlap into consideration. If two predictive criteria have virtually no overlap and are equally important, then they can be assigned weights of

1.00 apiece. If they have highly redundant overlap, then they should be assigned weights of about .50 apiece. If there is a small amount of overlapping correlation between the two predictive criteria, then they should be assigned weights of about .90 apiece. The overlap problem also occurs in chapter 8 on ''Generalizing from Facts.'' The problem can be handled in a simple commonsense manner or in a complicated mechanistic manner that has greater objectivity but less meaningfulness and validity.

CHAPTER 8

Generalizing from Facts

Chapter 8 will describe an alternative prediction system called "generalizing from facts" that may be even more applicable to lawyers than generalizing from cases.

COMPARING TWO PREDICTIVE APPROACHES

Both forms of generalizing or predicting can be dealt with from a spreadsheet perspective with alternatives on the rows, predictive criteria on the columns, and relation scores between the alternatives and the predictive criteria in the cells. At the far right (with both approaches) are overall scores that facilitate making predictions about future cases or events. Both approaches can also benefit from the kind of what-if analysis that is associated with spreadsheets and P/G%.

The essence of generalizing from cases in terms of a spreadsheet perspective is:

1. On the rows are cases, case types, or both. Table 7-1 involved only actual previously decided cases. Table 7-2 involved 12 case types, two of which corresponded to actual landmark cases.
2. The predictive criteria tend to be characteristics of the cases that can be determined by reading the cases or by reading background materials that are related to the cases.
3. With actual cases, the relations usually involve scoring the cases by reading the court opinions or court records. With case types that are not actual cases, the relations involve deducing scores from observing how other related cases have been handled that have different facts, but from which one can reason by analogy or through a fortiori reasoning. The relations tend to be scored on a 1–5, 1–3, or 1–2 scale.
4. One can add across each case in order to obtain an overall score for each case. One can then observe what overall scores are associated with a victory for the plaintiff and which ones with a victory for the defendant.

On the other hand, the essence of generalizing from facts in terms of spreadsheet perspective is:

1. On the rows are the alternative positions that the court could take, such as victory for the plaintiff on the first row and victory for the defendant on the second row. Victory generally refers to the case as a whole, but could refer to any specific issue.
2. On the columns are the predictive criteria. They can be any factual elements that may be relevant to the court's decision, regardless of whether they have occurred in previous cases.
3. The relations involve inserting probabilities into each column so the sum of probabilities adds to 1.00. For example, on the first criterion, one notes the probability of the plaintiff winning on this fact element alone as being .40. That means the probability of the defendant winning on this fact element alone has to be .60.
4. One then sums across the probabilities on each row, and divides by the number of predictive criteria. For example, suppose there are two predictive criteria and the plaintiff victory is .40 in light of the first criterion and .50 in light of the second. The plaintiff's overall probability is thus about .45 or .90 divided by 2. This assumes each criterion is equally important. If they are not equally important, then one calculates a weighted average taking the relative importance weights into consideration.

Either approach can generate probabilities as an end product, although the approach of generalizing from facts by aggregating probabilities is more direct. The way generalizing from cases does it is by noting the percent of the cases that the plaintiff won that had summation scores of 6, 7, and so on across the range of summation scores received. Likewise either approach can generate if-then statements as an end product. When predicting from cases, the statements tend to take the form, "If the summation score is 9 or greater, then the plaintiff will win." When predicting from facts, the statement tends to take the form, "If the probability is .40 on the first variable and .50 on the second variable, then the overall probability will be about .45."

Either approach can generate an equation as one of its end products or as a way of expressing a decision rule. When predicting from cases, the equation tends to take the form $Y = A + BX$. In such an equation, Y is the outcome to be predicted, X is the summation score of the case at hand, A is the value of Y when X is zero, and B is the increase in Y when X goes up one unit. When predicting from facts, the equation tends to take the form $Y = (W_1X_1 + W_2X_2)/N$. In such an equation, Y is the outcome to be predicted, W is the relative weight of each predictive criterion, X is the separate victory probability associated with each predictive criterion, and N is the number of predictive criteria, which in this example is 2.

The big advantage of predicting from cases is that is more explicitly draws on prior precedents, although the probabilities in generalizing from facts can also come from prior cases. The big advantage of predicting from facts is that it frees one from the constraint of having to work with a limited sample of prior cases, although one can do some deducing as to what would have happened in various case types for which there are no prior cases available.

It is easier to understand generalizing from facts through concrete examples, rather than abstract principles. This chapter presents three such examples, covering (1) a criminal case with two conflicting witnesses, (2) a civil case with conflicting lawyer perceptions, and (3) an international law case with multiple facts and weights.

A CRIMINAL CASE WITH TWO CONFLICTING WITNESSES

Table 8-1 provides an example of synthesizing a set of facts in a trial decision using the P/G% software. This is a criminal case in which the key question is whether the defendant is guilty or not. For the sake of simplicity, there are two pieces of evidence. One is a defense witness who offers an alibi for the defendant. That witness has an 80% probability of telling the truth, which would favor the defendant being found not guilty. The second piece of evidence is a prosecution witness who claims to have seen the defendant at the scene of the crime. There is a 70% probability that the witness is telling the truth when one just analyzes that witness alone without considering the testimony of related witnesses.

Not all witnesses or pieces of evidence are of equal importance. An alibi witness is more important than a witness who saw the defendant at the scene of the crime. If the alibi witness is telling the truth, then the defendant cannot be guilty. If the crime-scene witness is telling the truth, then the defendant could still be innocent, since being at the scene of the crime does not mean that the defendant committed the crime. Therefore, give the alibi statement a weight of 2 or a multiple of 2.

The synthesizing then involves adding .40 to .70 in order to obtain a weighted sum for the alternative that the defendant is not guilty. Those two weighted sums should then be divided by the sum of the weights (which are 2 and 1) in order to obtain probabilities that add to 1.00. The bottom line thus shows there is a .37 probability that the defendant is guilty in light of the analysis and a .63 probability that the defendant is not guilty. It would therefore be appropriate to acquit the defendant since the probability of guilt should be higher than about .90 in order to justify a conviction.

Studies on determining the probability of guilt or liability deal with how people ought to or do determine probabilities. There is an approximate consensus that people do not explicitly or implicitly use Bayesian probability calculations. Such calculations are too complicated, and information is not available on how each item of evidence relates to each other item of evidence, as well as how each item of evidence relates to the defendant being guilty. The complications are especially great when there are more than two items of evidence.

Table 8-1 does not explicitly deal with the relation between each item of evidence and the probability of guilt. Instead it deals with the easier matter of the

Table 8-1
Determining the Probability of Guilt

CRITERIA / ALTERNATIVES	(1) Defense Statement W = 2		(2) Prosecution Statement (Scene of Crime) W = 1	(3) SUM (1)+(22)	(4) SUM/N (3)/2	(5) Weighted Sum (1.5)+(2)	(6) Weighted Sum/Sum of Weights (5)/3
Defendant is Guilty	.20	(.40)	.70	.90	.45	1.10	.37
Defendant is not Guilty	.80	(1.60)	.30	1.10	.55	1.90	.63
	1.00	(2.00)	1.00	2.00	1.00	3.00	1.00

NOTES:

1. The numbers in columns 1 and 2 are probabilities. They indicate the degree of accuracy or truth associated with the statements in the direction of establishing the defendant's guilt. Thus, the .20 probability means that there is a .80 probability that the defense statement is true, and the .20 complement is in the direction of establishing the defendant's guilt. These are probabilities of truth, not probabilities of guilt.

2. The weights indicate the degree of importance of the evidence items. Thus an alibi statement is quite important (if true) in establishing innocence. A statement saying the defendant was at the scene of the crime is less important because even if it is true, it does not establish the defendant's guilt. The numbers in parentheses in column 1 are weighted probabilities.

3. The numbers in column 3 are the sum of the two unweighted probabilities. The numbers in column 5 are the sums of the two weighted probabilities.

4. The numbers in column 4 are unweighted average probabilities. The numbers in column 5 are weighted average probabilities. The numbers in column 6 are an approximation of Bayesian conditional probabilities especially when one only has probabilities of truthfulness and degrees of importance to work with.

5. If the probability in the upper right hand corner is greater than .90, then the judge, juror, or other perceiver of these two items of evidence should vote to convict assuming (1) .90 is accepted as the threshold probability interpretation of beyond a reasonable doubt, and (2) these are the only items of evidence. If the starred probability is .90 or less, then one should vote to acquit.

6. With two alibi witnesses, each might receive a weight of 1.5 if one witness receives a 2. They do not both receive a 2 because they partly reinforce each other.

7. No set of weights will cause the weighted average to exceed .90 with probabilities of .20 and .70. Thus, there is no threshold value for either W1 or W2.

8. The difficulty of obtaining a set of evidence items across the prosecution and the defense that average better than a .90 probability may indicate that jurors and judges generally operate below the .90 threshold, even though judges and commentators say that .90 is roughly the probability translation of "beyond a reasonable doubt".

probability that the evidence is accurate on the point it is making. The weights of each item of evidence mainly take into consideration how strongly the evidence relates to establishing guilt. The weights are relative weights that are easier concepts to handle than probabilities. The weights also consider the overlap between items of evidence. If two items of evidence are completely redundant, then they each would receive half the weight that each alone would otherwise receive. Table 8-1 purports to roughly approximate how jurors implicitly synthesize facts, and it implicitly recommends this weighted summation method as a meaningful and feasible approach to synthesizing facts.[1]

A CIVIL CASE WITH CONFLICTING OPINIONS

Determining the Probability of Liability Being Established

Table 8-2 shows the P/G% analysis that was actually used in a product liability case in the federal district court of the Northern District of Illinois. The case involved a U.S. insurance company suing a foreign electronics manufacturer for damages that allegedly occurred as a result of an appliance catching fire. The resulting fire caused approximately $950,000 in damages to a restaurant and other business establishments that were insured by the U.S. insurance company

Table 8-2
Determining Liability in a Civil Case

A. THE PREDICTIVE CRITERIA

CRITERIA	MEAS. UNIT	WEIGHT
1 P's Prediction	Prob. Win	1.00
2 D's Prediction	"	1.00
3 Combustible?	"	1.00
4 No Break Circuit?	"	1.00
5 Prior Occurrence?	"	2.00

B. THE PROBABILITY OF LIABILITY IF EACH PREDICTIVE CRITERION WERE THE ONLY ONE

ALTERNATIVES	CRITERIA				
	P's Prediction	D's Prediction	Combustible?	No Break?	Prior Occurrence?
D Liable (Pro P)	0.70	0.10	0.40	0.40	0.30
No Liable (Pro D)	0.30	0.90	0.60	0.60	0.70

C. COMBINING THE PROBABILITIES ON THE PREDICTING CRITERIA

ALTERNATIVES	COMBINED WTD. P/W%'s	Percents
1 D Liable (Pro P)	220.00	36.67
2 No Liable (Pro D)	380.00	63.33

and other insurance companies. They had already paid the injured parties, and they were now seeking to be reimbursed from the foreign manufacturer.

A key issue in this case and in a high percentage of civil cases was whether liability would be established. There are thus basically two alternative positions that the court could take on this issue as is shown in the alternatives column of Table 8-2B. Either the defendant will be found liable, which is the decision that favors the plaintiff, or the defendant will be found not liable, which is the decision that favors the defendant.

Five predictive criteria are shown in section A of the table. They are:

1. The plaintiff's prediction as to the probability of victory. This is shown in section B as a .70 probability that the plaintiff will win. The plaintiff is thus predicting that there is a .30 probability the defendant will win. Those probabilities were determined by talking with the plaintiff's attorneys and translating their words, gestures, and emotions into predictive probabilities.
2. The defendant's prediction as to the victory probability. This is shown as a .10 probability that the plaintiff will win, and thus a .90 probability that the defendant will win. All the probabilities are expressed in the top row of section B in terms of plaintiff victory and in the bottom row in terms of defendant victory. The defendant was more confident of victory in this case than the plaintiff, as indicated by comparing the .90 and the .70 probabilities.
3. A key subissue or predictive criterion within the larger issue of liability probability was a question as to whether the appliance could be combustible, meaning whether it was capable of burning. The plaintiff argued that it was, but the defendant argued that it was not. Their arguments translated into a .40 probability that the plaintiff would win and a .60 probability that the defendant would win on the overall liability issue if combustibility were the only factual element. Note that the .40 does not say that there is a .40 probability that the appliance is combustible. Instead, it says that if the only evidence present in this case were combustibility evidence, then the plaintiff would have about a .40 probability of winning the case.
4. A related subissue was whether the circuit breaker in the appliance might not have worked in the presence of intense heat as it was supposed to do. The plaintiff argued that it was possible that the electrical circuit did not immediately break when it was supposed to. The defendant argued that was virtually impossible to not occur. Their respective arguments led to saying on the part of the mediator in his analysis that if we had evidence only on the circuit breaker, the plaintiff would also just have a .40 probability of winning.
5. The last factual element or predictive criterion on this list is the question of whether there was a prior occurrence of this type of appliance having caused a fire. The plaintiff's lawyers argued that they were in the process of showing that there had been a prior occurrence, but they were reluctant to be specific in the pretrial proceedings, claiming that they wanted to save the evidence for trial. The defendant's lawyers argued that the company records and a thorough search of prior court cases showed no such prior occurrence. The plaintiff's lawyers were less convincing on this issue than on the previous two issues of combustibility and circuit breaking. Thus it was reasoned that if this were the only predictive criterion, then the plaintiff would have only a .30

> probability of winning. There seemed to be a consensus, however, that this was an especially important issue deserving more weight than the others. The first two predictive criteria were considered less weighty in view of the expected biases of the plaintiff's and defendant's predictions. The third and fourth factual elements are not that crucial, since even if it were shown that it is physically possible for the appliance to burn and physically possible for the circuit not to break, this does not indicate that burning or nonbreaking occurred in this instance or ever occurred in any previous instance. However, if a pattern of previous fires due to this appliance could be shown, that would be devastating to the product and practically assure victory to the plaintiff.

Section C of table 8-2 shows how the probabilities on the predictive criteria are combined. If each criterion were equally important, then we could add .70 + .10 + .40 + .40 + .30, and obtain a total of 1.90. We could then divide by five predictive criteria and get an average of .38. We would thus be saying, if on any one predictive criterion (such as the third) there is a .40 probability of plaintiff victory and we add a second predictive criterion (like the defendant's prediction) which is only .10, then it seems logical to average the two for an average of .25. This assumes both predictions are equally important and accurate. This is like averaging the allocation percentages between two different allocation criteria back in the estate allocation example in chapter 3 on "Computer-Aided Counseling." If, however, one criterion is about twice as important as the others, then we should logically count it twice or give it a weight or multiplier of 2 as with the fifth criterion. Doing so means adding another .30 to the 1.90 and obtaining a total of 2.20. We then divide that weighted total by the sum of the weights, which is 6, and we obtain a probability of .37, which is where the 36.67% comes from in the bottom line.[2]

Determining What It Would Take to Make the Loser into the Winner

One might ask for any given predictive criterion, How do the probabilities have to change in order to bring the victory probability for the plaintiff up to .50, .80, or any other probability in which one is interested? The algebra for answering that question is relatively simple and can be more explicitly programmed as part of the P/G% threshold analysis, although that has not yet been done. Suppose we want to know how high the plaintiff victory probability has to go on the combustibility criterion in order to make the plaintiff a winner given the scores and weights on the other four criteria. Being a winner in this context means having an overall probability of more than .50. An easy way to answer that question is by summing $.70 + .10 + X + .40 + .30 + .30$ for a total of $1.80 + X$. Notice that we added the .30 twice because the fifth criterion had a weight of 2. The next step is to divide that sum by 6 since the sum of the weights is 6. We then solve for X in the equation $(1.80 + X)/6 = .50$. The solution is $1.80 + X = 3.00$, and thus $X = 3.00 - 1.80$, which is 1.20.

As an alternative to this algebraic approach, one could use a reiterative guessing approach to arrive at the same result. Doing so would involve proceeding as follows:

1. The initial pair of probabilities on the third criterion are .40 and .60. In order for the plaintiff to come up to a 50–50 tie with the defendant, the .40 probability would have to be raised.
2. We might therefore try .80 and .20 as a new pair of probabilities. We would insert them into the data matrix in place of the .40 and .60. We would then ask for a new primary analysis.
3. The new primary analysis, however, would still show a probability of less than .50 for the victory probability of the plaintiff. We might then substitute a pair of probabilities equal to 1.00 and 0, and ask to see the new primary analysis.
4. Even doing that causes the overall plaintiff victory probability to be less than .50. We might then try 1.20 and −.20. If we then ask for the primary analysis, the overall or averaged probabilities are .50 and .50. That informs us that we have found the threshold probabilities for the combustibility predictive criterion.
5. On step 4, we might have easily overshot the mark by trying 1.30 and −.30. That would be indicated by the overall plaintiff probability being higher than .50. If so, then on the next step we would come back down a bit from 1.30 toward 1.00, and move up a bit from −.30 toward 0. Doing so would eventually converge on 1.20 and −.20.
6. Some people would consider that kind of reiterative guessing to be rather inelegant compared to the algebraic method, which goes immediately to the right answer. It is partly a matter of taste. The reiterative guessing method can be done quite fast with the P/G% program, which allows one to see experimental changes quickly. It also has the advantage of avoiding clerical errors that are made in algebra and arithmetic. It has the further advantage of being easier to conceptualize as to what is happening, and it quickly shows that the alleged threshold values realy are tie-causing values.

As for interpreting the 1.20, it tells us that the combustibility issue would have to generate a plaintiff victory probability of 1.20 in order for the overall probability to be .50 given all the other numbers. That in effect tells us that there is no way that the plaintiff can win in terms of the overall probability by increasing only the combustibility evidence since no probability can be higher than 1.00. The threshold analysis can give us a threshold probability for every cell and every weight so we can see what combinations of changes might lead to victory for the second-place alternative, which is the plaintiff winning. We know that if the threshold probability in the top row under combustibility is 1.20, then the threshold probability immediately beneath it would have to be −.20 since the two probabilities have to add to 1.00, although the current computer program does not know that. A probability of −.20 is just as impossible as a probability of 1.20. We can easily see that 1.20 makes sense because if we substitute 1.20 for the .40 that is now in that cell and add across, we then obtain a figure of .70 + .10 + 1.20 + .40 + .30 + .30. That sum adds to 3.00. If we then divide by 6, we obtain .50. We would also see proof if we substitute a −.20 for the .60 in the second row and then add across, since we will then also obtain a sum of 3.00. If we think merely getting above .50 is not sufficient insurance, we can change the equation we were working with to $(1.80 + X)/6 = .60$, rather than .50, or change the right-hand side to whatever high or low probability we are interested in. This helps clarify how the idea of threshold analysis applies to generalizing from facts by aggregating probabilities.

Generalizing from Facts to Determine Damages Likely to Be Awarded

The most common way that lawyers determine victory probabilities may be to start with an average figure like .65 in personal injury cases, and then ask whether the present case is above, below, or at the average regarding the probability that the plaintiff will win. If the lawyer decides this is an average or below-average case, then he or she has to decide roughly how much above or below .65. That method is cruder than either predicting from cases or predicting from facts. It does not explicitly consider prior cases, although it may be implicitly doing so. It does not explicitly consider the factual elements that go into determining liability, although it may implicitly do that too.

One interesting and useful aspect of that approach is that .65 seems to be the average probability of plaintiff victory regardless of the type of cases involved. It is the average probability by which the prosecutor wins in criminal cases according to the University of Chicago Jury Project. It is the average probability by which plaintiffs win in personal injury cases according to the Jury Verdict Research Service. It is also the percentage of international law cases that the United States wins according to the analysis that will be described shortly. The explanation for why .65 is such a common victory probability or percentage regardless of subject matter is:

1. If the victory probability is substantially below .50, then the plaintiff is not so likely to go to trial, but will be willing to settle or to withdraw.
2. If the victory probability is substantially above .75, then the defendant is not so likely to go to trial, but will be willing to settle.
3. If the victory probability is between .50 and .75, then the case is more likely to go to trial. A typical case in that set is likely to have a .65 victory probability.

Likewise, the most common way of predicting damages is probably through various rules of thumb like multiply the specials by 5, 10, or some other figure depending on whom one talks to. The specials consist of the out-of-pocket medical expenses and the lost wages. Thus, if the out-of-pocket medical expenses are $2,000 and the lost wages are $8,000 and the multiplier is considered to be 5, then the predicted damages would be $50,000 if the case is won. This is also cruder than predicting from prior cases, although the multiplier may be implicitly based on prior cases. It is also cruder than predicting from specific facts, which may include more relevant items than just the specials.

When one systematically predicts damages from prior cases, the most common approach may be to average the damages from similar cases. Thus suppose one knows of two similar cases. One was awarded $40,000 in damages, and the other was awarded $30,000. One might then predict the damages in the case at hand will be $35,000. That approach has the fault of relying on a small or large sample that may be unrepresentative. It also has the fault that the concept of "similar cases" may be highly subjective. In addition, it does not explicitly consider any facts that go into determining damages, although it may be implicitly saying something about what facts are relevant in how one defines or determines similarity.

As for a higher step in the quantitative prediction of damages, one can do a statistical regression analysis like that based on prior cases, such as the analysis described in discussing table 7-1 and especially table 7-4. The big drawback to doing so is that one is dependent on the prior cases that have occurred and especially on the variables that can be measured as having occurred within those prior cases. That may exclude important variables that are present in the case at hand that do not occur very often or that are difficult to measure quantitatively when they do occur. That is where predicting or generalizing from facts has an advantage since this method is not dependent on what is in the prior cases or what is conveniently measurable.

Table 8-3 provides an illustration of generalizing from facts in order to determine the damages that are likely to be awarded. The left side of section A shows alternative damage amounts for the case concerning the U.S. insurance company and the foreign electronics manufacturer. Seven rows of alternatives are listed. The first alternative is from $600,000 up to $700,000, and so on up to the fifth alternative which is $1,000,000 and up. The sixth row is blank. The seventh row refers to damages without providing for intervals. It is only the seventh alternative in which we are interested in this context.

The right side of section A shows the predictive criteria with which the mediator was actually working in this case. The predictive criteria did not include medical expenses or lost wages since this was a property damage case. The main damages involved a burned-out restaurant and some burned-out offices. This illustrates that a rule of thumb for predicting damages based on medical specials and lost wages would not have much applicability in this relatively common type of property damage case. The most important predictive criteria were considered to be the estimates of the knowledgeable lawyers on both sides of the case. They were not only knowledgeable in the sense of being specialists in product liability cases, including appliance-fire cases, but they were also knowledgeable about the facts of this specific case. The mediator discussed the likely damages with the lawyers separately, together with each other, and together with their clients. From these discussions one could roughly determine (1) the plaintiff's lowest prediction as to the damages likely to be awarded if the plaintiff wins, (2) the plaintiff's highest prediction, (3) the plaintiff's most likely prediction, (4) the defendant's lowest prediction, (5) the defendant's highest prediction, and (6) the defendant's most likely prediction.

Table 8-3
Determining Damages Likely to Be Awarded

A. THE DAMAGES ALTERNATIVES AND THE PREDICTIVE CRITERIA

Alternative	Criterion	Meas.Unit	Weight
1 $600,000	1 P'S LOW PRED.	$1,000'S	1.00
2 $700,000	2 P'S HIGH PRED.	$1,000'S	1.00
3 $800,000	3 P'S MOST LIKELY	"	2.00
4 $900,000	4 D'S LOW PRED.	"	1.00
5 $1,000,000	5 D'S HIGH PRED.	"	1.00
6	6 D'S MOST LIKELY	"	2.00
7*DAMAGES			

B. SCORES OF THE KEY ALTERNATIVE ON THE CRITERIA

ALTERNATIVE / CRITERIA SCORING

	P'S LOW	P'S HIGH	P'S MOST	D'S LOW	D'S HIGH	D'S MOST
DAMAGES	600.00	950.00	750.00	600.00	900.00	750.00

C. THE OVERALL OR AGGREGATE SCORE OF THE KEY ALTERNATIVE

Alternative	Combined Rawscores	%
7DAMAGES	6050.00	100.00

The measurement-unit column shows that these predictions are measured in $1,000 units to keep the numbers small and manageable. The weight column shows that extra weight is logically given to the plaintiff's most likely prediction and the defendant's most likely prediction, rather than to their lowest or highest predictions. We could also adjust the weights for the relative credibility of each side if one side seems to be perceiving the damages more accurately than the other side, possibly based on more experience or inside information. In this case there was no reason for giving more weight to one side than the other.

Section B of table 8-3 shows how the key alternative of "Damages" scored on each of the six criteria. The plaintiff's lowest prediction was about $600,000, and the highest was about $950,000. The plaintiff's most likely prediction was about $750,000. The most likely prediction is not necessarily the midpoint between the lowest and the highest. A person can estimate that somebody could be as young as 20 and as old as 50, but is probably 30. The defendant's lowest prediction was about $600,000 and the highest about $900,000, with the most likely prediction also at $750,000. One might wonder why the plaintiff's and defendant's predictions were so close here when they were so far apart regarding the victory probabilities. The answer is that victory probabilities are much more subjective. That was especially so in this case where the insurance company had already made payments to the injured parties. Those payments thus constituted liquidated damages, and thereby reduced some of the subjectivity that otherwise would have been present if the plaintiff insurance company were still arguing with the injured parties over the amount of property damage they had suffered.

Section C of table 8-3 provides an overall figure by summing eight separate figures, which come from the six basic figures shown in section B plus counting the plaintiff's and defendant's most likely predictions twice since both those criteria are given extra weights of 2. The sum of those eight figures is $6,050,000. That figure is then divided by 8, which is the sum of the weights, to arrive at an overall prediction of $756,250. That is the figure with which the mediator worked in seeking to bring about a fair settlement. The settlement involved considering more than just the damages. It also involved taking into consideration the possibility of the electronics manufacturer giving computers to the insurance company for use by its agents, also TV sets as sales bonuses, and claims against Americans that the manufacturer's foreign insurance company was willing to part with as described in chapter 4 dealing with "Computer-Aided Mediation." In seeking a settlement, the mediator tended to emphasize the plaintiff's lowest prediction when dealing with the plaintiff, and the defendant's highest prediction when dealing with the defendant.

AN INTERNATIONAL LAW CASE WITH MULTIPLE FACTS AND WEIGHTS

One can now combine what has previously been developed on predicting from cases and predicting from facts in order to obtain the benefits of both approaches. Table 8-3 provides such an illustration. It contains data from a set of 137 cases obtained from leading international law case books in which the United States was a party. The object here is to use those cases to develop a set of probabilities that can be aggregated to predict future cases that have various combinations of characteristics. The alternative positions in the past or future cases are the United States either wins or loses.

The Contents of an Empirical Probabilities Table

Table 8-4 works with seven predictive criteria. They include:

1. The main source of law. It could either be U.S. domestic law, international law or custom, a treaty, or the domestic law of another country.
2. The main subject matter. It could involve national territory, jurisdiction, hostilities between countries, diplomatic interaction, individuals in international law, treaty interpretations, responsibilities of the United States, or the responsibilities of other countries. This predictive criterion contains 14 subcategories based on various subject matters and what the U.S. position is for or against.

Table 8-4
Generalizing a Victory Probability from Factual Elements in Cases

Variables, Weights, and Categories (Arranged in rank order)	*Quantity of Cases in Category*	*Percent of Cases Won by U.S. in Category*
1. Main Source of Law ($r = .35$, $k = .24$)		
a) U.S. domestic law	53	85%
b) International law and custom	63	56
c) Treaty	17	47
d) Domestic law of other country	4	25
2. Main Subject Matter and U.S. Position ($r = .30$, $k = .27$)		
a) National territory and U.S. seeking change	3	100
b) National territory and U.S. seeking status quo	1	100
c) Jurisdiction and U.S. seeking it	26	85
d) Hostilities between countries and U.S. repelling interference	6	67
e) Diplomatic or consular intercourse and U.S. seeking redress	3	67
f) Individual in international law and U.S. seeking curtailment of his rights (e.g., deportation and alien rights)	26	65
g) Responsibility of other country asserted by U.S. generally for damages	17	65
h) Individual in international law and U.S. seeking to expand or maintain his rights (e.g., U.S. representing citizen in suit)	20	60
i) Treaty and U.S. seeking broad definition	10	60
j) Diplomatic and consular intercourse and redress sought from U.S.	2	50
k) Responsibility of U.S. asserted generally for damages	15	47
l) Treaty and U.S. seeking narrow definition	7	43
m) Hostilities between countries and U.S. seeking to interfere or obtain reparations	1	0
3. Decision-Making Tribunal ($r = .27$, $k = .17$)		
a) U.S. Supreme Court	41	76
b) Lower federal court	32	69
c) Ad hoc tribunals	56	61
d) British court	2	50
e) Non-British foreign court	3	33
f) Hague	3	0
4. Economic Interests and U.S. Position ($r = .24$, $k = .25$)		
a) U.S. liberal in antitrust cases	9	100
b) U.S. liberal in debtor–creditor cases	3	100
c) U.S. conservative in business v. labor cases	1	100
d) No economic interests involved or U.S. position neutral	119	61
e) U.S. conservative in debtor–creditor cases	5	60
5. Civil Liberty Interests and U.S. Position ($r = .23$, $k = .38$)		
a) U.S. liberal in noncriminal procedure matters	4	100
b) U.S. liberal in criminal procedure	6	83
c) U.S. conservative in noncriminal procedure matters	10	80
d) No civil liberty interest involved or U.S. position neutral	99	65
e) U.S. conservative in criminal procedure	16	44
6. Industrial Power of U.S. Opponent ($r = .21$, $k = .20$)		
a) Same	6	100
b) Not countries	70	70
c) Less	66	56
7. Nature of Plaintiff ($r = .19$, $k = .34$)		
a) State in U.S.	1	100
b) Alien in U.S.	10	80
c) Resident of foreign country	11	73
d) U.S. itself	75	68
e) U.S. citizen	14	57
f) Business firm	18	50
g) Other country	8	50

3. The decision-making tribunal. It could be the U.S. Supreme Court, a lower federal court, an ad hoc tribunal, a British court, a non-British foreign court, or The Hague. Under each predictive criterion, the subcategories are arranged in the order of the frequency of the cases that are found in those subcategories in the sample of 137 cases.
4. The economic interests, which could relate to antitrust, debtor-creditor, business-labor, or no economic interest. The U.S. position is also coded in these subcategories, which could be either liberal or conservative.
5. The civil liberties interest, which could relate to noncriminal procedure or criminal procedure. The U.S. position can either be liberal or conservative in these cases as well.
6. The industrial power of the U.S. opponent, which can be about the same as the United States, or less, or not a country.
7. The nature of the plaintiff in terms of being a U.S. state, a U.S. alien, a resident of a foreign country, the United States itself, a U.S. citizen, a business firm, or another country.

Table 8-4 is basically the same kind of table for aggregating probabilities as is table 8-2B, although at first glance they do not look alike. Table 8-2B shows its five predictive criteria on the columns. Table 8-4 has 43 predictive criteria arranged in seven groups. The first group refers to the source of law and includes four predictive criteria. The second group refers to the main subject matter and the U.S. position, and it includes 13 predictive criteria. The third through seventh groups contain 26 predictive criteria among those groups. That adds to 43 predictive criteria, which would be too much to show on the columns of an 8½ by 11 sheet, but not too much to show on the rows.

Table 8-2B has two rows. The top row shows the probability of the plaintiff winning and the bottom row shows the probability of the defendant winning for each criterion. Table 8-4 combines those two rows into one column labeled percent of cases won by the United States in the category or criterion to the left. To determine the probability or percent of the cases lost by the United States in the category to the left, just subtract the percentage shown from 100%. Thus the first percentage indicates that the United States won 85% of the cases that involved U.S. domestic law and thereby lost 15%. That is the same as saying the United States has a probability of .85 of winning in the U.S. domestic law cases and a .15 probability of losing.

A column is also included in table 8-4 showing the quantity of cases in each category. Thus the 85% in the top row translates into 45 cases won out of the 53 that involved U.S. domestic law, and the 15% translates into 8 cases lost. There is no such column showing the quantity of cases in table 8-2B. The reason is that the probabilities in table 8-2B are what might be called impressionistic probabilities. They are not based on any specific cases, but on a general impression that, for example, given the facts offered on combustibility the plaintiff seems to have about a .40 probability of winning. The probabilities or percentages in the international law table are sometimes referred to as empirical probabilities because they are based on actual prior cases. That is an unfortunate terminology because the so-called impressionistic probabilities are likely also to be based on prior empirical or observable experience. They may be even more valid (depending on whose observations are involved) than the small sample sizes and subjective category definitions that are associated with the international law probabilties. On the other hand, the empirical probabilities of table 8-4 could be more valid. The validity in predicting case outcomes depends on (1) how powerful the chosen predictors are in either situation, (2) how perceptive the person or group is who is scoring the impressionistic probabilities, and (3) how representative the samples of cases are from which the empirical probabilities come.

There is an important difference between table 8-2 on predicting the probability of victory in the product liability case and table 8-4 on doing likewise in the international dispute cases. Table 8-2 is constructed in such a way that all the predictive criteria apply to the case at hand because the table was constructed specifically for predicting that case. Most of the 43 predictive criteria in table 8-4 are likely to be not applicable to any given international law case. In fact, only seven of the 43 categories are likely to be applicable because the categories within each group are mutually exclusive. It does not have to be that way. One could develop a list of groups in which more than one category could apply to a given case. The mutual exclusivity of these lists within each group reflects one of the constraints of working with traditional survey research and mainframe computers for which these data were originally developed.

Applying an Empirical Probabilities Table

To apply table 8-4 to a specific case that is to be decided or that has already been decided, one first determines what seven categories apply to the case. One then adds the seven probabilities that are associated with those categories and divides by seven when the predictive criteria are considered equally important. One can, however, weight the predictive criteria in terms of their relative importance, and then sum the products of the weights and the probabilities, rather than add the probabilities alone. One would then divide by the sum of the weights in order to obtain an overall weighted probability.

As a concrete example, let us take the I. G. Farben case, 45 *Schweizerische Juristen-Zeitung* 341 (1949). The case involved a creditor of the I. G. Farben Company bringing suit in Switzerland to stop the confiscation of the I. G. Farben Swiss assets by the United States and the Allied Powers unless payments were first made to the legitimate creditors of the I. G. Farben Company. In terms of the seven variables in table 8-4, the case involves:

1. The domestic law of another country, namely Switzerland. The United States wins about 25% of such cases, although the sample size is only four cases in which the domestic law of another country was involved.
2. The United States is seeking reparations. The U.S. victory probability in such cases is

0%. One should, however, note that we are not basing the overall prediction on any one criterion. We could also weigh the criteria on the basis of the sample size for each criterion on the theory that the bigger the sample size the more reliable is the predictor up to a sample of about 30.

3. A non-British foreign court is involved in which the United States won 33% of the three past cases. There were not enough Swiss cases to have a special category for just those cases. We know, however, that one of the three cases is a Swiss case since the I. G. Farben case is part of the larger sample of 137 cases.
4. This case is one that involves economic interests between a debtor and a creditor. The debtor is the I. G. Farben Company, which is not a litigant in this case. The creditor is the plaintiff. The United States is the defendant, but the United States is not defending the I. G. Farben Company. The United States is seeking to take the assets away from both the creditor and the I. G. Farben Company and give them to people who were slave labor to the I. G. Farben Company, or give them to be used as part of the general reparations of Nazi Germany to the Allied Powers. The United States is thus neutral between the creditor and the debtor since it is taking a position contrary to both of them. That category involves a .61 probability of victory.
5. There are no civil liberty interests involved in this case, such as freedom of speech, equal protection under the law, or fair criminal procedure. In the 99 cases like that, the United States wins 65% of the time and loses 35% of the time.
6. The sixth predictive criterion relates to the industrial power of the U.S. opponent. The data tend to indicate that the United States does better when its opponent is an industrialized country like the United States, rather than a less-developed country. The explanation might be that international law may favor weaker countries who are not so likely to win on the battlefield or in other forms of international interaction. That is like the fact that minority groups do better before the U.S. Supreme Court than they do on the battlefield of a mob scene or before a legislature. In this I. G. Farben case, the U.S. opponent was a noncountry. This was an international law case involving a lot of countries, but no country was a plaintiff. In such cases, the United States wins 70% of the time.
7. The seventh predictive criterion allows for seven categories regarding tne nature of the plaintiff. In this case, the plaintiff is a resident of a foreign country. The 11 cases of that type resulted in a victory probability for the United States of .73.

If we add those seven probabilities, we obtain a sum of 3.27. If we divide that sum by seven, we obtain an overall average probability of .47. Since that number is closer to a probability of 0.00 than to a probability of 1.00, we would predict that the United States is more likely to lose this case than to win. That is what did happen in the I. G. Farben case. We can improve upon that predictive analysis by taking into consideration that the seven predictive criteria are not all equally important. This set of predictive criteria, like many sets in predicting law cases, can be divided into four general types of predictors. Those predictors in order of importance are:

1. The nature of the law, which is covered by the first criterion.
2. The nature of the facts, which is covered by the second criterion.

3. The nature of the decision-makers, which the third criterion covers.
4. The nature of the litigants, which criteria 4-7 cover.

If we give these criteria weights of 4, 3, 2, and 1, respectively, then the summation score for the I. G. Farben case would be (4)(.25) + (3)(0) + (2)(.33) + (1)(.61) + (1)(.65) + (1)(.70) + (1)(.73). The sum of those products is 4.36. If we divide that figure by the sum of the weights, which is 13, then we obtain an overall probability of .34. That is closer to the figure of 0.00, which represents a loss in the case for the United States. If instead of using those weights that are based on a knowledge of the subject matter, we use weights based on a mechanistic regression analysis, then the seven weights are 3.50, 3.00, 2.70, 2.40, 2.30, 2.10, and 1.90. Using those seven weights or multipliers, we get a new overall sum of 7.58. If we divide that sum by the sum of the weights, which is 17.90, we obtain an overall probability of .42. This is further away from the 0.00 figure than the .34 obtained using the commonsense weights.[3]

SOME CONCLUSIONS

Further Summarizing the Methods

Chapters 7 and 8 have discussed various prediction methods. Chapter 7 emphasized generalizing from cases by relating the summation scores of the cases in a P/G% table to the outcomes of the cases. That relating can be done in two ways. One way is largely verbal in the form of if-then statements. An example would be a set of statements saying (1) if the summation score is 3 or below, then the defendant is likely to win, (2) if the summation score is 6 or above, then the plaintiff is likely to win, and (3) if the summation score is 4 or 5, then the case at hand is temporarily unpredictable until we do more processing or obtain more information.

The second way of relating the summation scores to the case outcomes is in the form of an equation like $Y = A + BX$. In that equation, Y is sentence length, damages, or winning (expressed as a 1) or losing (expressed as a 0), and X is the summation score. From the P/G% data matrix, the computer can generate a numerical value for the A coefficient showing the value of Y when X is zero, and for the B coefficient showing how much Y moves up when X moves up one unit.

Chapter 8 emphasizes generalizing from facts by aggregating probabilities or averaging continuum outcomes. An example of the averaging of probabilities might be a set of statements saying (1) if the only information we have were X_1, then the plaintiff would have a .70 probability of winning, (2) if the only information we have were X_2, then the plaintiff would have a .20 probability of winning, and (3) since we have information on both X_1 and X_2 and they are equally important subjects, then we say the overall probability of the plaintiff winning is .45, which is 70 + .20 divided by 2.

An example of the averaging of continuum outcomes might be a set of statements saying (1) if the only information we have were Z_1, then the damages would be about $2,000, (2) if the only information we have were Z_2, then the damages would be about $4,000, and (3) since we have information about both Z_1 and $_2$ and they are equally important subjects, then we say the overall damages when the plaintiff wins are likely to be about $3,000, which is $2,000 + $4,000 divided by 2.

Further Comparisons

There are some additional comparisons concerning these two methods that have not already been made, especially in the first part of Chapter 8. Both methods can rely on cases to some extent. This can be seen in the use of the international law cases as an illustration of predicting from facts in Chapter 8. That example was used in Chapter 8 because it involves averaging probabilities or outcomes, which is really the essence of the method of predicting from facts.

Both methods can rely on facts if facts refer to predictive criteria. Along related lines, one might note that predicting from cases does not necessarily involve much in the way of cases. This can be seen in the use of cases in predicting the outcome of welfare proceedings. Twelve case types were used, but only two corresponded to actual cases. The other case types were hypothetical combinations of facts whose outcomes could be deduced from the cases that were actually decided or from quotations within those cases.

The method of predicting from cases may often be superior to traditional multivariate regression analysis because it is simpler and less confounded by interactions that result in weights that conflict with known facts. However, the method of prediction from cases or P/G% prediction does use regression analysis as a useful way of relating the summation scores to the case outcomes.

The method of predicting from facts or P/G% probability analysis may often be superior to traditional Bayesian probability analysis becaause it is simpler and makes better use of the limited information that is available. However, the method of predicting from facts does make use of a fundamental principle of Bayesian analysis: namely, that a probability can legitimately be a kind of gut feeling so that probabilities of 0, .25, .50, .75, and 1.00 are roughly the equivalent of attitude scores on a 1, 2, 3, 4, and 5 scale. This is in contrast to narrower notions that probabilities have to be deductive (like the probability of two heads when flipping two coins is .25), or that they have to be inductive (like the probability of a plaintiff wining is .25 because plaintiffs won 1 out of 4 recent cases).

Either predicting from cases or from facts can be combined with legal retrieval systems like Lexis or WestLaw. Those systems can generate cases like the set of nine cases in table 7-1 dealing with legislative redistricting or the set of 137 cases in table 8-4 dealing with international law disputes in which the United States is a party. What both systems lack as of now is any provision for systematically processing the cases that they retrieve. A big step in the direction of enabling the cases to be more systematically processed would be to note within the data base for each case whether the plaintiff or the defendant won. Doing so can help provide the outcome column when predicting from cases. It can also provide useful information for calculating the probabilities of victory when predicting from facts.

At the beginning of the chapter, it was mentioned that predicting from cases has the advantage of explicitly drawing upon prior precedents, and predicting from facts has the advantage of freeing one from the constraint of having to work with a limited sample of prior cases. One can combine the two approaches by doing the same field of law in both ways separately. One can also combine the approaches by working with a set of cases to generate probabilities for facts or predictive criteria. The probabilities can then be averaged for the case at hand, as was done with the international law cases.

Perhaps the most important point is that both methods of predicting from cases or facts using the P/G% system or related spreadsheet-based systems are simple and valid enough for lawyers to use without any technical training in statistics or mathematical probability. Both methods reflect a kind of common sense among lawyers regarding how case outcomes are to be predicted. In that sense, P/G% prediction (like P/G% choosing and allocating) seeks to reflect what good decision-makers implicitly do. This is in contrast to telling lawyers what statisticians or mathematicians think they ought to do as if they were operating in a world in which there are only algebraic symbols, hypothetical numbers, or complete information on all variables and cases. We need predictive methods for operating in the real world of multidimensionality and limited information to make predictions that relate to important decisions.[4]

OTHER EXAMPLES

Chapters 7 and 8 have used a variety of examples to illustrate predicting from cases and predicting from facts. Those examples have included predicting the outcomes of cases that relate to (1) legislative redistricting, (2) welfare proceedings, (3) criminal cases, (4) a product liability case, and (5) international law cases in which the United States is a party. Many of the applications in chapters 11, 12, and 13 are also relevant for providing examples that could involve either predicting from cases or from facts.

Especially relevant applications from those chapters include:

1. Predicting winners in civil cases on the basis of the characteristics of the decision-makers, the applicable law, the place where the case is tried, and the litigants (Chapter 11).
2. Predicting the outcomes of equal protection cases before the U.S. Supreme Court on the basis of the nature of the rights that are allegedly violated (including voting, criminal justice, schools, employment, housing, and consumer rights) and the nature of the groups who are allegedly being discriminated against (including race, gender, economic class, and region) (Chapter 12).

Other applications can easily be used to aid in predicting relevant case outcomes, especially the other applications from the private practice examples including:

3. Predicting who will win in a dispute over the division of the profits of a partnership (Chapter 11).
4. Predicting who will win in a dispute over the allocation of an estate (Chapter 11).
5. Predicting who will win in a divorce dispute over child custody, child support, or a property settlement (Chapter 11).

The applications involving legal policy disputes also lend themselves to predictive or explanatory analysis. In predictive analysis, we are trying to determine the combinations of predictive criteria or facts that will lead to various outcomes. In explanatory analysis, we are frequently trying to determine the goals or motives of the decision-makers. Thus, any one of the legal policy applications could be used as an example of predictive or explanatory analysis. Two examples that especially stand out are:

6. In discussing judicial review, the points are made that (a) societies that choose legislative supremacy probably place a high value on popular responsiveness; (b) societies that choose judicial review probably place a high value on sensitivity to minority rights; and (c) societies that provide for executive fiat with no constitutional review probably have a negative attitude (at least among the key decision-makers) toward popular responsiveness and sensitivity to minority rights (Chapter 12).
7. In discussing right to counsel, the point is made that the reason right to counsel was not provided in misdemeanor cases or felony cases from the start is because the key decision-makers were sensitive to the goal of not deviating greatly from prevailing precedent as well as sensitive to the goal of acquitting the innocent (Chapter 13).
8. In discussing arms control, the point is made that President Reagan's motivation in suggesting a bilateral reduction rather than a freeze could be explained by diametrically opposed considerations. On the one hand, he may have been trying to decrease the chances of an arms control agreement by proposing a drastic idea that the Soviet Union would be likely to reject, especially since they had more to lose by a nuclear arms reduction since they had less nuclear capability. On the other hand, he may have been sincerely seeking to go beyond a nuclear freeze partly because he liked playing the role of a peacemaker. Thus this kind of explanatory analysis often results in more than one explanation that is consistent with the alternative chosen and in a general way with the goals and relations (Chapter 12).
9. In discussing juries in civil cases, the alternatives of limited jury and full jury turn out to be approximately a tie. The explanation may be that this is common in controversial matters, which is partly what makes them controversial. There is often a trade-off or an ambivalence in the sense that one alternative does well on one goal, but another alternative does well on another goal. The same alternative may do well on some goals and poorly on others. Thus, part of the problem may be that liberals like the idea of 12-person unanimous juries, especially in criminal cases to protect

innocent defendants from being convicted. Such juries in civil cases, however, decrease the probability of injured plaintiffs collecting, as compared to having to convince only six jurors by a majority vote.

Another relevant kind of explanatory or predictive analysis involves knowing only some of the decision-making elements and seeking to deduce the nature of the remaining elements. The key elements in decision-making are the goals to be achieved, their relative weights, the alternatives available for achieving them, constraints on the alternatives, and relations between goals and alternatives in order to choose the best alternative, combination, or allocation. Any of the legal policy applications could be used as an example of that kind of deductive analysis, including:

10. Suppose we know a given decision-maker's goals, weights, and perceptions of the relations. Then we can predict which alternative or alternatives that decision-maker is likely to choose in the consumer protection example (Chapter 11).
11. Suppose we know that a decision-maker has decided in favor of private housing ownership with government rent subsidies as the best way of providing housing for the poor. Then we can offer some explanations for what that decision-maker's goals, weights, and perceptions of the relations are likely to be in the example of housing for the poor (Chapter 11).
12. Suppose we know a given decision-maker's goals, perceptions of the relations, and preferred choice in the no-fault divorce problem. Then we can deduce what relative weights the decision-maker might have for the goals in order to arrive at that preferred choice (Chapter 11).
13. Suppose we know a given decision-maker's goals, weights, and preferred choice in the problem involving alternative tort systems. Then we can deduce what he or she might be likely to perceive the relations between the alternatives and the goals to be (Chapter 11).
14. Suppose we know a given decision-maker's preferred choice or choices and how he or she perceives the relations in the problem involving crime reduction. Then we can deduce what the goals and their relative weights might be (Chapter 12).
15. Suppose we know for a given decision-maker everything except a single weight or a single relation, as in the problem of appropriate legislation for dealing with unemployment and inflation. In terms of a spreadsheet analysis like P/G%, that is an objective problem like solving for X in an equation of the form $2X = 6$. The computer can quickly inform us as to the threshold value for the missing weight or relation score. The computer can also tell us that the decision-maker would have to be above or below that threshold value for a certain alternative to be the preferred alternative, given that we know the values for the other weights and relations.

Explanatory analysis is not only of value to political and other social scientists interested in explaining the behavior of people in the legal system. It is also of value to practicing lawyers, especially in an advocacy context. If one can explain why judges tend to decide for the plaintiff in a certain type of case, then that information can be useful to a future plaintiff's lawyer regarding what to emphasize or to a future defendant's lawyer regarding what to deemphasize. Both explanatory and predictive analyses tend to have little value in themselves to practicing lawyers, but considerable value as inputs into other lawyer activities or skills. Both predicting and explaining are useful (1) in counseling clients as to what is likely to happen and why; (2) in deciding whether to go to trial or accept a settlement, which is closely associated with mediation as well as negotiation; and (3) in evaluating alternative legal policies.

NOTES

1. On the systematic synthesizing of facts in trial decisions to arrive at a probability of guilt of liability, see Charles Kingston, "Probability and Legal Proceedings," 57 *Journal of Criminal Law, Criminology, and Police Science* 93-98 (1966); Richard Lempert, "Modeling Relevance," *Michigan Law Review* 021-1057 (1977); Peter Lindsey and Donald Norman, *Human Information Processing* (Orlando, Fla.: Academic Press, 1972), 549-556; Martin Kaplan and Gwen Kemmerick, "Juror Judgement as Information Integration: Combining Evidential and Nonevidential Information," *Journal of Personality and Social Psychology* 493-499 (1974); and David Schum, "Contrast Effects in Inference: On the Conditioning of Current Evidence by Prior Evidence," 18 *Organizational Behavior and Human Performance* 217-253 (1977).

2. The traditional approach to aggregating probabilities is to use the formulas associated with Bayesian probability calculations. Those calculations are almost unbelievably complicated, especially with more than one predictive criterion. An analysis of what those calculations require in the context of predicting case outcomes is given by S. Nagel, "Alternative Predictive and Analytic Techniques Applicable to Multiple-Category Variables" in *The Legal Process from a Behavioral Perspective* (Homewood, Ill.: Dorsey Press, 1969), 169-171, and S. Nagel, D. Lamm, and M. Neef, "Decision Theory and Juror Decision-Making," in Bruce Sales (ed.), *The Trial Process* (New York: Plenum, 1981), 373-376.

Averaging the probabilities will get exactly the same result if there is only one predictive criterion. Averaging the probabilities will also give approximately the same result no matter how many predictive criteria there are if there is little overlap among the predictive criteria or if the overlap is taken into consideration by how the criteria are weighted. For example, if two criteria are highly redundant, then instead of giving each criterion a weight of 1.00, they should be given a weight of .50 apiece. If they are mildly redundant, then .90 apiece might be appropriate. Assigning weights does have an element of subjectivity to it, although there may be reasonable agreement among knowledgeable people. More important, the approach of averaging weighted probabilities is possible to do, whereas the approach of obtaining information on the degree of overlap using the Bayesian approach is virtually impossible in any real-world problem given the Bayesian emphasis on odds, likelihood ratios, priors, and conditional probabilities.

3. For further details concerning the analysis of the international dispute cases, see "Empirical Probability Tables: International Dispute Cases" in Nagel, *The Legal Process*, 157-172; and Martin Goodman, "United States as a Party in International Law Disputes" (Bachelor's Thesis in the University of Illinois Law Library, 1964). The unweighted summation method is related to the prediction system used by the Gluecks for

predicting delinquency and other forms of criminal behavior. Sheldon Glueck and Eleanor Glueck, *Predicting Delinquency and Crime* (1959), 18-32.

4. On systematic synthesizing of facts in trial decisions, see Jerome Frank, *Courts on Trial: Myth and Reality in American Justice* (Princeton, N.J.: Princeton University Press, 1950); Sales, *The Trial Process;* and Norbert Kerr and Robert Bray (eds.), *The Psychology of the Courtroom* (New York: Academic Press, 1982). Relevant software for calculating probabilities includes the Bayesian probabilities program in the package called "Computer Models for Management Science," from Addison-Wesley, Reading, Mass.

SECTION D

Law Administration

CHAPTER 9

Assigning Lawyers to Case Types

Table 9-1 shows how one can systematically view the problem of assigning lawyers to types of cases as an example of the more general problem of assigning people to tasks. This hypothetical problem involves two lawyers named Able and Baker. It involves the case types of criminal and civil cases. Each lawyer is expected to bill 30 hours in an average week. In such a week, there are about 24 criminal hours and 36 civil hours. The problem could be expanded to include more people and more tasks, but two people and two tasks can be used to illustrate the general methodology.

THE INPUT INFORMATION

The partners in the hypothetical law firm decide to score themselves on their degree of interest in each type of case. They do so using a 1–5 scale, where 5 = highly interested, 4 = mildly interested, 3 = neither interested nor disinterested, 2= mildly disinterested, and 1 = highly disinterested. The partners also decide to score each other anonymously on degree of ability in each type of case, where 5 = highly capable on this type of case, 4 = mildly capable, 3 = neither capable nor incapable but just average, 2 = mildly incapable, and 1 = highly incapable. As an alternative to scoring each other on ability, the partners could measure ability in terms of years of experience or quantity of previous cases handled within each case type. That scoring can also be converted into a 1–5 scale.

Each partner or associate then receives an overall score that is the sum of the separate scores on interest and ability. Each separate score can be given equal weight, or the ability scores can be doubled to show that they are twice as important. The overall score can then be divided by the number of scores or the

Table 9-1
The Problem of Allocating 60 Hours to Two Lawyers for Two Case Types

LAWYER \ CASES	CRIMINAL		CIVIL		
	Quality Score	Hours Assigned	Quality Score	Hours Assigned	Hours per Lawyer
ABLE	4	a	3	b	30
BAKER	2	c	3	d	30
Hours per Casetype		24		36	60

NOTES:

1. The allocation system is shown in its simplest form with two lawyers and two case types in the law firm.
2. Each lawyer is expected to put in 30 billable hours a week to satisfy the average weekly total of 60 hours of billable time for the firm.
3. Criminal cases constitute 40% of the total or 24 hours, and civil cases constitute 60% or 36 hours in an average week.
4. Lawyer Able receives scores of 4 and 3 on the two case types, and Lawyer Baker receives scores of 2 and 3.
5. Hours per case type and hours per lawyer refer to billable hours, as contrasted to hours that cut across cases and are thus not billable to any specific client, such as general background reading.
6. The problem is to decide approximately how many hours a week should Able do on criminal cases (a) and on civil cases (b), and approximately how many hours should Baker do on criminal cases (c) and on civil cases (d).

sum of the weights in order to give each person a 1–5 overall score. In the hypothetical data, Lawyer Able receives a score of 4 on criminal cases and a 3 on civil cases. Lawyer Baker receives a 2 on criminal cases and a 3 on civil cases.

THE OVERALL GOAL AND PROCEDURES

The object of the analysis is to determine how to assign the 60 hours to the two lawyers so as to provide the best allocation of the lawyers to the case types, or more generally the best allocation of people to tasks. "Best" in this context means an allocation or assignment that will result in a maximum overall quality sum of each product of a lawyer's quality score times the hours assigned for a given case type. In this context, the overall quality score is equal to 4a + 2c + 3b + 3d. The object is to solve for a, b, c, and d so as to maximize that overall score while satisfying the constraints.

The best way to proceed if one does not have a computer is to give as few hours as possible to those cells that have quality scores of 1, or 2, and as many hours as possible to those that have quality scores of 5 or 4 while still satisfying the constraints. Doing so results in an allocation of 0 hours to cell c, 8 hours to a, 2 hours to b, and 10 hours to d.

MICROCOMPUTERS AND MODIFICATIONS

The method just described can be meaningful for a substantial number of judges and case types. One can, however, solve big judicial assignments faster and with more accuracy by using a linear programming routine. Such routines are easy to use on microcomputers. One simply informs the computer of the row totals, the column totals, and the quality scores. The computer then generates the optimum allocations.

The program, will also indicate (1) how much each quality score can vary without affecting the optimum result, (2) how much each row total and column total can vary, and (3) how much of a change in the overall quality score would occur as a result of a one-unit change in the hours assigned or in any of the inputs. In most problems that involve assigning people to tasks, the quality scores can vary substantially without affecting the results, thereby allowing considerable leeway for error. Knowing which changes will have the most effect on the overall output can be helpful in deciding how to change the constraints or other inputs.[1]

OTHER EXAMPLES

This short example involves assigning lawyers to cases. The same kind of analysis, although with different goals, could be used to assign judges to cases to promote courthouse efficiency, or to assign clerical personnel to various tasks to promote law firm efficiency. Rather than assigning lawyers to cases in terms of general ability and interests, one can think in terms of the more specific skills discussed in Part II of this book, such as ability and interest concerning counseling, negotiating, trial technique, mediating, legal policy evaluation, appellate advocacy, or case analysis-prediction. One can also think in terms of more specific case types than simply criminal and civil, such as those discussed in Part III, which include contracts, property, family disputes, torts, constitutional law, economic regulation, and international law, as well as criminal and civil substance and procedure.

NOTE

1. On computer-aided assignment of people to tasks, see Sang Lee et al., *Management Science* (Dubuque, Iowa: Wm. C. Brown, 1981), 177-235; Samuel Richmond, *Operations Research for Management Decisions* (New York: Ronald Press, 1968),

277-285; Warren Erikson and Owen Hall, *Computer Models for Management Science* (Reading, Mass.: Addison-Wesley, 1986), 1-86; and S. Nagel and M. Mills, "Allocating Attorneys to Casetypes," 15 *Capital University Law Review* 223-242 (1986).

CHAPTER 10

Case Sequencing and Law Firm Efficiency

The purpose of this chapter is to describe how the methods of optimum sequencing can improve the efficiency and profits of law practice. Optimum sequencing refers to the order in which cases or other jobs are handled so as to maximize benefits minus costs or income minus expenses. Different arrangements of the cases or jobs can have different degrees of benefits, costs, and profitability.

Table 10-1 shows an example of optimum sequencing applied to law cases. The illustrative problem is: "What is the best order in which to handle three cases that involve an estimated 10, 20, and 30 hours and that are predicted to generate $21, $61, and $80 in billing?" To make the problem more exciting, consider each billing as being measured in $1,000 units, although we will see that optimum sequencing works with any monetary units and any set of hypothetical or real cases. For the sake of simplicity, assume we have a one-lawyer firm who works a 40-hour week. With three cases labeled A, B, and C, there are six ways in which they can be ordered: ABC, ACB, BAC, BCA, CAB, and CBA. Which is the best order?

THE ALTERNATIVES AND THE CRITERIA

A more general way to view the problem is in terms of five different methods that are frequently proposed for ordering cases in a law firm, a government agency, or elsewhere. Those alternative methods arranged randomly are:

1. Take the cases in the order of the highest benefits first. That means CBA.
2. Look to the cases with the lowest costs first. That means ABC.
3. Take them first come, first served. That also means ABC.

Table 10-1
Law Firm Administration: Sequencing Cases
(PROBLEM: What is the best order to handle three cases that involve 10, 20, and 30 hours and that generate $21, $61, and $80 in billing?)

A. The Alternatives: Five Sequencing Methods

	Alternative
1	Highest B's First
2	Lowest C's First
3	1st Come, 1st Serv
4	Highest B-C First
5	Highest B/C First

B. The Criteria: Two Weeks of Profit

	Criterion	*Meas. Unit*	*Weight*
1	1st Week Profit	$	2.00
2	2nd Week Profit	$	1.00

C. The Profit Obtained by Each Alternative for Each Week

	Alternative/Criteria Scoring	
	1st Week	*2nd Week*
Highest B's Fir	70.50	31.50
Lowest C's Firs	68.67	33.33
1st Come, 1st S	68.67	33.33
Highest B-C Fir	70.50	31.50
Highest B/C Fir	74.33	27.67

D. The Overall Score for Each Sequencing Method

	Alternative	*Combined Rawscores*
1	Highest B's First	172.50
2	Lowest C's First	170.67
3	1st Come, 1st Serve	170.67
4	Highest B-C First	172.50
5	Highest B/C First	176.33

NOTES:

1. The above computer printout shows that by taking the first three cases in the order of the highest benefit/cost ratio first, one thereby maximizes overall benefits minus costs.

2. This is so because the B/C order results in more profit being earned earlier, and that profit is thus available to draw interest or to be reinvested more so than if it earned later.

3. In the above example profit from the first week is given twice the weight or importance as profit of the second week. An alternative approach would be to weight the weeks equally, but to time-discount the second week more so than the first week.

4. The reasonable assumption is that the 60 hours of work involved in doing the first three cases means 40 hours in the first week and 20 hours in the second week. The assumption is also that there is billing every week, not just at the end of the cases, and that the bills are paid promptly.

4. Prefer the most profitable first, meaning the ones with the highest benefits minus costs. That means C ($80-30), B ($61-20), and then A ($21-10).
5. Take them in the order of their benefit/cost ratios. That means B ($61/20, or 3.05), C ($80/30, or 2.67), and then A ($21/10, or 2.10).

We want to pick the best ordering criterion in terms of maximizing the profits of the law firm, while operating within ethical constraints. At first glance, one might think the order of the cases will make no difference in the profit that can be made from these three cases. The cases are going to consume a total of 60 hours regardless of the order in which they are handled. Likewise, the order will not affect the fact that they will collectively bring in $162 in billings. If we assume that one hour is worth $1 or one monetary unit, then their net profit will be $162 minus $60, or $102 regardless of the order in which they are processed.

At second glance, however, we realize that one method may bring in more money earlier than another method. The method that brings in the most money as early as possible is the most profitable because that early money can be invested in the firm or elsewhere, thereby drawing interest that might otherwise be a missed opportunity. Table 10-1B shows that the criterion for judging these methods should be how much profit they generate in the first week, the second week, and so on, with more weight given to the profit of the first week than the second week.

HOW THE ALTERNATIVES COMPARE

Table 10-1 shows for each method how profitable it is in terms of the separate weekly profits, rather than the overall profit, which is the same $102 for all methods. The winning method is taking the cases in the order of their benefit/cost ratios. That method generates $74.33 in the first week, which is about $4 higher than its nearest competitor. If we assume that these numbers are $1,000 units, then by not taking the cases in their B/C order, the firm may be losing the interest that could have been made on $4,000 invested for one week. If that kind of loss is multiplied by 52 weeks and 30 cases rather than three cases, then a lot of money may be needlessly lost.

The $74.33 is calculated by noting that case B has the highest B/C ratio, and thus comes first. Case B takes 20 hours and generates a net profit of $41. We then go to case C, which has the second best B/C ratio. It takes 30 hours, but we only have 20 hours left in the week. We, therefore, do two-thirds of the case, and thus earn two-thirds of the $50 profit, which is $33.33. If we add that to $41, the first week generates $74.33 profit. The second week brings $27.67 in profit, or the remainder of the $102.

One can contrast that optimally profitable sequencing with any of the other less profitable methods. For example, if the cases are processed in terms of their individual profitability, we would take case C first, rather than case B. Doing so would consume 30 hours for a profit of $50. We would then have time for only

10 of 20 hours of case B, which is the next most profitable case. That would earn half of the $41 profit, or $20.50. If we add $50 to $20.50, then we get only $70.50, or $70,500, rather than $74.33, or $74,333.

To be more exact we could time discount the profits of the second week using the time-discounting provisions of the P/G% program. That would give a more accurate overall score than giving the first week's profits a weight of 2. The time discounting, however, would not change the rank order as to which is the best sequencing method.

IMPLICATIONS FOR COMPUTERS AND CLIENTS

A computer can aid in implementing the B/C sequencing method by questioning the relevant lawyers as the cases come in about their estimates of the expenses and income for each case. The computer can then arrange the cases each week in the order of the B/C ratios, and then display that order to aid in deciding which case to take next. To prevent cases with a low B/C ratio from being unreasonably delayed, the computer can flag cases for immediate processing in time to meet the statute of limitations, other deadlines, or an ethical constraint that says no case should have to wait more than a given time to reach a certain stage.

By following such procedures, the law firm administration will not only be maximizing the law firm's profits, but it will also be maximizing the happiness of the clients collectively. This is so if we assume that $1 in billing activity generates the equivalent of one happiness unit. That way the B/C method thus generates more client happiness earlier than the alternative methods do. The estimated total happiness units per week can be calculated by adding 40 to the numbers given in the first column of Table 10-1C and adding 20 to the numbers in the second column. The B/C method thus generates 114.33 happiness units, which is higher than any of the other methods. It is pleasing when law firm administrative methods can be found that maximize both the interests of the law firm and the interests of the clients.[1]

OTHER EXAMPLES

The example used to illustrate case sequencing in this short chapter is a general example that does not specify the type of case. That is largely because the general rule that it presents is applicable to all types of cases regardless of whether they involve contracts, property, family disputes, torts, criminal law, constitutional issues, economic regulation, international law, or other subjects. The general rule is that one will maximize overall benefits minus costs for the set of cases by arranging the cases in the order of their benefit/cost ratios, where cost mainly refers to time consumption. One exception might be where the shortest cases have to be taken first in order to obtain payment for them given a severe cash flow problem. Normally it would not make sense to take a short case that involves only a small return in favor of a slightly longer case that involves a much larger return. Another exception is where certain nonmonetary benefits must be received quickly, such as establishing a precedent on which the other cases depend. The rule of proceeding in the order of the benefit/cost ratios may also have to be deviated from in order to satisfy the statute of limitations or other timely performance rules. They require that certain actions must be taken within a certain time frame backed by such negative sanctions as a malpractice action or a reprimand.

Mentioning cash flow and nonmonetary benefits implies that there are at least two types of cases for purposes of applying the methodology of optimum sequencing. They are those in which all the benefits are monetary, and those in which some of the benefits are nonmonetary. When all the benefits are monetary, one can easily add the separate benefits within each case in order to obtain a total income or total benefits figure for each case. When some of the benefits are nonmonetary, one has to change all of the benefits into a common measurement unit in order to be able to add them for a total benefits figure for each case. The common measurement unit might be money if the nonmonetary benefits can be meaningfully monetized. An alternative where monetizing is not so available is to convert the raw numbers for each case into percentages by summing all the raw numbers on a given type of benefit and then dividing each raw number by the sum. That generates a set of part/whole percentages. They are useful in dealing with the problem of multidimensionality, not only for sequencing but also for choosing, allocating, predicting, and other forms of reasoning that involve multiple goals or multiple predictive criteria. Part/whole percentaging is a key aspect of Policy/Goal Percentaging, which is partly how it derived its name.

NOTE

1. On computer-aided sequencing (CAS) of law firm cases and other jobs, see S. Nagel "Sequencing and Allocating Attorney Time to Cases," 13 *Pepperdine Law Review* 1021-1039 (1986); and S. Nagel, Mark Beeman, and John Reed, "Optimum Sequencing of Court Cases to Reduce Delay," 37 *Alabama Law Review* 583-638 (1986). Also see the more general literature on efficient sequencing, such as Richard Conway et al., *Theory of Scheduling* (Reading, Mass.: Addison-Wesley, 1967). On allocating time per case regardless of the order of the cases, see S. Nagel, "Attorney Time Per Case: Finding an Optimum Level," 32 *University of Florida Law Review* 424-441 (1980). For general materials on computer-aided law decisions, see S. Nagel, *Microcomputers as Decision Aids in Law Practice* (Westport, Conn.: Greenwood-Quorum, 1987). The software that is most relevant to optimum sequencing is probably docketing software such as "Docket" by Micro-Craft, 2007 Whitesburg Drive, Huntsville, AL 35801. Such software is useful for keeping track of appointments, court dates, and other dates that are important to individual cases. Such software, however, does not have any provision for aiding lawyers in optimally docketing cases so as to maximize cash flow considerations or minimize average time from start to finish.

PART III

Applications to All Fields of Law

CHAPTER 11

Private Law

The P/G% software can be applied to all fields of law. For a starter, we begin with private law where only private parties are generally involved and not the government as a party. That includes the fields of contracts, property law, family law, and tort law. Within each field of law, we have one example from private practice and one example from legal policy.

CONTRACTS

Private Practice: Dividing Law Firm Profits

Table 11-1 illustrates a P/G% application to the field of contracts that has special interest to lawyers. The type of contract involved is that of a law partnership. The immediate issue is how to divide this year's profits. The partners should be listed by name along the rows. The screen display allows for listing the alternative budget categories in an allocation problem like this. It also has a column for listing the minimums per category or person and the previous actual allocations.

The minimum per partner may be a dollar amount, a percentage of last year's allocation, or some other minimum. Generally, the best way of handling minimums is to ignore them until after the funds available have been allocated in accordance with the merit or other criteria. One then observes which partners would not be receiving their minimums if only the allocation criteria were used to determine the allocations. Those partners are then given their minimums and removed from the allocation analysis. The residue of the profits available for allocation is then allocated to the remaining partners in proportion to how well they score on the allocation criteria.

Table 11-1
Contracts: Law Firm Partnership

A. LISTING OUT THE PARTNERS

	Alternative
1	PARTNER #1
2	PARTNER #2
3	
4	
5	
6	
7	
8	
9	
10	
11	
12	
13	
14	
15	PARTNER #15

B. LISTING OUT THE ABBREVIATED CRITERIA

	Criterion		Criterion
1	YEARS AS PARTNER	1	ATTRACT CLIENTS
2	AGE	2	RETAIN CLIENTS
3	YEARS AS LAWYER	3	MANAGEMENT
4	YEARS WITH FIRM	4	COMMITTEES
5	BILLABLE HOURS	5	TEACHING
6	BILLINGS THIS YEAR	6	PUBLISHING
7	BILLINGS LAST YEAR	7	BAR ACTIVITIES
8	COLLECTIONS THIS YEAR	8	COMMUNITY ACTIV.
9	COLLECTIONS LAST YEAR	9	REL.W/ASSOCIATES
10	$ MANAGED THIS YEAR	10	REL.W/STAFF
11	$ MANAGED LAST YEAR	11	RESPECT/COMMUNITY
12	TURNOVER TO CASH		
13	REALIZATION ON UNB		
14	REALIZE ON BILLED		
15	TECHNICAL ABILITY		

The reason for showing previous allocations is to stimulate questions as to why this year's allocation is so much higher or lower than last year's allocation for those partners in which there is a substantial difference. Answering questions like that may help indicate what additional criteria should be included, how the weights of the criteria should be changed, or other changes designed to make the allocations more meaningful in terms of what the partners might collectively prefer and in terms of providing appropriate incentives.

Table 11-1 lists 26 criteria in abbreviated form. For further details concerning these criteria, see the article on "Partner Compensation" by John Iezzi in the March/April 1985 issue of *Legal Economics.* Notice that the criteria can be measured in years, dollars, 1–5 scales, or whatever seems meaningful. That means each partner cannot be given an overall score by simply adding the 26 separate scores because those separate scores are measured differently. The criteria can be weighted equally at least at first. Otherwise some criteria can be given a weight of 2 or 3 depending on how important they are considered to be relative to other criteria by the partners deciding collectively.

On any given criterion, each partner receives a score. Those scores can be converted into part/whole percentages by simply adding the column scores and dividing each score by the total. If that criterion were the only criterion, then it would be meaningful to divide the profits among the partners in accordance with those percentages. In this hypothetical situation, however, there are 26 criteria. If they are weighted equally, then each partner should receive the average of his or her 26 allocation percentages. If they are weighted unequally, then each partner should receive the weighted average of his or her 26 allocation percentages.[1]

Legal Policy: Consumer Protection

Table 11-2 deals with the legal policy problem of how to provide consumer protection concerning matters of price, quality, and safety while at the same time stimulating business to greater productivity and avoiding an undue burden on the taxpayer. An additional criterion is that of equity, which refers to the extent to which the policy chosen facilitates buying power by poor people who otherwise would not be able to afford essential products.

Five general policy alternatives are discussed:

1. Doing nothing on the part of the government, which may be appropriate in a highly competitive market like pricing airline passenger service.
2. Government aid and subsidies, which may be appropriate for stimulating new technologies such as the development of airline service in the 1920s. It was in those years that the U.S. government paid for airmail delivery much more than the expenses of the airlines in order to stimulate airline development.
3. Litigation, which can often encourage greater safety where large and embarrassing damage suits might otherwise be likely.
4. Regulation, which may be especially relevant to preventing the occurrence of dangerous situations, such as requiring that pilots pass certain tests and not fly more than a certain number of consecutive hours.
5. Government ownership, which may be applicable to provide essential services that private enterprise is not so willing to provide, especially at low prices. An example is the government ownership of large airports, which cities are willing to undertake in order to attract visitors and which the airlines prefer over privately owned airports.

Table 11-2 shows how each of those five alternative policies is scored on each of the four criteria using a 1–5 scale. With such a scale, a 5 means strongly conducive to the goal, a 4 means mildly conducive, a 3 means neither conducive nor

Table 11-2
Contracts: Consumer Protection

GOALS / POLICIES	Stimulate Business to Greater Productivity	Protect Consumer	Taxpayer Expense	Equity	Sum
Doing Nothing	4	2	4	2	12
Govt. Aid & Subsidies	5	5	1	2	13
Litigation	3	4	4	2	13
Regulation	2	4	2	4	12
Government Ownership	2	4	2	4	12

adverse, a 2 means mildly adverse, and a 1 means strongly adverse. The scoring here is not for any particular industry but for business-consumer relations in general. In that regard, the various alternatives score about equally at 12 or 13 points. That does not mean they are equally desirable in all situations, but rather that each alternative has different advantages.

A set of general principles concerning the comparative advantages of the alternatives might include the following:

1. Doing nothing works best where marketplace competition provides consumer benefits and productivity incentives, as with airline deregulation.
2. Government aid works best where private enterprise cannot raise enough large long-term capital to take advantage of the potential of techological innovation.
3. Litigation works best to provide injured individuals with compensation, but is generally not as good a preventive approach as regulation is.
4. Regulation works best where the marketplace cannot adequately protect the consumer, as with products that do not have brand names but could be unsafe.
5. Government ownership works best for essential industries where the public demands equity, but private enterprise cannot profitably provide the services under an equitable arrangement.

The score of a policy may depend on greater details than are provided in this table. For example, the extent to which government ownership is protective of consumers depends on whether the government base is democratic or dictatorial. The idea of protecting the consumer might also be more meaningfully divided into the three separate criteria of price, quality, and safety. Regulating the hours of pilots may be relevant to safety protection, but not price protection. Likewise, stimulating competition may help lower prices, but could jeopardize safety protection if there is no regulation.[2]

PROPERTY LAW

Private Practice: Estate Allocation

A good property law application with regard to private law practice is the estate allocation example given in chapter 3 on "Computer-Aided Counseling." Table 3-2 back in chapter 3 shows how spreadsheet analysis and multicriteria decision-making can be used to help in allocating an estate. A 1–5 scale can be used unless more precise measurement is available. The scores on each criterion are then converted into part/whole percentages. Those percentages show how much should be allocated to each beneficiary if only that criterion were being considered. Since there are two or more criteria, the allocations associated with each beneficiary are averaged. If the criteria have different degrees of importance, then the allocations associated with each beneficiary are averaged taking those weights into consideration.[3]

Legal Policy: Housing for the Poor

A good property law application with regard to legal policy in the public sector is the problem of providing housing for the poor. Table 11-3 shows six alternative policies and six criteria. In light of the scores of the policies on the goals, the condominium arrangement seems best for existing government-owned public housing. That policy is, however, resisted partly because the present public-housing management does not want to become the employee of the tenants.

In light of the scores of the policies on the goals, the rent supplements seem best for providing housing for the poor outside of government-owned public housing projects. That policy is, however, resisted partly because it means appropriating new federal funds. The program of home ownership for the poor might have been effectively administered if the intermediary were Department of Housing and Urban Development (HUD) employees who have no commission incentive to deemphasize maintenance costs or to bribe property assessors as part of repeated foreclosure schemes with the federal government covering the mortgages.

One could add the policy of doing nothing to provide housing for the poor. Such a policy at first glance looks good with regard to the burden on the taxpayer. It could, however, result in unacceptable slum living conditions that could be an even greater burden on the taxpayer than helping to provide affordable housing.[4]

Table 11-3
Property Law: Housing for the Poor

GOALS / POLICIES	Affordable Housing for the Poor (Low Prices)	Low Burden on the Taxpayer		Incentives for Work and Law Compliance	Stimulate Housing Development	Likely to be Effectively Administered	SUMS
		Building Cost	Maintenance Cost				
Rent Control	4	3	3	3	1	2	15
Govt.-Owned High-Rise Housing	4	1	1	2	3	2	13
Govt.-Owned Low-Rise Housing	4	2	2	2	3	2	15
Private Ownership with Govt. Rent Subsidies	4	5	4	4	4	5	26
Govt.-Built with Condo Ownership	4	1	3	4	3	3½	18½
Private Ownership with Govt. Purchase Subsidies and Private Sector Intermediaries	4	4	4	5	4	1	22

FAMILY LAW

Private Practice: Divorce Issues

Table 11-4 provides what are referred to as four P/G% shells. They are shells in the sense that they just give alternatives and criteria. It is up to the attorney and client to indicate how the alternatives score on the criteria or to add additional alternatives or criteria for any specific case.

The first shell relates to deciding whether to get a divorce. It was discussed in further detail in chapter 3 on "Computer-Aided Counseling." The essence of that shell is to reach a decision among the alternatives of stay married as is, develop an agreement of some kind, live apart, or obtain a divorce. Eight sample criteria are listed, although in any specific case other criteria may also be appropriate. The first criterion relates to reducing an alcohol or addiction problem. The second criterion relates to reducing violence, and so on. Whichever alternative receives the highest overall score is the alternative to be chosen at least tentatively. That alternative should be subjected to a threshold analysis to see what it would take to bring a second-place or other-place alternative up to first place.

The second shell involves deciding on a property settlement. The alternatives are (1) sell everything and divide the proceeds equally or in some other way, (2) the wife keeps the house and the husband gets the rest of the property, (3) divide the property in half without first converting the property into cash, (4) keep some property intact and convert other property into cash, or (5) whatever other alternatives seem appropriate to the circumstances. The criteria include (1) coming close to an equal division between the husband and the wife, (2) taking the interests of the children into consideration, and (3) taking special needs of the husband or wife into consideration.

The third shell involves deciding on child custody. Some of the options include (1) the mother gets all the custody, (2) the mother gets custody of some children and the father gets custody of other children, (3) the mother gets custody of all the children at certain times of the year and the father gets custody at other times, or (4) the father gets all the custody. The criteria can include (1) the interests of the children, which is given an extra weight of 2, (2) the mother's interest, and (3) the father's interest. As with the other shells, whichever alternative scores the highest is tentatively the winner, subject to threshold analysis or other kinds of what-if analysis.

The fourth shell involves deciding on child support. The alternatives include different dollar amounts per week or per month. The criteria refer to (1) not being less than the needs of the children, (2) not being more than the needs of the children, (3) not being less than the ability of the parent who is paying support, and (4) not being more than ability of the parent who is paying support. As with the other shells, the scoring of each alternative on each criterion can be on a 1–5 scale, 1–3, or whatever scoring is comfortable.[5]

Table 11-4
Family Law: Divorce Issues

A. DECIDING WHETHER TO GET A DIVORCE

ALTERNATIVES	CRITERIA	MEAS. UNIT	WEIGHT
1 Stay Married As Is	1 -Alcohol/Addict	1-5 Scale	1.00
2 Develop Agreement	2 -Violence		1.00
3 Living Apart	3 Remarriage		1.00
4 Full Divorce	4 Privacy/Ind.		1.00
	5 Economic Status		1.00
	6 Colleagues/Rela.		1.00
	7 Children		1.00
	8 Companionship		1.00

B. DECIDING ON A PROPERTY SETTLEMENT

ALTERNATIVES	CRITERIA	MEAS. UNIT	WEIGHT
1 Sell All/Div. 1/2	1 Equal Division	1-5 Scale	1.00
2 House Kept / $ Rest	2 Child Interests		1.00
3 Keep All/Div. 1/2	3 H or W Needs		1.00
4 Keep Some/Pay $			

C. DECIDING ON CHILD CUSTODY

ALTERNATIVES	CRITERIA	MEAS. UNIT	WEIGHT
1 Mother Gets All	1 Child Interests	1-5 Scale	2.00
2 Some Kids to Each	2 Mother Interests		1.00
3 Some Time to Each	3 Father Interests		1.00
4 Father Gets All			

D. DECIDING ON CHILD SUPPORT

ALTERNATIVES	CRITERIA	MEAS. UNIT	WEIGHT
1 $50/2 Weeks	1 - Child Needs	1-5 Scale	1.00
2 $100	2 - Spouse Ability		1.00
3 $150			1.00
4 $200			1.00
5 $250			
6 $300			
7 $350			
8 $400			
9 $450			
10 $500			

Legal Policy: No-Fault Divorce

Table 11-5 provides an example of legal policy evaluation on a private law matter: the grounds required for obtaining a divorce. The alternatives are:

1. No divorce allowed, as was the case in South Carolina until about 1950, and as is the case now in Ireland.
2. Divorce only on grounds of adultery, as was the case in New York until about 1960.
3. Divorce only on grounds of adultery or physical cruelty, as in Illinois until about 1970.

Table 11-5
Family Law: No-Fault Divorce

A. THE ALTERNATIVES AND THE EVALUATIVE CRITERIA

ALTERNATIVES	CRITERIA	MEAS. UNIT	WEIGHT
1 No Divorce Allowed	1 =Public Opinion	1-5 Scale	1.00
2 Adultery Div. Only	2 +Honest Hearings		1.00
3 Phys. Cruelty Reqd.	3 Free Choice		1.00
4 Mental Cruelty	4 -Wrong Divorces		1.00
5 Incompat. W/O Fault	5 -Wrongly Stay Mrd.		1.00
	6 +Two Parents		1.00
	7 -Taxpayer Cost		1.00
	8 +Remarriage		1.00

B. HOW THE ALTERNATIVES SCORE ON THE CRITERIA

ALTERNATIVES	CRITERIA			
	=Public Opinion	+ Honest Hearings	Free Choice	-Wrong Divorces
No Divorce Allowed	1.00	1.00	1.00	5.00
Adultery Div. Only	2.00	2.00	2.00	4.00
Phys. Cruelty Reqd.	3.00	3.00	3.00	3.00
Mental Cruelty	4.00	4.00	4.00	1.00
Incompat. W/O Fault	5.00	5.00	5.00	1.00

ALTERNATIVES	CRITERIA			
	-Wrongly Stay Mrd.	+ Two Parents	- Taxpayer Cost	+Remar-riage
No Divorce Allowed	1.00	5.00	5.00	1.00
Adultery Div. Only	2.00	4.00	3.00	2.00
Phys. Cruelty Reqd.	3.00	3.00	3.00	3.00
Mental Cruelty	4.00	2.00	3.00	4.00
Incompat. W/O Fault	5.00	1.00	4.00	5.00

C. THE OVERALL SCORES OF THE ALTERNATIVES

ALTERNATIVES	COMBINED RAWSCORES	PERCENTS
1 No Divorce Allowed	20.00	16.16
2 Adultery Div. Only	21.00	17.07
3 Phys. Cruelty Reqd.	24.00	19.51
4 Mental Cruelty	27.00	21.95
5 Incompat. W/O Fault	31.00	25.20

D. WHAT IT WOULD TAKE TO BRING THE LAST PLACE ALTERNATIVE UP TO FIRST PLACE

CRITERIA	ALTERNATIVES		
	No Divorce Allowed	Incompat. W/O Fault	Weight
=Public Opinion	12.00	-6.00	-1.750
+Honest Hearings	12.00	-6.00	-1.750
Free Choice	12.00	-6.00	-1.750
-Wrong Divorces	16.00	-10.00	3.750
-Wrongly Stay Mrd.	12.00	-6.00	-1.750
+Two Parents	16.00	-10.00	3.750
-Taxpayer Cost	16.00	-7.00	12.000
+Remarriage	12.00	-6.00	-1.750

4. Divorce on adultery, physical cruelty, or mental cruelty, as in Illinois until about 1985.
5. Divorce on the former grounds plus incompatibility without fault, as is now the rule in virtually all 50 states.

The criteria for judging those alternatives include the following:

1. Having a law more congruent with public values.
2. Encouraging honest hearings, rather than perjured testimony.
3. Allowing more freedom as to whether a couple wants to stay married or not.
4. Discouraging wrongful divorces that are regretted later by the spouses and/or the children.
5. Discouraging spouses from wrongly staying married to their detriment and/or the detriment of the children.
6. Encouraging two-parent families.
7. Decreasing taxpayer cost.
8. Increasing the possibility of remarriage to form a better family relation.

The scoring of the alternatives on the criteria is on a 1–5 scale. By coincidence, there are five alternatives that move in approximately five notches from the most severe to the most lenient grounds for divorce. That causes the scores of the alternatives on the criteria to generally go from 1 to 5 or from 5 to 1 depending on the criterion. For example, the alternatives go from 1 to 5 on the criteria of public opinion, honest hearings, free choice, discouraging wrongly staying married, and encouraging remarriage. The alternatives, however, go from 5 to 1 on discouraging wrongful divorces and encouraging two-parent families. On the matter of saving the taxpayer money, allowing no divorces means no judicial expenses for divorce proceedings. Allowing no divorces, though, may cause some women to stay on public aid because they cannot get a divorce to marry a more responsible husband, but that taxpayer expense is not considered here. Allowing divorces on grounds of incompatibility does result in divorce hearings, but they tend to be simpler and less expensive than divorces on grounds that are more difficult to establish.

If each goal is treated as being equally important, then incompatibility without fault comes out the winner as shown in Table 11-5C. One might ask why incompatibility was not adopted as divorce grounds earlier if it now seems to be the best grounds. The answer may be the influence of a ninth goal that is not shown, namely minimizing deviation from past law. As of 1940, incompatibility would have been too much of a deviation from past law and from the law of other states. By 1980, intervening changes made incompatibility no longer much of a deviation from the mental cruelty law of Illinois and other states. Indeed, Illinois as of 1980 was the deviant state for not changing to incompatibility, whereas it would have been a deviant state for changing to incompatibility as of 1940.

Table 11-5D shows what it would take to make no divorce allowed as desirable as no-fault divorce in light of the eight criteria and the scores of the alternatives on the criteria. If only one score at a time were to change, no divorce would have to move up to score higher than the 1–5 scale allows, or no-fault would have to move down to a negative score lower than the 1–5 scale allows. Another possibility is if the decision-makers were to become convinced that the goals are substantially undesirable of public opinion, honest hearings, free choice, discouraging wrongful marriages, or encouraging remarriage. That, however, seems unlikely. The place of greatest vulnerability for an attack on no-fault divorce in this analysis is arguing that discouraging wrongful divorces or encouraging two-parent families is four times more important than any of the other six goals.[6]

TORT LAW

Private Practice: Predicting Winners in Civil Cases

Table 11-6 deals with predicting who will win in civil cases and with what damages. For illustrative purposes section A shows data from five hypothetical cases. The defendant won in two of the five cases, and the plaintiff won in three, for amounts of $70, $65, and $78. For the sake of discussion, four predictive criteria are shown:

1. Whether the judge is elected or appointed. It is hypothesized that elected judges are more likely to side with the plaintiff in damage suits when the political party is held constant. This is so because elected judges are more likely to rise up within the party ranks as doorbell ringers and as lawyers with small practices. Appointed judges may be more likely to be chosen for their financial contributions to the party and to come from larger law firms.
2. Whether the area provides for no-fault liability or for liability only if the plaintiff is completely or substantially free from contributory negligence.
3. Whether the place where the case is heard is urban or rural.
4. Whether the plaintiff is male or female. Elected judges, no-fault liability, and urban places tend to be associated with plaintiffs winning. Male plaintiffs are not more likely to win than female plaintiffs, but they are likely to be awarded higher damages if they do win.

Section B shows how the hypothetical cases score on these four criteria. One could use any criteria that are meaningful in light of the specific subject matter of the cases being analyzed. These four criteria are representative of the four types of predictive criteria that are frequently referred to in the judicial decision analyses of social scientists. The first criterion relates to who the decision-makers are. The second criterion relates to what the law is. The third relates to a factual element, although not necessarily an evidentiary one. The fourth

Table 11-6
Torts: Predicting Who Will Win in Civil Cases

A. THE PREVIOUS CASES, THEIR OUTCOMES, AND THE PREDICTIVE CRITERIA

ALTERNATIVES	PREVIOUS OUTCOME	CRITERIA	MEAS. UNIT	WEIGHT
1 Johnson (D)	D - $0	1 Elected Judge	1/No - 2/Yes	1.00
2 Park (P)	P - $70	2 No-Fault Law		1.00
3 Dixon (D)	D - $0	3 Urban Place		1.00
4 Crawford (P)	P - $65	4 Male Plaintiff		1.00
5 Hudson (P)	P - $78			

B. HOW THE CASES SCORE ON EACH OF THE PREDICTIVE CRITERIA

ALTERNATIVES	CRITERIA			
	Elected Judge	No-Fault Law	Urban Place	Male Plaintiff
Johnson (D)	1.00	1.00	1.00	1.00
Park (P)	2.00	1.00	2.00	2.00
Dixon (D)	2.00	1.00	1.00	1.00
Crawford (P)	2.00	2.00	2.00	1.00
Hudson (P)	2.00	2.00	2.00	2.00

C. THE OVERALL SCORES OF THE CASES

ALTERNATIVES	COMBINED RAWSCORES	PREVIOUS OUTCOME
1 Johnson (D)	4.00	D -$0
2 Park (P)	7.00	P -$70
3 Dixon (D)	5.00	D -$0
4 Crawford (P)	7.00	P -$65
5 Hudson (P)	8.00	P -$78

D. BRINGING THE HIGHEST LOSER UP TO THE LEVEL OF THE LOWEST WINNER

CRITERIA	ALTERNATIVES		WEIGHT
	Dixon (D)	Park (P)	
Elected Judge	4.00	0.00	??
No-Fault Law	3.00	-1.00	??
Urban Place	3.00	0.00	-1.000
Male Plaintiff	3.00	0.00	-1.000

criterion relates to who the litigants are. Normally the law and the facts are by far the most important, but when they are held constant the nature of the decision-makers and the litigants may have some predictive value.

Section C shows the overall results. These results lead to a decision rule that says if the total score of a case is 7 or more, the plaintiff is likely to win. If the total score is 5 or less, the defendant is likely to win. Section C also leads to saying that if the plaintiff wins with 7 points, the average damages are likely to be about $67.50. If the plaintiff wins with 8 points, the average damages are likely to be about $78. That kind of reasoning can be extended to a much larger sample of cases. In order to get good separation between the winners and the losers, it may be necessary to give different weights to the predictive criteria. To obtain better precision in predicting the amount of damages from the total scores, it may also be helpful to have the computer develop an equation in which damages are shown as a function of the total scores.

This kind of analysis can be useful not only for predictive purposes, but also for advocacy purposes. Suppose, for example, that a lawyer is representing the plaintiff in the Dixon case, and suppose the Dixon case is not included in the set of cases that have already been decided. Section D of the table shows what changes it would take to bring the Dixon case up to the level of the Park case, which was one of the winning cases with a relatively low score. The answers include:

1. If the lawyer for Dixon could convince the court that the urban place factor or the male plaintiff factor deserve lowered importance, that could help Dixon since it does not do so well on those two criteria, assuming those are relevant criteria to argue in court as contrasted to nonevidentiary predictive criteria.
2. The lawyer for Dixon might try to convince the court to perceive that the Dixon case deserves a higher score on each of the predictive criteria. In this situation that might be difficult to do since the cases are just scored No or Yes. Moving some of the No answers in the Dixon case up to Yes answers could bring Dixon up to the level of Park.
3. One should note that Park received a score of 7, and Dixon received a score of 5. We are thus looking for ways to raise the overall score of the Dixon case by 2 points. That can be done by (a) raising the weight or importance of the criteria on which Dixon does well, or (b) lowering the weight or importance of the criteria on which Dixon does poorly. It can also be done by (c) increasing the scores of the Dixon case on the criteria.
4. The Park column of section D shows that by lowering the scores in the Park case, one can generate a tie between Park and Dixon. It may be possible to convince the court that the Park case did not score so well but still deserved to win. One normally does better, though, by arguing that one's client deserves to win than by arguing that some previous plaintiff who was a winner was really not so deserving.
5. The question marks in the upper right-hand corner of section D show that no changes in the relative importance or weight of the elected judge factor or the no-fault law factor will make any difference, since both the Dixon and Park cases received the same scores of Yes on elected judge and No on no-fault liability.[7]

Legal Policy: Alternative Tort Systems

Table 11-7 uses the P/G% system to evaluate alternative tort law systems. The alternatives are:

1. The traditional common law system where the plaintiff collects nothing if the plaintiff has contributed any negligence to causing whatever injuries have occurred. A more liberal variation allows the plaintiff to collect if immediately prior to the injury, the defendant had the last clear chance to avoid having the injury occur.

Table 11-7
Torts: Evaluating Alternative Tort Law Systems

A. THE ALTERNATIVES AND THE EVALUATIVE CRITERIA

Alternative	Criterion	Meas.Unit	Weight
1 CONTRIB.NEGL.	1 INJURED RECOVER	1-5 SCALE	2.00
2 COMPARATIVE NEGL.	2 -LITIGATION COSTS		1.00
3 NO-FAULT ADD-ON	3 DETER ACCIDENTS		2.00
4 PURE NO-FAULT	4 -LAWYER FEES		1.00
	5 POLIT.FEASIBLE		3.00

B. THE SCORES OF THE ALTERNATIVES ON THE CRITERIA

	INJURED	-LITIGAT	DETER AC	-LAWYER	POLIT.FE
CONTRIB.NEGLIGE	2.00	1.00	4.00	1.00	2.00
COMPARATIVE NEG	3.00	2.00	3.50	2.00	4.00
NO-FAULT ADD-ON	4.00	3.00	2.50	4.00	4.00
PURE NO-FAULT	4.50	5.00	2.00	5.00	2.00

C. THE OVERALL SCORES OF EACH ALTERNATIVE

Alternative	Combined Rawscores	%
1CONTRIB.NEGL.	20.00	18.18
2COMPARATIVE NEGL.	29.00	26.36
3NO FAULT ADD-ON	32.00	29.09
4PURE NO FAULT	29.00	26.36

D. BRINGING COMPARATIVE NEGLIGENCE UP TO THE LEVEL OF NO-FAULT ADD-ON

	NO-FAULT A	COMPARATIV	Weight
INJURED RECOVER	2.50	4.50	-1.000
-LITIGATION COSTS	0.00	5.00	-2.000
DETER ACCIDENTS	1.00	5.00	5.000
-LAWYER FEES	1.00	5.00	-0.500
POLIT.FEASIBLE	3.00	5.00	??

E. BRINGING PURE NO-FAULT UP TO THE LEVEL OF NO-FAULT ADD-ON

	NO-FAULT A	PURE NO FA	Weight
INJURED RECOVER	2.50	6.00	8.000
-LITIGATION COSTS	0.00	8.00	2.500
DETER ACCIDENTS	1.00	3.50	-4.000
-LAWYER FEES	1.00	8.00	4.000
POLIT.FEASIBLE	3.00	3.00	1.500

2. The system whereby the plaintiff is allowed to collect if the plaintiff has been less than 50% responsible for the injuries, but then the plaintiff can collect only a percentage of the damages equal to the percentage for which the defendant was responsible. A more liberal variation allows the plaintiff to collect a percentage of the damages equal to the percentage for which the defendant was responsible even if the defendant was responsible for less than 50%.
3. The pure no-fault system, which allows the plaintiff to collect if the plaintiff is injured regardless of who is at fault. Such a system began in the early 1900s in industrial accident situations where workmen's compensation insurance covers on-the-job injuries regardless of whether the responsible individual is the worker, the employer, a fellow worker, or someone else. Such a system also began shortly thereafter in consumer situations or product liability where the consumer collects by showing the product was responsible for the injury without showing that the manufacturer was negligent. Such a system is being increasingly adopted in the automobile accident field where injured drivers and passengers can collect from their own or the other side's insurance company regardless of who is negligent. This is the way one collects on fire insurance so long as the person collecting did not intentionally cause the fire or the injuries.
4. The no-fault add-on system involves various forms of compromise between a system in which negligence by the plaintiff or defendant is relevant and a system in which such negligence is irrelevant. The common compromise is to allow the plaintiff to choose between a system in which negligence by the plaintiff or defendant is relevant and a system in which such negligence is irrelevant. The common compromise is to allow the plaintiff to choose between the two systems under vairous conditions. The advantage of going the no-fault route is the ease of establishing liability. The advantage of going the negligence route is that one does not thereby waive any rights as to the amount of damages that can be collected.

Table 11-7 works with five criteria in seeking to evaluate those four alternatives. The criteria (and roughly how each alternative scores on them) include:

1. *To what extent do 100% of the injured recover for 100% of their damages?* On a 1–5 scale, pure no-fault does the best at about 4.5, although it is not perfect partly due to limitations on what can be collected and because there will always be people who will not exercise their rights no matter how easy they may be to exercise. Contributory negligence does the worst at a score of 2, although it is not as bad on this criterion as it could be since juries tend to award damages in cases in which they are theoretically not supposed to do so.
2. *Reducing litigation costs.* Pure no-fault does the best on that since it comes close to eliminating litigation as in the workmen's compensation field. Contributory negligence does the worst on that criterion since it encourages litigation over administrative decision-making by agencies like workmen's compensation boards, and also over out-of-court settlements by holding open the possibility that the defendant will not have to pay anything.
3. *Accident deterrence.* Contributory negligence does the best on this criterion because in theory people supposedly will drive and behave more carefully if they know they are going to have to pay damages for their negligence. The converse for pure no-fault is that they will behave not so carefully if their negligence is irrelevant to paying damages. In practice, the occurrence of automobile accidents is about the same in

contributory negligence states as it is in no-fault states when driving circumstances are held constant. People drive carefully to a considerable extent because they do not want to get injured, not because they are trying to avoid paying damages to other people.

4. *Reducing lawyer fees.* This is closely related to reducing litigation costs, but not identical, as the scoring indicates. Thus, the no-fault add-on system allows for the greater possibility of substantial lawyer fees than pure no-fault, but may reduce litigation more than a negligence system does. Even if the scoring were the same on both criteria, they are conceptually and functionally different. Litigation costs are a public taxpayer cost. Lawyer fees are mainly a cost to the individual plaintiff.
5. *Political feasibility.* Comparative negligence and the no-fault add-on system are both relatively noncontroversial compared to the less moderate systems. Contributory negligence continues to exist largely out of inertia. It would have a difficult time being incorporated into the statutory codification of common law torts. Pure no-fault has a difficult time being adopted largely because of the opposition of the influential legal profession. It is interesting to note, though, that the insurance companies tend to support pure no-fault even though it increases the probability that liability will be established. Their support stems from the money they save on decreased lawyer fees and decreased damage amounts. They do not benefit directly from the decreased costs of the judicial process.

Section C of table 11-7 shows that the overall winner is the no-fault add-on system. Contributory negligence is a distant loser. Comparative negligence and pure no-fault are tied for second place. Those overall scores for each alternative are based on the relation scores shown in section B and the weights shown in section A. Normally the weights in the P/G% analysis are all set equal to 1.00 until it has been determined what weights would make a difference in the bottom line of which alternative is the winner. In this situation, it seems reasonable to say that at least from a public policy perspective, political feasibility is the most important goal. In fact, it can be considered a constraint in the sense that if it is not met, it makes no difference how well an alternative does on the other goals. Likewise from a societal perspective, the criteria of enabling the injured to obtain compensation and rehabilitation and of deterring accidents do seem to be more important goals than reducing litigation costs or lawyer fees.

Sections D and E of table 11-7 show what it would take to bring either of the second-place alternatives up to first place. Section D shows that comparative negligence would be the winner if more weight were placed on deterring accidents, assuming that comparative negligence does do more accident-deterring than no-fault add-on. Comparative negligence would also be the winner if negative weight were placed on having the injured recover, reducing litigation costs, or reducing lawyer fees. Changing the weight of political feasibility would make no difference since comparative negligence and no-fault add-on are considered equally politically feasible. Comparative negligence can also become a winner if it can score higher on some of the criteria or if no-fault add-on were to score lower.

Section E shows that pure no-fault would be the winner if a different set of changes were to occur. Pure no-fault would benefit if more weight were placed on having the injured recover, decreasing litigation costs, or decreasing lawyer fees. Likewise pure no-fault would benefit if we gave a negative weight to deterring accidents or cut the weight of political feasibility in half from 3.0 to 1.5. Increasing the score of pure no-fault on any one criterion would not help much given 5.0 as the maximum on a 1-5 scale and given that pure no-fault is not that different in many of its scores as compared to no-fault add-on. There is more room for the scores of no-fault add-on to go down enough to make pure no-fault a winner, but those decreases seem contrary to empirical reality.[8]

NOTES

1. For relevant literature on contract law from a private practice perspective, see John Calamari, *Hornbook on Contracts* (St. Paul: West, 1987); Ian Macneil, *Contracts: Exchange Transactions and Relations* (Mineola, N.Y.: Foundation, 1978); Gordon Schaber, *Contracts in a Nutshell* (St. Paul: West, 1984); and Alan Schwartz and Robert Scott, *Sales Law and the Contracting Process* (Mineola, N.Y.: Foundation, 1982).

2. For literature dealing with the law of contracts from a public policy perspective, see Marian Benfield, *New Approaches in the Law of Contracts* (Mineola, N.Y.: Foundation, 1970); Carol Katz (ed.), *The Law and the Low Income Consumer* (New York: New York University School of Law, 1968); Homer Kripke, *Consumer Credit* (St. Paul: West, 1970); Mark Nadel (ed.), *Consumer Protection Policy* (Urbana, Ill.: Policy Studies Organization, 1983); and Anthony Kronman and Richard Posner (eds.), *The Economics of Contract Law* (Boston: Little, Brown, 1979).

3. For relevant literature on property law from a private practice perspective, see Roger Cunningham, Dale Whitman, and William Stoebuck, *Hornbook on the Law of Property* (St. Paul: West, 1987); Ralph Boyer, *Survey of the Law of Property* (St. Paul: West, 1981); Roger Bernhardt, *Real Property in a Nutshell* (St. Paul: West, 1981); and John Cribbet, *Principles of the Law of Property* (Mineola, N.Y.: Foundation, 1975).

4. For literature dealing with property law from a public policy perspective, see David Hill, *Landlord and Tenant Law in a Nutshell* (St. Paul: West, 1986); Bruce Ackerman (ed.), *Economic Foundations of Property Law* (Boston: Little, Brown, 1975); Sheldon Plager (ed.), *New Approaches in the Law of Property* (Mineola, N.Y.: Foundation, 1970); Anthony Downs, *Urban Problems and Prospects* (Chicago: Markham, 1970); Leonard Freedman, *Public Housing: The Politics of Poverty* (New York: Holt, Rinehart, and Winston, 1969); and Jon Erickson and Charles Wilhelm (eds.), *Housing the Homeless* (New Brunswick, N.J.: Center for Urban Policy Research, 1986).

5. For relevant literature on family law from a private practice perspective, see Homer Clark, *Hornbook on Domestic Relations* (St. Paul: West, 1968); Harry Krause, *Family Law in a Nutshell* (St. Paul: West, 1977); and Judith Areen (ed.), *Cases and Materials on Family Law* (Mineola, N.Y.: Foundation, 1985).

6. For literature dealing with family law from a public policy perspective, see American Enterprise Institute, *The New Consensus on Family and Welfare* (Washington: AEI, 1987); Albert Wilkerson (ed.), *The Rights of Children: Emergent Concepts in Law and Society* (Philadelphia: Temple University Press, 1973); and Walter Wadlington (ed.), *Statutory Materials on Family Law and Children in the Legal System* (Mineola, N.Y.: Foundation, 1981).

7. For relevant literature on tort law from a private practice perspective, see Clarence Morris, *Text on Torts* (Mineola, N.Y.: Foundation, 1980); William Prosser et al., *Hornbook on Torts* (St. Paul: West, 1984); Edward Kionka, *Torts in a Nutshell: Injuries to Persons and Property* (St. Paul: West, 1977); and Wex Malone, *Torts in a Nutshell: Injuries to Family, Social, and Trade Relations* (St. Paul: West, 1979).

8. For literature dealing with tort law from a public policy perspective, see Robert Rabin (ed.), *Perspectives on Tort Law* (Boston: Little, Brown, 1976); Dan Dobbs, *Torts and Compensation: Personal Accountability and Social Responsibility for Injury* (St. Paul: West, 1985); Peter Huber, *Liability: The Legal Revolution and Its Consequences* (New York: Basic Books, 1988); Walter Olson (ed.), *New Directions in Liability Law* (New York: Academy of Political Science, 1988); and Marc Franklin and Robert Rabin, *Injuries and Remedies: Tort Law and Alternatives* (Mineola, N.Y.: Foundation, 1983).

CHAPTER 12

Public Law

The P/G% software can be applied to public law as well as to private law. In public law situations, the government is generally a party. This includes criminal law, constitutional law, economic regulation, and international law. One can define economic regulation law broadly enough to include tax law, patent law, and other ways in which the government through law seeks to regulate the economy.

As with chapter 11 on "Private Law," the public law examples are divided into those that relate to private practice and to legal policy. At first glance it seems inconsistent to talk about private practice in the field of public law. Private practice, however, refers to representing specific clients as in an adjudication, negotiation, or counseling. Legal policy, on the other hand, refers to evaluating alternative rules that are existing or proposed, as in a hearing or other proceeding that relates to administrative rule-making, appellate law-making, or the statute-making of a legislature. One of the most important aspects of representing clients is being able to predict how cases are likely to be decided for purposes of trial technique, negotiation, or counseling.

CRIMINAL LAW

Private Practice: Predicting Winners in Criminal Cases

A good example of the use of the P/G% software for private practice in the field of criminal law is predicting criminal case decisions regarding whether a defendant will be found guilty or innocent. Table 7-3 back in chapter 7 provides data for showing how the software can be used to generalize from past cases in order to predict how a present or future case is likely to be decided. The alternatives are five past cases that relate to the subject in question. In two of the cases, there was a conviction, whereas three resulted in acquittal. The key problem is explaining why some defendants get convicted and others get acquitted so that one can make meaningful predictions.

Four explanatory factors are offered for this set of hypothetical cases. They relate to whether (1) the charge was a misdemeanor or a felony, (2) the area was poor or prosperous, (3) the judge was a Republican or a Democrat, (4) the defendant was black or white. Those criteria would not necessarily have any explanatory power in a different set of cases, although they might.

Observing how the cases score on the criteria, one can generalize concerning the relation between the overall scores of the cases and their outcomes. If the criteria are given equal weight, then the best predictive decision-rule is that cases with 7 or more points are likely to result in a conviction, whereas cases with 5 or less points are likely to result in an acquittal. Cases with 6 points are at first unpredictable. If, however, extra weight is given to whether the area is poor or middle-class, then the new best decision-rule is that 8 or more points lead to a conviction and 7 or less points lead to an acquittal.[1]

Legal Policy: Crime Reduction

Table 12-1 deals with the basic and highly controversial problem of how to reduce crime, as contrasted to the previous tables, which emphasize how to process defendants in terms of police searches, pretrial release, right to counsel, and sentencing. Table 12-1 also differs in terms of methods (as well as substance) by working with policies that are not mutually exclusive. In Tables 11-4 to 11-7, the criminal justice system was faced with choosing one of three alternatives in each table or problem. In Table 12-1, six policies are shown, all of which could be simultaneously adopted.

The six policies are not arranged from liberal at the bottom to conservative at the top. Instead, they are arranged in three pairs. The first pair is especially directed toward the goal of increasing the probability of guilty defendants being arrested, convicted, and punished. The first policy of decreasing legal technicalities is a conservative approach to that goal. The second policy of increasing the professionalism of criminal justice (CJ) decision-makers is a relatively liberal approach to that goal, especially through educational prerequisites and expensive training progams. The second pair of policies is directed toward decreasing the benefits of crime. Hardening the crime targets by making potential theft victims less vulnerable is a relatively conservative approach. Working with gang members to change their peer group values toward political action, rather than antisocial displays of manliness, is a liberal approach. The third pair of policies is directed toward increasing crime costs. Having longer sentences and more severe prisons is a conservative emphasis, as contrasted to a liberal emphasis on providing career opportunities that one risks losing by committing crimes.

The relations in Table 12-1 are not rank-order relations. Instead, the numbers showing the relation between each policy and each goal are degree categories, from 0, which indicates no relation, to 3, which indicates a high positive relation. Using that scoring system, many of the relations are 0 relations since only some of the policies are directed toward increasing punishment probability, increasing crime benefits, or increasing crime costs. All the policies, however, bear some relation to the expenditure of money, with a decrease in legal technicalities being the least expensive alternative. Likewise, all the policies bear some relation to separating the innocent from the guilty with increasing professionalism scoring the highest.

As for weighting the goals, the protection of the innocent is something liberals are especially sensitive to, although so are conservatives but with less emphasis. Saving money is something conservatives are especially sensitive to, although so are liberals but with less emphasis. Both ideological orientations favor decreasing the benefits of crime, increasing the costs of crime, and increasing the probabilty that those costs will be imposed. They differ, however, in how they would achieve those three goals, as was mentioned above.

Increasing the professionalism of the criminal justice decision-makers scores first among all three ideological orientations. Three policies are tied for second place in looking at the total votes column: hardening crime targets, changing peer-group values, and increasing the opportunity costs. At the bottom in adoptability are decreasing legal technicalities and increasing sentence length/ prison hardship. Since all six policies are potentially capable of being adopted, one needs to determine where the line should be drawn when the six policies are arranged in rank order on the total votes column. Doing that is like determining where there is a breakpoint on a grading curve between passing and failing students. One might say the breakpoint here seems to be at 36, meaning policies with less than 36 votes are considered failing as to whether they should be adopted. Table 12-1 thus illustrates how a policies-goals table can be used to deal with either finding an optimum combination of policies or choosing one out of a set of alternatives.[2]

CONSTITUTIONAL LAW

Private Practice: Equal Protection

Table 12-2 provides a P/G% spreadsheet analysis of the equal protection cases of the U.S. Supreme Court for the purpose of predicting future cases and explaining past cases. Two predictive criteria are involved. One is how high the case situation scores regarding the rights that are allegedly being denied. The highest score (meaning the more severe denial of equal protection) occurs when voting rights are involved. These include the right to vote, to be a candidate, to be in a districting system with equal population per district, or related rights. Next in line are rights that relate to criminal justice. These include right to

Table 12-1
Criminal Law: Crime Reduction

ALTERNATIVE POLICIES (X's)	GOALS TO BE ACHIEVED (Y's)				
	Protect the Innocent (L)	Increase probability of arrest, conviction, or punishment (N)	Decrease Crime Benefits	Increase Crime Costs (N)	Save Money (C)
Decrease legal technicalities	1	1	0	0	3
Increase the professionalism of CJ decision-makers	3	2	0	0	2
Harden Crime Targets	2	0	2	0	2
Change peer group values	2	0	2	0	2
Increase sentence length & prison hardship	1	0	0	2	2
Increase the opportunity costs, i.e. the lost opportunities from committing crimes	2	0	0	3	1
TOTAL	11	3	4	5	12

counsel, trial by jury, direct examination, cross-examination, right to appeal, or the right to have illegally seized evidence excluded from the courtroom. The third category of rights relates to education, including various aspects of school segregation and school financing. The fourth, fifth, and sixth rights tend to emphasize the private sector, as contrasted to the public sector. They include rights that relate to housing ownership and rental, employment hiring and promotion, and consumer rights, especially the right to be served by a business firm that is open to the public.

The second predictive criterion relates to how high the case situation scores regarding the group that is allegedly being given unequal treatment. The highest category is race, toward which the Supreme Court has shown the most sensitivity. Race could be broadly defined as including any kind of ethnic or cultural group, which would cover race, religion, and ancestral nationality. The religion cases, however, tend to be covered under the religion clauses of the first amendment, and ancestral nationality cases independent of race have not come before the Supreme Court. The second category is referred to as sex in Table 12-2, but

Table 12–1 (continued)

ALTERNATIVE POLICIES (X's)	OVERALL SCORES Liberal Score	Neutral Score	Conservative Score	Total Score
Decrease legal technicalities	8	10	12	30
Increase the professionalism of CJ decision-makers	15*	14*	13*	42
Harden Crime Targets	12	12	12	36
Change peer group values	12	12	12	36
Increase sentence length & prison hardship	9	10	11	30
Increase the opportunity costs, i.e. the lost opportunities from committing crimes	13	12	11	36
TOTAL	69	70	71	210

NOTES:

1. The goals are arranged from relatively liberal (L) on the left, neutral (N) in the middle, and conservative (C) on the right. Within each ideological category the goals are randomly arranged.

2. Alternative policies are arranged in a list from relatively liberal to neutral to conservative to be consistent with the arrangement of the goals.

3. The numbers showing the relation between each policy and each goal are degree categories. A "0" indicates no relation. A "1" indicates a relatively low positive relation. A "2" indicates a medium positive relation. A "3" indicatets a high positive relation.

4. Conservatives are considered as giving the relatively conservative goals a weight of 3, neutral goals a weight of 2, and liberal goals a weight of 1. Liberals are considered as giving the conservative goals a weight of 1, neutral goals a weight of 2, and liberal goals a weight of 3. Neutrals are considered as giving all the goals a weight of 2.

5. An overall score is calculated by summing the products of the relation scores multiplied by the weights across each row or policy.

6. A star in one of the overall-score columns shows which policy in the column scored the highest.

Table 12-2
Constitutional Law: Equal Protection

Criteria / Case Types	*Score On Rights*	*Score On Groups*	*Sum*	*Outcome*
1. Consumers/Region	1	1	2	D
2. Consumers/Economic Class	1	2	3	D
3. Employment/Region	2	1	3	D
4. Consumers/Sex	1	3	4	D
5. Employment/Economic Class	2	2	4	D
6. Housing/Region	3	1	4	D
7. Employment/Sex	2	3	5	D
8. Housing/Economic Class	3	2	5	D
9. Schools/Region	4	1	5	D
10. Housing/Sex	3	3	6	D
11. Schools/Economic Class	4	2	6	D
12. Consumers/Race	1	6	7	P
13. Criminal Justice/Region	6	1	7	?
14. Schools/Sex	4	3	7	?
15. Criminal Justice/Economic Class	6	2	8	P
16. Employment/Race	2	6	8	P
17. Voting/Region	7	1	8	P
18. Criminal Justice/Sex	6	3	9	P
19. Housing/Race	2	6	9	P
20. Voting/Economic Class	7	2	9	P
21. Schools/Race	4	6	10	P
22. Voting/Sex	7	3	10	P
23. Criminal Justice/Race	6	6	12	P
24. Voting/Race	7	6	13	P

should be called gender to distinguish it from sexual orientation or sexual behavior. The third category is economic class. It mainly deals with cases in which there is alleged discrimination against the poor, although those cases may also involve criminal procedure rights or first amendment advocacy. The fourth category is region. It includes arbitrary distinctions that relate to being urban or rural, north or south, inner city or suburban, or to other geographical distinctions. We could add a fifth category called miscellaneous. It would include cases that relate to discrimination against the elderly, the young, the handicapped,

Table 12-2 (continued)

1. The above data can generate two compatible decision rules. One rule is:
   (1) If an equal protection case has a summation score of 7 or higher, then the plaintiff will win.
   (2) If the case has a score of 6 or lower, then the defendant will win.
2. The alternative decision rule is:
   (1) If an equal protection case has a summation score greater than 7, then the plaintiff will win.
   (2) If the case has a score of exactly 7, then the outcome is questionable.
   (3) If the case has a score of 6 or lower, then the defendant will win.
3. Each case type is defined in terms of:
   (1) The rights that are allegedly being denied, which can relate to voting, criminal justice, schools, housing, employment, or consumer rights in that order of importance.
   (2) The group that is allegedly being given unequal treatment, which can relate to race (which generally means being black), sex (which generally means being female), economic class (which generally means being poor), or region (which generally means being urban, inner city, or poor) in that order of importance.
4. To determine the score of each case type on the rights, the six rights are arranged in rank order with the most important right receiving a score of 6. Slight adjustments are then made to recognize there is more distance between the top two rights and the bottom four than there is between the other rights.
5. To determine the score of each case type on the groups, the four groups are arranged in rank order with the most important group receiving a score of 4. Slight adjustments are then made to recognize there is more distance between the top group and the bottom three than there is between the other groups.
6. The first decision rule implies that the court would decide in favor of the plaintiff if the state provided grossly unequal right to counsel from one county to another, or if women were denied admission to an all-male public school, although the court has not yet done so.
7. The second decision rule implies that being black scores slightly higher than a 6. That causes case type 12 to score slightly higher than a 7, and thus to be distinguishable from the questionable case.
8. Landmark cases or constitutional amendments that correspond to the case types include Gomillion v. Lightfoot (case type 24), Powell v. Alabama (23), Nineteenth Amendment (22), Brown v. Board of Education (21), Harper v. Virginia (20), Shelley v. Kramer (19), Taylor v. Louisiana (18), Reynolds v. Sims (17), Jones v. Mayer (12 and 16), Gideon v. Wainwright (15), and Rodriguez v. San Antonio (9 and 11).
9. The data for this table come from S. Nagel, "Case Prediction by Staircase Tables and Percentaging," 25 Jurimetrics Journal 169-196 (1985).

gays, or other groups not covered by race, gender, class, and region. We could likewise add a miscellaneous set of rights beneath the category of consumer rights, including rights that relate to marital relations or nonmarital sexual relations.

With six types of rights and four types of groups, there are 24 possible case types, as listed in the right-hand column of Table 12-2. They are arranged from the case type about which the Supreme Court is the least sensitive to the case type about which the Court is the most sensitive. If the Court is most sensitive about rights that relate to voting and about groups that relate to race (especially blacks), then it follows that the voting rights of blacks would be the case type with the highest overall score and the greatest likelihood of receiving a favorable decision from the Supreme Court concerning denial of equal protection. At the opposite extreme would be rural consumers complaining to the Supreme Court that they do not have adequate shopping centers, and that the state governments should do something about that kind of inequality.

If each right is given a rank-order score from 1 to 6, and each group is given a rank-order score from 1 to 4, then the highest case type would receive a score of 10 and the lowest would receive a score of 2. Using that kind of rank-order scoring would, however, generate some inconsistencies among the 24 case types. For example, all the case types with scores of 8 or more would be represented by famous Supreme Court cases declaring the alleged discrimination to be unconstitutional. The six cases with 8 or more points include (1) case type 24, which is represented by *Gomillion v. Lightfoot* declaring racial discrimination in reapportionment to be unconstitutional; (2) case type 23 represented by *Powell v. Alabama* declaring racial discrimination in criminal justice to be unconstitutional, especially in jury representation; (3) case type 22 represented by the nineteenth amendment declaring gender discrimination in voting to be unconstitutional; (4) case type 21 represented by *Brown v. Board of Education* declaring compulsory racial separation in education to be unconstitutional; (5) case type 20 represented by *Harper v. Virginia* declaring the poll tax to be unconstitutional voting discrimination against the poor; and (6) case type 18 represented by *Taylor v. Louisiana* declaring gender discrimination in jury selection to be unconstitutional. Likewise, all the case types with scores of 4 or less are ones that have not even come before the Supreme Court, let alone resulted in victories for the side arguing unconstitutional discrimination.

Using rank-order scoring would result in inconsistencies for the cases that score 5, 6, or 7 total points. For example, the case of *San Antonio v. Rodriguez* involved education and inequalities on the basis of both economic class and one city versus another. It is a 5- or 6-point case depending on whether one emphasizes the geographical discrimination or the economic-class discrimination. It was a big loser before the U.S. Supreme Court in 1973 and reaffirmed in the Minnesota school busing case of 1988. On the other hand, the case of *Jones v. Mayer* is also either a 5- or 6-point case. It involved private-sector discrimination against blacks as either employers or consumers. It is worth 6 total points in the rank scoring by virtue of 4 points for race and 2 for employment, or 5 total points by virtue of 4 for race and 1 for consumer rights. It was a big winner before the U.S. Supreme Court in 1968 as a landmark in establishing that private discrimination can be unconstitutional. Obviously there is something wrong with the scoring system if some cases lose with 5 or 6 points and others win with 5 or 6 points.

The remedy in order to get perfect separation of the cases is to recognize that in this situation, rank order of the categories on each of the two predictive criteria is not sufficiently precise. Race is the highest of the four groups in the eyes of the

Supreme Court, but it is not simply 4, 3, 2, and 1. The Court has held on numerous occasions that the equal protection clause was especially designed to protect blacks. A more appropriate scoring might be 5, 3, 2, and 1, or even 6, 3, 2, and 1, as is shown in Table 12-2. Likewise, voting and criminal justice are the top two sets of rights in the eyes of Supreme Court in the list of six types of rights, but they are not simply 6, 5, 4, 3, 2, and 1. Those first two stand out as being especially important, and thus the scoring might more meaningfully be 7, 6, 4, 3, 2, and 1, as is shown in Table 12-2.

With that more meaningful scoring, in all the case types where there are 7 or more points, the plaintiff has either already won an important victory or the area is still not fully decided. The two case types that have 7 points that are still questionable can be considered as leaning in the direction of the plaintiff eventually winning when appropriate test cases are decided. The first category is inequalities within different regions of a state in the realm of criminal justice. For example, in many states indigent defendants are well represented by public defender systems in the relatively large cities, but not so well represented by volunteer attorneys or assigned counsel in rural areas. The Supreme Court may someday require the states to raise the level of court-appointed counsel in those rural areas to a minimum standard. Doing so could be considered a declaration that the previous system represented a denial of equal protection. It could also be considered as a declaration that the due process clause of the Constitution was not being adequately satisfied. The other ambiguous case type is inequalities in education based on gender. The courts have already declared unconstitutional discriminatory admissions practices. Public school sports is the key area in which there are still diverse opinions at the lower court level concerning unequal opportunity to participate on high school and college teams. There may, however, be a trend in the direction of judging each female or male applicant on the basis of their individual characteristics. A female applying to play on a high school basketball or even football team could thus not be constitutionally denied the right to play merely on the grounds that she is a female. One thing this kind of analysis illustrates is how it can be applied to cases or case types that have not yet been decided, as well as to explaining differences among those that have been decided.

At the bottom of the list of case types (in the sense of those cases with the lowest scores), are a number in which there have been no Supreme Court decisions, yet the outcome column shows them as being likely to be decided in favor of the defendant. For example, consumers complaining about regional discrimination is shown as involving a defendant outcome. The reasoning is that if school children complaining of regional discrimination lose, then consumers with a related complaint are even more likely to lose. Another example that is higher in terms of its total points is economic class discrimination with regard to housing. That is listed as a case type in which the defendant is likely to win, partly because poor people lost in the *Rodriguez* education class and the Supreme Court has indicated that education is more important than housing. One could also reason that poor people complaining about economic discrimination in housing are also likely to lose because the courts tolerate sexually segregated dormitories at public universities, and the courts are generally less sensitive to poor people being discriminated against than the courts are to women. The reasoning involved here is sometimes referred to as a fortiori reasoning. Its essence is that if one loses with X and Y in one's favor, then one is likely to lose even more with only X in one's favor. The converse is that if one wins with X and Y in one's favor, then one is likely to win even more with X, Y, and Z in one's favor. That kind of reasoning can be translated into the numerical concepts that are associated with P/G% prediction by saying that if one loses with N points in a P/G% predictive analysis, then one is likely to lose even more with N − 1 points. Likewise, if one wins with N points, then one is likely to win even more with N+1 points.

Since reasoning by analogy is so often used in law-case analysis, it should be distinguished from a fortiori reasoning. The essence of reasoning by analogy is saying:

1. A case was decided in Y manner that had facts A and B present.
2. Along comes a case that has facts A and C present.
3. If C is similar or analogous to fact B, then one would predict that the second case will be decided like the first case.

Reasoning by analogy often involves deciding whether a new case is more analogous or more similar to one set of cases than another set, where the two sets involve different bottom-line decisions. A fortiori reasoning, on the other hand, involves situations where fact C is known to be inferior or superior in determining Y outcome over fact B. This can be contrasted with the different (but related) question of whether fact C is sufficiently or insufficiently similar to fact B on whatever is relevant, such that the second case will be decided the same as the first case.[3]

Legal Policy: Judicial Review

Table 12-3 provides an example of using the P/G% software to arrive at a conclusion as to what policy ought to be adopted in light of a set of goals to be achieved. The subject matter is what is the best institutional structure for determining whether governmental acts comply with or violate the constitution. The table shows three alternatives:

1. *No constitutional review at all.* In practice, that means the chief executive can largely do as he or she pleases. It thus means constitutional determination by the president, the king, the prime minister, the dictator, or whatever the chief executive is called. This is the prevailing practice in many developing countries, in Eastern Europe, and in some American states prior to the U.S. Supreme Court's determination that the states have an obligation to comply with the federal constitution.

Table 12-3
Constitutional Law: Judicial Review

GOALS / POLICIES	Popular Responsiveness W = 1	Sensitivity to Minority Rights W = 3	SUM	WEIGHTED SUM
1. No Constitutional Review	3	1	4	6
2. Concurrent Constitutional Review	4	2	6	10
3. Judicial Constitutional Review	2	4	6	14

NOTES:

1. Judicial review is especially important if one gives more weight to minority rights than to popular responsiveness in this context.

2. One does not have to weight minority rights three times as much as popular responsiveness. Just twice as much would mean that judicial review would have a weighted sum of 10 versus 8 for concurrent review.

3. The threshold weight (where they are tied) is equal weight for both goals.

2. *Concurrent constitutional review.* This means in theory that the legislature or parliament and the courts have an equal say in determining constitutionality. In practice it means legislative supremacy, since the legislature generally has more power to enforce its interpretation than the courts. This is the system that prevails in Great Britain and to some extent in countries that have been influenced by Britain. It is also the prevailing system in other West European democracies.
3. *Judicial constitutional review.* Here the courts, especially the national supreme court, have the last word on what is constitutional regardless of the subject matter. That system exists only in the United States and to some extent in West Germany and Japan as a result of U.S. occupational influence. The wording of some Latin American constitutions provides for judicial review, but in practice the courts tend to bow to the will of the chief executive and the legislature.

Table 12-3 shows two key goals that are relevant to deciding among the three alternatives. They are popular responsiveness and sensitivity to minority rights. Each alternative policy is scored on each of those goals using a 1–5 scale. On such a scale, a 5 means highly conducive to the goal, 4 means mildly conducive, 3 means neither conducive nor adverse, 2 means mildly adverse, and 1 means highly adverse to the goal.

On the goal of popular responsiveness, concurrent review receives a higher score than the other two alternatives. This is so in view of its emphasis on legislative supremacy and democratically chosen legislatures. Judicial review receives a lower score than the other two alternatives. This is so in view of its association in the United States with a federal judiciary that is appointed for life and thus not so responsive to public opinion. Having no constitutional review at all is generally between the other two alternatives on popular responsiveness, although some chief executives may be less or more responsive to public opinion than others.

On the goal of sensitivity to minority rights, judicial constitutional review does better than the other two alternatives. This is so because in the U.S. context, appointment for life has enabled federal judges to be more capable of deciding in favor of minority free speech, minority equal treatment, and due process rights for people on trial who otherwise would have few rights if left to the legislatures or public opinion. This is defining minority rights in a broader sense than just rights for blacks or nondominant ethnic groups. It is defining minority rights as being synonymous with the civil liberties aspects of free speech, equal protection, and due process. On that goal, no constitutional review tends to be highly adverse, and concurrent constitutional review tends to be at least mildly adverse.

Thus we have a trade-off problem with some alternatives doing better on one goal and some doing better on the other goal. If the goals are weighted equally, then the first summation column shows a tie between concurrent review and judicial review. If, however, sensitivity to minority rights is given slightly more weight than popular responsiveness, then judicial review wins over concurrent review. On the other hand, if popular responsiveness is given slightly more weight than minority rights, then concurrent wins over judicial review. The weighted sum column shows the results if sensitivity to minority rights is considered more important than popular responsiveness and "more important" is interpreted as a weight of 2, rather than a weight of 1. Under those circumstances, judicial review is the winner over both other alternatives.

The problem thus reduces to the question of which is more important, sensitivity to minority rights or popular responsiveness. One does not have to decide how much more important one goal is than the other, just which is more important. A weight of 1 for each goal can be considered a threshold weight or a tie-causing weight, because at that weight there is a tie between the two top alternatives. The question thus becomes whether the more desirable weight for sensitivity to minority rights is greater than 1 or less than 1 if popular responsiveness is anchored at a weight of 1.

This kind of analysis can not only be used for deciding among alternative public policies, but also for explaining why one policy rather than another is adopted. In this context, there are three policies to be explained. The explanations that the table generates are:

1. A country is likely to adopt or retain judicial review if it considers sensitivity to minority rights to be more important than popular responsiveness. That is more likely to be the case in a country that has many religions, ethnic groups, and other pluralistic social divisions, as does the United States.
2. A country is likely to adopt or retain legislative supremacy if it considers popular responsiveness to be more important than sensitivity to minority rights. That is more likely to be the case in a country that has one dominant religion and ethnic group, as England traditionally has.
3. A country is likely to adopt or retain the approach of having no constitutional review if it places a negative value on popular responsiveness and a negative value on minority rights. If both those goals are given weights of −1 apiece, then the weighted summation scores are −4, −6, and −6. That makes no constitutional review the winner since −4 is a higher number than −6. This is more likely to be the case in dictatorships where the dictator puts his or her own will ahead of public opinion, and where the dictator is insensitive to minority rights, especially free speech but also ethnic minority rights as part of a possible divide-and-conquer policy.[4]

ECONOMIC REGULATION

Private Practice: Welfare Proceedings

Table 7-2 back in chapter 7 is a good example of an application of the P/G% software to an economic regulation matter that emphasizes the case-prediction perspective of the practicing lawyer, as contrasted to a legal policy evaluation. The table deals with attempting to generalize from prior cases a predictive decision-rule as to when a welfare recipient is likely to win in a welfare proceedings case.

The table deals with 12 case types as contrasted to a set of specific cases. Case type 8 is *Goldberg v. Kelly,* which held that a welfare recipient could not be terminated from welfare without being provided with a hearing. The hearing should include the right to receive notice of alleged wrongdoing, present witnesses, cross-examine accusers, and have a judge who is not one of the accusing welfare workers. Case type 7 is the *Argersinger* case, where the Supreme Court held that an indigent defendant in a criminal proceeding is entitled to a court-appointed lawyer, including a defendant who is accused of criminal welfare cheating.

The other 10 case types involve various combinations of procedural matters such as not being given reasons, not being given a hearing, or not being given a lawyer, and various substantive matters such as being denied eligibility, receiving reduced benefits, being terminated from welfare, or being criminally prosecuted. Each case type is scored on the criteria of substantive and procedural rights denied. Using a 1–4 scale for substantive rights and a 1–3 scale for procedural rights results in some inconsistencies because a case type that has a summation score of 4 could be a loser or a winner for the welfare recipient.

There is, however, complete separation between the winners and the losers when the scoring system on procedural rights is made more precise. It needs to recognize that not being given reasons is more serious than just a 3 to 2 ratio with a hearing denial. It also needs to recognize that not being given a lawyer is less serious than a 1 to 2 ratio with a hearing denial. In other words, by expanding the 1–3 scale up above 3 and down below 1, the overall scores can now indicate that case type 4 is likely to be a loser, case type 6 is likely to be a winner, and case type 5 falls into an unpredictable category, as contrasted to all three case types receiving the same overall score.[5]

Legal Policy: Unemployment-Inflation

Table 12-4 illustrates P/G% applied to economic problems including that of reducing unemployment and inflation while preserving equity and free enterprise. This table, like all the others, analyzes multiple policies, meaning three or more. Too often people see policy problems in terms of conflicting dichotomous choices that tend to distort the alternatives available. One example is thinking in terms of a capitalistic approach versus a socialist approach for economic problems. Sometimes decision-makers further distort policy problems by reducing them to one alternative in the form of a go/no-go decision. That does not even involve comparing two oversimplified alternatives. This table also works with multiple goals. Too often people see policy problems only in terms of benefits or only in terms of costs and not sufficiently in terms of both multiple benefits and multiple costs.

For the sake of simplicity the relations in Table 12-4 are measured on a 1-5 scale. The numbers on such a scale mean:

Table 12-4
Economic Regulation: Unemployment-Inflation

POLICIES \ GOALS	Reduce Unemployment to 3%	Reduce Inflation to 3%	Equitable Distribution of Unemployment and Inflation	Free Enterprise	Sum
1. Doing Nothing	3	3	2	4	12
2. Increase Money Supply Decrease Interest Rates	4	2	3	3	12
3. Decrease Money Supply Increase Interest Rates	2	4	3	3	12
4. Increase Govt. Spending Decrease Taxes	4	2	3	3	12
5. Decrease Govt. Spending Increase Taxes	2	4	3	3	12
6. Job Creation Price Control	4	4	4	1	13
7. Decrease Taxes Decrease Domestic Spending	4	4	3	3	14
8. Tax Breaks & Subsidies Decrease Defense Spending	5	5	3	3	16

NOTES:

1. **Policy 1 of doing nothing causes too much harm at least in the short run.**
2. **Policies 2-3 and 4-5 assume that periods of high unemployment and inflation do not occur simultaneously, which is no longer so.**
3. **Policy 6 is too expensive and too restrictive on marketplace incentives compared to the alternatives.**
4. **Policy 7 has the defect that merely decreasing taxes will not necessarily stimulate productivity without strings attached. Decreasing domestic spending may not be enough to avoid large government deficits which can stifle low interest rates needed for technological and business innovation.**
5. **Policy 8 presumes that tax breaks and subsidies will increase productivity which will reduce the work week and thereby make more jobs available while not reducing take-home pay. Increased productivity also means reduced inflation since workers and producers will be giving more for the increased wages and prices charged.**
6. A score of 5 in a cell means the policy is highly conducive to the goal; a score of 4 means the policy is mildly conducive to the goal; a 3 means the policy is neither conducive nor adverse to the goal; a 2 means the policy is mildly adverse to the goal; and a 1 means the policy is highly adverse to the goal.

1. A 1 is the equivalent of a double minus, and means the policy has a highly adverse relation to the goal.
2. A 2 is the equivalent of a single minus, and means the policy has a mildly adverse relation to the goal.
3. A 3 is the equivalent of a zero in direction, and means the policy is neither adverse nor conducive to the goal.
4. A 4 is the equivalent of a single plus, and means the policy has a mildly conducive relation to the goal.
5. A 5 is the equivalent of a double plus, and means the policy has a highly conducive relation to the goal.

Such a scoring system is more sophisticated than a yes-no dichotomy, but less sophisticated than working with absolute units like dollars, years, crimes, deaths, and so on. More sophisticated units are generally difficult to obtain and to work with, and they are usually unnecessary since they do not affect the bottom-line results.

Table 12-4 is worked out in class by the instructor in collaboration with the students. That kind of development generally involves some trial and error before there is agreement on the policies, the goals, and the relations. The usual sequence is:

1. Start out with some policies and then some goals.
2. Add to the policies and the goals in light of the initial set.
3. Consolidate policies and goals that heavily overlap, as indicated by the fact that they are likely to have the same relation scores.
4. Divide policies and goals when one realizes that the initial wording may have been too gross.
5. Insert relation scores using pluses and minuses. Go down one column or goal at a time in order to promote consistency within each goal.
6. Convert the pluses and minuses into numbers on 1–5 scales. Revise the relation scores if one thinks that finer distinctions are sometimes necessary, as where scores of 3.5 might appear.
7. Decide on tentative weights for the goals by giving the least important goal a weight of 1, and expressing the weights of the other goals as multiples of the first goal. Do not weight the goals if they all seem about equally important, or if the weighting seems too difficult. The weighting can be postponed until after seeing the results, because one then often realizes that different weights will not change the results. The results may also help clarify how much difference there has to be in order to change the results.
8. Sum across each policy in order to determine its overall score. If the goals have different weights, then sum the products across each policy. Each product involves the relation score multiplied by the weight of the goal to which it pertains.
9. Observe the unweighted or weighted summation scores to see if there is one outstanding policy, a scattered combination of outstanding policies, or an optimum level pattern where doing too little or too much is undesirable.

Applying the above procedures to Table 12-4, one could conclude that the problem tends to reduce to a choice between (1) the President Reagan approach of decreasing tax rates and decreasing domestic spending versus (2) the industrial policy approach associated with Gary Hart of providing selective tax breaks, selective subsidies, and decreasing defense spending. One can argue that selective incentives are more likely to reduce unemployment and inflation than across-the-board tax decreases, especally if those tax decreases are aggravated by increased defense spending. That might lead a student supporter of the Reagan position to suggest an additional goal of administrative feasibility, arguing that it is impossible to administer selective tax breaks and subsidies rationally, just as it is supposedly impossible to administer wage/price controls or socialistic pricing. In other words, the results of Table 12-4 tend to stimulate the students into thinking about more fundamental problems than the immediate problems dealt with by the table. The tables also stimulate further ideas concerning additional variations on the policies, goals, and relations, and thus new summation scores. The tables thereby tend both to facilitate the acquisition of knowledge and to stimulate new creative ideas.[6]

INTERNATIONAL LAW

Private Practice: The United States As a Party

Table 12-5 contains data for predicting international law cases where the United States is a party. The object is to predict the probability that the United States will win from at least two predictive criteria. The predictive criteria are the source of law and the industrial power of the U.S. opponent. They are two criteria from a larger list of seven, which also includes (1) the international law subject matter and the U.S. position on it, (2) the decision-making tribunal, (3) the economic interests that may be involved and the U.S. position on them, (4) the civil liberty interests that may be involved and the U.S. position on them, and (5) the nature of the plaintiff as a legal entity.

The source of the law refers to the four categories of (1) domestic law of another country (the United States is victorious in only 25% of such cases), (2) an international treaty (47% victorious), (3) international law/custom (56%), and (4) U.S. domestic law (85%). The industrial power of the U.S. opponent refers to the three categories of (1) less industrial power than the United States (the United States is victorious in only 56% of such cases), (2) non-countries (70% victorious), and (3) about the same in industrial power (100% victorious although that subsample is small). The victory probabilities are based on an analysis of the 137 cases contained in four leading international law casebooks.

With four categories on one criterion and three categories on the second criterion, there are 12 case types, as shown at the left side of Table 12-5. The summation column sums the raw scores for each case type across the variables. Technically speaking, part/whole percentages should be used since the predictive variables are measured differently via a 1–4 scale and a 1–3 scale. The

Table 12-5
International Law: The United States as a Party

Case types / *Criteria*	*Source of Law*	*U.S. Opponent*	*Sum*	*Outcome*
1. Foreign Law and Less Industrial Opponent	1	1	2	40%
2. Foreign Law and Non-Country Opponent	1	2	3	48
3. Treaty and Less Industrial Opponent	2	1	3	51
4. Foreign Law and Equal Opponent	1	3	4	62
5. International Law and Less Industrial Opponent	3	1	4	56
6. Treaty and Non-Country Opponent	2	2	4	58
7. International Law and Non-Country Opponent	3	2	5	63
8. Treaty and Equal Opponent	2	3	5	73
9. U.S. Law and Less Industrial Opponent	4	1	5	70
10. International Law and Equal Opponent	3	3	6	78
11. U.S. Law and Non-Country Opponent	4	2	6	78
12. U.S. Law and Equal Opponent	4	3	7	92

NOTES:

1. The decision rule that the above data generate is $Y = .20 + .10(X)$, where Y is the probability of the United States winning and X is the summation score.

2. The above decision rule could also be expressed as a series of if-then statements like (1) If X is 1, then Y is .30; (2) If X is 2, Y is .40; (3) If X is 3, Y is .50; (4) If X is 4, Y is .60; (5) If X is 5, Y is .70; (6) If X is 6, Y is .80; and (7) If X is 7, Y is .90.

3. Table 12-5 only deals with two of the seven variables in the international law cases. The two are the main source of law and the industrial power of the U.S. opponent. The source of law includes U.S. law, international law, a treaty, and foreign law. The U.S. opponent can be equal to the United States, not a country, or less than the United States in industrial power.

4. Only two variables are used in Table 12-5 rather than seven, partly because of the temporary limitation to 15 alternatives. One can handle all seven variables through multiple runs with 15 case types per run. The number of case types, however, is 163,800 since the number of categories per variable is 4, 13, 6, 5, 3, and 7, respectively. Under those circumstances, one would not want to list all the case types. Instead, one would want to know what the probability of U.S. victory is for any combination of seven categories. To estimate that, simply average the seven probabilities of U.S. victory.

5. The outcome figures shown above come from averaging the two probabilities from the two variables used for each case type. Thus, the combination of U.S. law and equal power has a .92 probability because U.S. law has an .85 probability and equal power has a 1.00 probability. This gives an approximation to a Bayesian conditional, especially where we only have the main probabilities to work with.

6. The above prediction equation comes from observing the relation between the summation scores and the outcome probabilities in Table 12-5. One can determine the prediction equation more accurately by using a statistical calculator that can easily arrive at such an equation for 12 pairs of inputs. One can also think in terms of six pairs of inputs for the summation scores from 2 to 7. Thus a score of 4 has an average outcome of .57 since case type 6 has an outcome of .56 and case type 8 had an outcome of .58.

7. Table 12-5 provides a good illustration of an outcome that is not a dichotomy of win or lose, but rather a continuum outcome of 9 to 1.00.

scales, however, are close enough to justify working with raw scores at least for this methodological illustration.

Each probability in the outcome column is arrived at by averaging the probabilities for the relevant categories on each predictive variable. Thus, case type 1 involves foreign law (25% U.S. victory rate) and a less industrial U.S. opponent (56% U.S. victory rate). The average between 25% and 56% is 40% rounded to the nearest even number. There are more sophisticated ways of combining probabilities in accordance with Bayesian probability analysis. They are, however, highly complicated, especially when more than two predictive variables are involved. The information for a Bayesian analysis is also almost never available since it requires knowing various details on how the predictive variables relate to each other. Simply averaging the basic probabilities should provide a sufficient approximation to an overall probability, especially if each predictive criterion is worded in the direction of winning and does not greatly overlap the other criteria. Even if the criteria do overlap, the weights can take that into consideration. Two duplicative criteria, for example, can each be given about half the weight it would otherwise receive if the other criterion in the pair were not also being used.

After determining the criteria, case types, relations, summation scores, and outcomes, one should develop a decision-rule indicating for various summation scores what outcomes are likely to occur. This example, however, differs from the previous examples in that the outcome is a range between 40% and 92% rather than just a dichotomy of winning versus losing. Having an outcome range is common in most court cases as well as a win-lose dichotomy. In damage cases, the dichotomous liability decision is followed by a continuum damages decision when liability is established. Damages can range from a low of $1 in some libel cases to millions of dollars in treble-damage antitrust suits. In criminal cases, the conviction decision is followed by a sentencing decision when there is a conviction. Sentences can range from a low of no jail time to life imprisonment or the death penalty.

In Table 12-5, one could bypass the summation score and formulate a decision-rule that specifies for each case type or case what the outcome is likely to be. That approach is likely to lead to inconsistencies, as was shown with the redistricting cases and the housing discrimination cases. It is also much more clumsy to have to specify how each case or case type will be decided, especially if there are many case types. With a win-lose dichotomy, the decision-rule simply specifies what summation score separates the winners from the losers. In predicting a range outcome, there is no such threshold summation score. Instead, one would like to know the likely outcome at a base summation score of 0 or 1, and how much the outcome is likely to increase for each 1-unit increase or 1% increase in the summation score.

Looking at the last two columns of Table 12-5 tends to generate a decision-rule that $Y = .20 + .10(X)$, where Y is the probability of the United States winning, and X is the summation score. One can see that the two case types with summation scores of 3 average about a .50 probability; the three case types that score 4 average about .60; and the three case types that score 5 average about .70. Extending those relations downward implies or extrapolates that a summation score of zero would have a probability of about .20. One cannot, however, score less than a 2 on the two predictive criteria together. At the other end, the eyeballing approach implies that a summation score of 8 would have a probability of about 1.00. One cannot, however, score more than 7 on the predictive criteria. Thus the eyeballed or linear relation is not subject to the criticism that it leads to probabilities below zero or above 1.00 since all the possible summation scores lead to reasonable probabilities when using the decision rule $Y = .20 + .10(X)$.

Greater precision may sometimes be required than the eyeballing approach provides. Under those circumstances, one can insert into a statistical calculator the 12 pairs of numbers, consisting of 2 and .40, 3 and .48, and so on. After keying in those 24 numbers, one can read out the value of the constant, which is .19 rather than .20, and the value of the slope, which is slightly more than .10. The computer program will do that kind of statistical regression analysis directly when the P/G% program is further developed.

One can also obtain a decision rule which reflects diminishing returns of the from $Y = .24(X)^{.65}$ by inserting the same 24 numbers and asking for diminishing returns output. With that equation, a summation score of 1 predicts a probability of .24, and a summation score of 2 predicts a probability of .38. Each successive increment on the summation score increases the probability, but at a diminishing rate. The .65 means that if the summation score doubles (i.e., increases by 100%), then the probability will increase by about 65%. For example, if the summation score doubles from 1 to 2, then the predicted probability goes up from .24 to .38. The .14 difference is about 65% of the .24 base. Diminishing returns is a fact of life in the relation between most inputs and most outputs, but linear relations often give good enough predictability. With the aid of the microcomputer program, one can request how one wants the summation scores related to the range outcomes with equal ease, regardless of whether one chooses constant returns, diminishing returns, or other available options.[7]

Legal Policy: Arms Control

Table 12-6 provides a good legal policy example from the field of international law with regard to evaluating alternative approaches to arms control. These are alternatives on a high level of generality, as contrasted to more narrowly focused issues like what to do about specific weapons systems, including the MX system of long-range land-based missiles, the B1 system of long-range strategic bombers, the "star wars" system for shooting down incoming missiles, or even narrower issues that relate to the number of missiles of varous kinds that should be allowed in specific places starting at certain times under various conditions.

Table 12-6 shows nine such alternatives on a high level of generality. They are arranged from the most war-oriented perspective to the most pacifist perspec-

Table 12-6
International Law: Arms Control

POLICIES \ GOALS	Low Burden on the Economy	Avoidance of Nuclear War	Avoidance of Being Conquered	Political and Technological Feasibility	SUM
1. Encourage War to Bring an Armageddon	2	1	2	1	6
2. First Strike With No Retaliation	1	2	4	1	8
3. Arms Buildup	1	1	4	3	9
4. Wait for Bilateral Reducation Without Stimuli	2	2	4	4	12
5. Wait for Bilateral Reduction With Stimuli	2 (4)	3 (4)	4	4	13 (16)
6. Supervisable Freeze	3	4	3	4	14
7. Temporary Unilateral Freeze	3	4	3	3	13
8. Permanent Unilateral Freeze	4	4	2	1	11
9. Unilateral Disarmament	4	3	2	1	10

1. This table originated in 1986. The numbers in parentheses show changes in the scores as of 1988.
2. The policy alternatives are arranged from the most war-oriented at the top to the most pacifist at the bottom. The criteria are arranged in random order.
3. The criteria are tentatively given equal weight. If they were given liberal weights, then the second criterion would be given more weight than the third criterion. If they were given conservative weights, then the third criterion would be given more weight than the second criterion. Either way, Alternative 5 would still receive the highest summation score.

tive, although some of the middle-range alternatives are less easy to classify in terms of being more or less warlike or pacifist. The alternative (policy) approaches include:

Policy 1. *Encouraging war to bring on an Armageddon battle.* No one in the Reagan administration or the Democratic opposition proposed an alternative of that kind. This list of alternatives, however, is designed to provide a full range of the possibilities, even if some of them are not actively proposed by responsible people.

Policy 2. *First strike with no retaliation.* This is a position that has been taken but not so openly by some military and nonmilitary people, but decreasingly so as the possibility of no retaliation becomes more remote. The possibility, though, may be in the process of being revived by some of the more wild "star wars" talk that assumes there is a possibility that all retaliatory action by the Soviet Union subsequent to a U.S. first strike could be neutralized. Even the people who are most optimistic about "star wars" do not believe such a possibility is presently here or likely to occur in the near future.

Policy 9. Moving to the opposite extreme is *unilateral disarmament.* No one associated with the Dukakis candidacy or anyone who was a possible contender for the Democratic nomination in 1988 has proposed unilateral disarmament. There are fervent pacifists who do make such proposals, just as there are fervent anti-communists who talk in terms of getting the war over already with the United States having more survivors.

Policy 8. Short of unilateral disarmament is the position that argues in favor of a *permanent unilateral freeze.* That means the United States would stop the development of new weapons systems and stop adding to its arsenal of nuclear bombs on a long-term basis, regardless of what the Soviet Union does. There are people who are not too far to the left who do argue such a position on the grounds that if we already have 10,000 nuclear bombs, and it only takes 1,000 to totally destroy the Soviet Union, why do we need to push toward 11,000. The answer is partly that there is little to be gained in simply adding more of the same, but there may be something to be gained in developing new delivery systems (such as Stealth bombers, which can fly below radar levels unlike the B1 bombers) or new defenses to enemy nuclear missile submarines (which may be more of a threat and more capable of being dealt with than a rain of land-based missiles).

Looking at the alternatives in the middle, we might first note that these are not mutually exclusive. Even the most extreme alternatives could be meaningfully adopted to some extent. For example, we can unilaterally stop building new B1 bombers regardless of what the Soviet Union does. We could do so on the grounds that it is a waste of money to build any new B1 bombers when the better Stealth bomber is about to become operational. Likewise, one can make a case for doing research on the subject of establishing a first-strike capability in order to obtain a better idea of what the other side might come up with without necessarily using the results.

As for the middling positions:

Policy 3. The first of the middling positions on the conservative side is to engage in an *arms buildup*. If that alternative were done exclusively, then it probably should not be considered a middling position but instead above the warlike constraint, which is shown as a double line between the second and third alternatives. The Reagan administration advocated an arms buildup, but also advocated looking for ways of developing meaningful arms control agreements. This is partly from recognizing that concentrating exclusively on an arms buildup is extremely expensive in terms of the national deficit, the possibility of having to raise taxes, the pressure of increasing interest rates in order to borrow defense money, and the distraction of federal funds away from uses that could be more stimulating to national industrial productivity.

Policy 4. *Wait for a bilateral reduction without trying to stimulate one to occur.* The idea of a bilateral reduction was first proposed by the Reagan administration in about 1985. At first, it was treated by most Democrats as a phony proposal designed to generate no arms control at all. It was thought of as being analogous to the sometimes-used southern civil rights strategy of attaching what were then considered extreme amendments to civil rights legislation in anticipation that nothing would then pass. An example was attaching equal rights for women to the 1964 Civil Rights Act in anticipation that doing so would cause the whole bill to fail, but instead the whole bill passed. Another example was arguing in 1965 that a statute prohibiting poll taxes was not good enough given the bad image liberals gave to the poll tax. Southern senators therefore proposed a constitutional amendment to prohibit the poll tax, figuring that nothing would then happen to the preservation of the poll tax. The amendment, however, passed faster than almost any other amendment. Likewise, when liberals were advocating a freeze, Reagan said a freeze is not good enough, let's have a reduction in arms. Alternative 4 was thus ambiguous as to whether this was just a conservative ploy to continue the arms race, or in some sense really further to the left than the liberal freeze proposals.

Policy 5. There are two main versions of the *bilateral reduction* alternative. One that is referred to as Alternative 4 involves waiting for a bilateral reduction, but not doing anything very actively to encourage the Soviet Union to enter into such an arrangement. Alternative 5 does involve the United States taking the initiative to propose a summit meeting to get into the details of a bilateral arms reduction. Table 12-6 was largely developed in about 1986. The way the bilateral reduction turned out was a bit like the southern civil rights strategy. President Reagan talked about a bilateral reduction as a counter to the liberal freeze idea, but did not propose a summit meeting to implement it. Mikhail Gorbachev virtually leaped at the idea of a bilateral reduction, and he proposed a specific summit meeting. President Reagan accepted either out of sincerity, embarrassment, or both. As a result, meetings were held in Finland, Iceland, and Washington that resulted in a meaningful bilateral reduction on some strategic weapons.

Policy 6. The *freeze proposal* took three forms. The least drastic involved a mutually supervised freeze. As of 1986, that was considered a more liberal alternative than waiting for a bilateral reduction because the feeling was that the waiting time might be many years.

Policy 7. If a mutually supervised freeze could not be developed, then many liberals were willing to have a *temporary unilateral freeze*. That would involve the United

States at least stopping the increase of nuclear bombs subject to going back to the arms race if the Soviet Union failed to take reciprocal action.

In judging these nine alternatives as of 1986 or as of any earlier or later point in time, one might want to bear especially in mind four relevant criteria:

1. If there is a tie among the alternatives on all the other criteria, the best alternative is the one that provides the *lowest burden on the economy.* That is like saying the alternative with the lowest cost, but cost here means more than just the direct expenses of the arms race. One might note in this context that the United States and the Soviet Union over the last ten years or so have been first and second among major industrial countries in the percent of the gross national product spent on defense, whereas West Germany and Japan have been at the bottom of that list. Closely related is the fact that the United States and the Soviet Union over the last ten years have been close to the bottom of the list showing increases in national industrial productivity, whereas West Germany and Japan have been at the top of that list. Massive defense expenditures are clearly a high burden on the economy.
2. The second criterion is *avoidance of nuclear war.* These criteria are arranged in random order; it is not meaningful to arrange the criteria from conservative to liberal. All the criteria are supported by both conservatives and liberals, although not necessarily to the same extent. No reasonable person is likely to say that avoidance of nuclear war is not a goal, assuming everything is held constant on the other criteria. In other words, if two alternatives are tied on a low burden on the economy, avoidance of being conquered, and political-technological feasibility, then clearly the alternative that scores best on avoidance of nuclear war is the best alternative. Because one has avoidance of nuclear war as a goal does not mean avoidance at all costs.
3. *Avoidance of being conquered.* Some conservatives like to argue that liberals believe in the idea of "better red than dead." There may be a lot of conservatives who also would be willing to forsake a lot of their values if their lives depended on it. This though is clearly a false dichotomy. It is possible to be nonred and alive. The key consideration here as with the other criteria is that if two alternatives are tied on the other criteria, then the one that avoids the United States being conquered by the Soviet Union is the better alternative.
4. The fourth criterion is *political and technological feasibility.* No alternative is worth much consideration let alone adoption if it is not politically and technologically feasible. Political feasibility in this context means that the alternative is capable of winning on a roll-call vote in Congress and passing a presidential veto if necessary, which is not the case with alternatives 1, 2, 8, and 9. Technological feasibility in this context means physically possible given the state of scientific knowledge and the engineering and economic ability to implement that knowledge, which is lacking in the alternative of having a first strike with no retaliation.

As for how the alternatives score on these criteria:

1. With regard to low burden on the economy, as one goes from Alternative 1 up to Alternative 9, the scores get better with regard to low burden. The lowest burden on a 1–5 scale is unilateral disarmament with virtually no defense expenditures.

2. Avoidance of nuclear war, on the other hand, has a curved relationship with the nine alternatives in the sense that the highest or best scores are in the middle. At the conservative extreme of encouraging war or of trying to develop a first-strike capability, the occurrence of nuclear war is almost guaranteed, rather than avoided. At the other extreme, unilateral disarmament can encourage the Soviet Union to be more willing to risk a first strike if the United States is incapable of retaliating, although under total unilateral disarmament the Soviet Union could defeat the United States without having to resort to nuclear war.
3. Avoidance of being conquered also has the highest scores in the middle. Encouraging war could easily lead to the Soviet Union conquering whatever is left of the world since the Russians have shown an ability to survive massive destruction better than the United States as indicated by surviving Stalin, Hitler, Ivan the Terrible, and Genghis Khan, among others. Encouraging unilateral disarmament is clearly contrary to the idea of avoiding being conquered. The Soviet Union may not be as evangelistic in spreading its values as it was shortly after the Russian Revolution, but it still shows a high degree of interest in supporting communist movements throughout the world.
4. As already mentioned and almost by definition, the extremes lack political feasibility and some may also lack technological feasibility.

In light of these relations between the alternatives and the criteria, the leading contenders are Alternatives 4 through 7. The arms buildup idea as an exclusive policy is barely above the unfeasible conservative alternatives, although it may be applicable to some aspects of conventional arms or Trident submarines. We should refer to "additional bilateral reduction," rather than just bilateral reduction since we have already had some as of 1988. The bilateral reduction we have had in itself provides a stimulus by way of establishing momentum for future bilateral reductions, especially if the systems for mutual inspection work out as they seem to be doing. Thus the alternatives get reduced to numbers 5, 6, and 7.

Among those alternatives, the bilateral reduction idea with stimuli seems to be a clear winner since it received conservative support from the Reagan administration, and the freeze idea of the liberals now seems less liberal and less ambitious than the bilateral reduction idea, which has been shown to be feasible and not just a phony alternative to avoid more realistic alternatives. One might then ask why does Alternative 5 not come out with the highest overall score. The main reason is that the scoring on Alternative 5 in table 12-6 largely reflects perceptions as of about 1986. As of that time, the alternative was not taken as seriously as it now is. Thus the new scores for Alternative 5 might be that it can have a positive effect on reducing the burden on the economy. That would give it a 4 on the first criterion (as is shown in parentheses). As for avoiding nuclear war, it was considered neither conducive nor adverse as of about 1986. It now seems to have a realistic positive relation with reducing the possibility of nuclear war, and it should therefore also be scored a 4 on the second criterion. That means that its new overall score is a 16 (as is shown in parentheses), which makes it a clear winner over the alternative proposals. In fact, the leading competition of a nuclear freeze almost disappeared from the political activities of 1988.

One methodological aspect of P/G% analysis that this example illustrates beyond the important substance is the need for flexibility in discussing the relations between alternatives and criteria. The relations must be viewed as subject to change such that a losing alternative can become a winning alternative due to changes in the circumstances. Another methodological aspect is that no matter how emotional the problem and the issues might be, there tends to be considerable agreement on what the criteria should be, although not necessarily on their relative weight. In this situation, one might say that liberals would place more weight on avoidance of nuclear war, and conservatives more weight on avoidance of being conquered, at least by the Soviet Union. Both sides would probably place about equal weight on economic burden although conservatives might think more in terms of cost to the taxpayer and liberals more in terms of cost to international competitiveness. Both are likely to agree that political and technological feasibility is a must for meaningful policy alternatives.

A third methodological aspect is that often an alternative can be developed that will be better than the best expectations of either liberals or conservatives, or in P/G% terms that will be capable of winning with either liberal or conservative weights. That is the case with the alternative of stimulating additional bilateral reductions. It comes out a clear winner with liberal weights of 2, 3, 1, and 2 for the four criteria, or with conservative weights of 2, 1, 3, and 2. The liberals (at least in private and sometimes in public) have admitted surprise at how well arms control developed in the Reagan administration beyond their advocacy of a mere freeze as contrasted to a real reduction. Conservative Republicans (in private and sometimes in public, especially President Reagan) have admitted it feels pretty good to have the image of being an effective peacemaker. In fact, arms control agreements of the Reagan administration may be the key element in giving the Reagan presidency respectability in U.S. history that it might not otherwise have, as partly was the case with the Nixon administration and its role in détente and opening relations with the People's Republic of China. On a still higher level of methodological generality, this example can be used to illustrate the idea of arriving at superoptimum solutions that are better than the best original expectations of all sides involved. That includes liberals and conservatives arguing over what has been the highly emotional issue of international arms control.[8]

NOTES

1. For relevant literature on criminal law from a private practice perspective, see Wayne LaFave and Austin Scott, *Hornbook on Criminal Law* (St. Paul: West, 1986); Arnold Loewy, *Criminal Law in a Nutshell* (St. Paul: West, 1975); Rollin Perkins and Ronald Boyce, *Text on Criminal Law* (Mineola, N.Y.: Foundation, 1982); and Neil Cohen and James Gobert, *Problems in Criminal Law* (St. Paul: West, 1976).

2. For literature dealing with criminal law from a public policy perspective, see Norman Abrams, *Federal Criminal Law and Its Enforcement* (St. Paul: West, 1986); James Levine, Michael Musheno, and Dennis Palumbo, *Criminal Justice: A Public Policy*

Approach (New York: Harcourt Brace Jovanovich, 1980); Samuel Walker, *Sense and Nonsense About Crime: A Policy Guide* (Monterey, Calif.: Brooks/Cole, 1985); James Wilson (ed.), *Crime and Public Policy* (San Francisco: Institute for Contemporary Studies, 1983); and Joseph Scott and Travis Hirschi (eds.), *Controversial Issues in Crime and Justice* (Beverly Hills, Calif.: Sage, 1988).

3. For relevant literature on constitutional law from a private practice perspective, see John Nowak, Ronald Rotunda, and Nelson Young, *Hornbook on Constitutional Law* (St. Paul: West, 1986); Jerome Barron and Thomas Dienes, *Constitutional Law in a Nutshell* (St. Paul: West, 1986); Norman Dorsen, Paul Bender, and Burt Neuborne (eds.), *Political and Civil Rights in the United States* (Boston: Little, Brown, 1976); William Lockhart et al., *Cases on the American Constitution* (St. Paul: West, 1986); and David Engdahl, *Constitutional Power: Federal and State in a Nutshell* (St. Paul: West, 1974).

4. For literature dealing with constitutional law from a public policy perspective, see Laurence Tribe, *American Constitutional Law* (Mineola, N.Y.: Foundation, 1978); Henry Abraham, *Freedom and the Court: Civil Rights and Liberties in the United States* (New York: Oxford, 1982); John Brigham, *Civil Liberties and American Democracy* (Washington, D.C.: Congressional Quarterly, 1984); Glenn Phelps and Robert Poirier, *Contemporary Debates on Civil Liberties: Enduring Constitutional Questions* (Lexington, Mass.: Lexington-Heath, 1985); and James Sundquist, *Constitutional Reform and Effective Government* (Washington, D.C.: Brookings, 1986).

5. For relevant literature on economic regulation from a private practice perspective, see Ernest Gellhorn, *Antitrust Law and Economics in a Nutshell* (St. Paul: West, 1986); Herbert Hovenkamp, *Hornbook on Economics and Federal Antitrust Law* (St. Paul: West, 1985); Ernest Gellhorn and Richard Pierce, *Regulated Industries in a Nutshell* (St. Paul: West, 1987); Thomas Hazen, *Hornbook on the Law of Securities Regulation* (St. Paul: West, 1985); and Arthur LaFrance, *Welfare Law: Structure and Entitlement in a Nutshell* (St. Paul: West, 1979).

6. For literature dealing with economic regulation from a public policy perspective, see Ira Magaziner and Robert Reich, *Minding America's Business: The Decline and Rise of the American Economy* (New York: Harcourt Brace Jovanovich, 1982); Gar Alperovitz and Jeff Faux, *Rebuilidng America* (New York: Pantheon, 1984); Kenneth Meier, *Regulation: Politics, Bureaucracy, and Economics* (New York: St. Martin's, 1985); and Eugene Bardach and Robert Kagan (eds.), *Social Regulation: Strategies for Reform* (San Francisco: Institute for Contemporary Studies, 1982).

7. For relevant literature on international law from a private practice perspective, see John Jackson and William Davey, *Legal Problems of International Economic Relations* (St. Paul: West, 1986); Donald Wilson, *International Business Transactions in a Nutshell* (St. Paul: West, 1984); Henry Steiner and Detlev Vagts, *Transnational Legal Problems* (Mineola, N.Y.: Foundation, 1986); and Thomas Buergenthal and Harold Maier, *Public International Law in a Nutshell* (St. Paul: West, 1985).

8. For literature dealing with international law from a public policy perspective, see Myres McDougal and Michael Reisman, *International Law in Contemporary Perspective* (Mineola, N.Y.: Foundation, 1981); Samuel Kim, *The Quest for a Just World Order* (Denver: Westview, 1984); Marvin Soroos, *Beyond Sovereignty: The Challenge of Global Policy* (Columbia: University of South Carolina Press, 1986); Richard Falk and Saul Mendlovitz (eds.), *The Strategy of World Order* (New York: World Law Fund, 1966); and John Tessitore and Susan Woolfson (eds.), *Issues Before the 43rd General Assembly of the United Nations* (Lexington, Mass.: Lexington-Heath, 1981).

CHAPTER 13

Procedural Law

The P/G% software can be applied to procedural law as well as substantive law. In procedural law problems, the main consideration is seeing to it that the proper steps are followed in order to satisfy due process as defined by the Constitution, statutes, or common law rules. This is contrasted to matters of substance that relate to whether a defendant is guilty, liable, or otherwise deserving to lose or win. Procedural law problems tend to be divided into criminal procedure and civil procedure, roughly corresponding to the substantive aspects of chapters 11 and 12 on "Private Law" and "Public Law," respectively.

CRIMINAL PROCEDURE

Private Practice: Plea Bargaining

In this example, we are concerned with the decision of whether to go to trial or accept a plea bargain. Table 13-1 shows the basic data for illustrating sensitivity analysis as applied to prosecution strategy in a criminal case. The problem here is one of deciding whether to accept a plea bargain or to go to trial from a prosecutor's perspective. The overall criterion is to maximize benefits minus costs, but here the benefits are nonmonetary and the costs are monetary.

Table 13-1A shows that the alternatives are either to accept the settlement or go to trial. The criteria from the prosecutor's perspective for judging between those two alternatives are:

1. The average sentence that is likely to occur if the case goes to trial and results in a conviction, discounted by the probability of that conviction occurring.

Table 13-1
Criminal Procedure: Plea Bargaining as an Example

A. THE ALTERNATIVES AND THE CRITERIA

	Alternative	Criterion	Meas.Unit	Weight
1	SETTLE	1*AVG.SENT.(P)	YEARS	0.70
2	TRIAL	2*TRIAL HOURS(P)	HOURS	−20.00
		3 AVG.SENT.(D)	YEARS	−0.60
		4 TRIAL HOURS(D)	HOURS	−18.00
		5*D'S OFFER TO P	YEARS	1.00
		6 P'S DEMAND OF D	YEARS	−1.00
		7*SET.HOURS(P)	HOURS	−20.00
		8 SET.HOURS(D)	HOURS	−18.00

B. THE UNWEIGHTED AND WEIGHTED SCORES OF EACH ALTERNATIVE ON EACH CRITERION

	AVG.SENT	TRIAL HO	D'S OFFE	SET.HOUR
SETTLE	0.00	0.00	2.00	12.00
TRIAL	5.00	36.00	0.00	0.00

	AVG.SENT	TRIAL HO	D'S EFFE	SET.HOUR
SETTLE	0.00	−0.00	2.00	−240.00
TRIAL	3.50	−720.00	0.00	−0.00

C. THE ADJUSTED SCORES SHOWING THAT ONE INCREMENTAL YEAR IS WORTH $400

	AVG.SENT	TRIAL HO	D'S OFFE	SET.HOUR	Combined Rawscores
SETTLE	0.00	−0.00	800.00	−240.00	560.00
TRIAL	1400.00	−720.00	0.00	−0.00	680.00

D. WHAT IT WOULD TAKE TO MAKE SETTLING AS ATTRACTIVE AS GOING TO TRIAL

	SETTLE	TRIAL	Weight
AVG.SENT.(P)		1828.57	0.640
TRIAL HOURS(P)		42.00	−23.333
D'S OFFER TO P	920.00		
SET.HOURS(P)	6.00		−10.000

2. The quantity of working hours if the case goes to trial multiplied by $20 an hour for calculating the trial costs.
3. The defendant's offer to the prosecutor regarding the maximum quantity of prison time the defendant is willing to serve in return for a plea of guilty.
4. The quantity of working hours if the case is settled multiplied by $20 an hour for calculating the settlement costs.

Table 13-1B shows the predicted scores for each alternative on each criterion:

1. If the case goes to trial and there is a conviction, the prosecutor predicts a 5-year sentence.
2. If the case goes to trial, the prosecutor predicts 36 working hours.

3. The defendant has offered to plead guilty if the prosecutor will recommend no more than a 2-year sentence.
4. If the offer is accepted, the prosecutor predicts 12 working hours to close the case.

Table 13-1B also shows each predicted score multiplied by its corresponding weight. That yields four weighted scores as follows:

1. The 5 years discounted by the .70 probability of victory gives an expected value of 3.5 years.
2. The 36 trial hours multiplied by $20 an hour gives a predicted trial cost of $720.
3. The 2-year offer is not discounted by any probability.
4. The 12 settlement hours multiplied by $20 an hour gives a predicted settlement cost of $240.

With those data the prosecutor can meaningfully decide whether to go to trial or accept the plea bargain. The incremental gain in going to trial is 1.5 years for the average case under these circumstances, or 3.5 years minus 2 years. The incremental gain of settling is $480, or $720 minus $240. The data thus reduce to the question of which is more desirable: to obtain an extra 1.5 years on a 2-year sentence, or to save $480 off what otherwise would be $720 in cost? If the prosecutor in this specific case would prefer to have the extra 1.5 years than an extra $480 in the prosecution budget, then go to trial since it is likely to give the additional years. If, however, the prosecutor prefers to have the $480 over the 1.5 years, then accept the plea bargain since it saves the $480.

A useful purpose that this kind of analysis can serve is not only to aid in deciding which is better between settling or going to trial, but also to aid in deciding what it would take to bring the second-place alternative up to first place. Sections C and D are useful in that regard. Table 13-1C is the same as Table 13-1B except the years in Table 13-1B have been converted into their dollar equivalent. If the prosecutor says that a gain of 1.5 years is worth more than a saving of $480 in this case, then the prosecutor is saying that a gain of 1 year is worth *more* than $320, since 1.5 is to $480 as 1 is to $320. If pressed further, the prosecutor might be able to say that an extra year beyond the 2 years offered is worth about $400 of prosecutor time and expense in this particular case. We can thus translate the 3.5 years of Table 13-1B into $1,400 and the 2 years into $800.

With those substitutions, the benefits minus costs of settling are $560, or $800 minus $240. Likewise, with those substitutions, the benefits minus costs of going to trial are likely to be about $680, or $1,400 minus $720. Table 13-1D shows what it would take to make settling as attractive as going to trial. In other words, it shows what it would take to eliminate that gap of $120, or $680 minus $560. There are seven possible changes and various combinations of them that could make settling the more desirable alternative. Those changes include from the right-hand column to the left:

1. If the probability of prosecution victory is only .64 rather than .70, then the settlement is the better alternative.
2. If the cost per hour of trial hours is $23.33 instead of $20, then the settlement is better.
3. If the settlement cost can go down from $20 to only $10, then settling is better.
4. If the average sentence upon conviction drops from $2,000 worth or 5 years down to about $1,800 worth or 4.5 years, then settling is better.
5. If the quantity of trial hours rises from 36 to 42, then settling is better.
6. If the defendant's offer can be pushed up from $800 worth or 2 years to about $1,000 or 2.5 years, then settling is better. Knowing this settlement threshold value is an especially helpful aspect of computer-aided negotiation.
7. If the quantity of settlement hours drops from 12 to only 6, then settling is better.

If any of those threshold values are inserted into the computer in place of the original weights or scores of the alternatives on the criteria, then an exact tie will occur with regard to the combined raw scores shown at the right side of Table 13-1C. The P/G% software is especially useful for making those kinds of calculations. It informs negotiators how far wrong they can be on any of the input values and still arrive at the right decision as to whether to settle or go to trial. The calculations show the tie-causing, threshold, or break-even values for each input item where going slightly higher or lower will shift which is the more desirable alternative.[1]

Legal Policy: Right to Counsel

Table 13-2 deals with the important criminal procedure issue of the extent to which indigent defendants should have court-appointed counsel. The five alternatives have the following meanings:

1. No right to free counsel for indigent defendants, only hired counsel. This was the prevailing rule prior to 1932.
2. Right to free counsel only in capital cases as established in 1932 in *Powell v. Alabama,* 287 U.S. 45.
3. Right to free counsel in both capital and felony cases as of 1963 in *Gideon v. Wainwright,* 372 U.S. 335.
4. Right to free counsel in capital, felony, and misdemeanor cases as of 1972 in *Argersinger v. Hamlin,* 407 U.S. 25.
5. Right to counsel in all three types of criminal cases based on crime severity and also in pretrial interrogation (as of 1964 in *Escobedo v. Illinois,* 378 U.S. 478 for hired counsel and 1966 in *Miranda v. Arizona,* 384 U.S., 436, for indigent defendants) and in posttrial appeals (as of 1963 in *Douglas v. California,* 372 U.S. 353).

There are five criteria shown in Table 13-2. They relate to the desirability of (1) acquitting the innocent, (2) convicting the guilty, (3) decreasing governmental expense, (4) increasing respect for the legal system, and (5) facilitating

Table 13-2
Criminal Procedure: Right to Counsel

ALTERNATIVES	CRITERIA				
	Acquit Innocent	Convict Guilty	Expense Reduce	Respect Law	Adversary Truth
Right to Counsel	1.00	5.00	5.00	1.00	1.00
Capital Cases	2.00	4.00	4.00	2.00	2.00
Capital & Felonies	3.00	3.00	3.00	3.00	3.00
Cap. Felony & Misd.	4.00	2.00	2.00	4.00	4.00
All, Pre/Post Trial	5.00	1.00	1.00	5.00	5.00

IOTES:

. The alternatives have the following meanings:

(1) No right to free counsel for indigent defendants, only hired counsel, prior to 1932.
(2) Right to free counsel in capital cases only, as of 1932.
(3) Right to free counsel in capital and felony cases, as of 1963.
(4) Right to free counsel in capital, felony, and misdemeanor cases, as of 1972.
(5) Right to counsel in all three levels of cases and also pre-trial and post-trial, as of 1963, 1966, and 1972.

:. The criteria have the following meanings.

(1) Acquit the innocent.
(2) Convict the guilty.
(3) Decrease governmental expense.
(4) Increase respect for the legal system.
(5) Facilitate adversary truth-finding.

l. The relations are scored on a 1-5 ranking system. Thus, no right to counsel ranks lowest on acquitting the innocent, and comprehensive right to counsel ranks highest, with the opposite rankings on convicting the guilty.

l. With those alternatives, criteria, and relations, comprehensive right to counsel is the winning alternative with the highest summation score, provided that the goals are given equal weight.

i. Any alternative involving less than comprehensive right to counsel could be the winner if enough extra weight is given to convicting the guilty and decreasing expense while the other three goals are held at weights of 1.00.

i. The reason comprehensive right to counsel was not adopted immediately is because the Supreme Court also includes a criterion which could be called decrease deviation from the prevailing law. As of 1930, Alternative 5 would have a highly negative score on that goal but not as of 1965 in view of the intervening changes in the law.

truth-finding under the adversary legal system. The scores of the alternatives on the criteria are ranks on a 1–5 ranking system, rather than scale scores on a 1–5 scale. For example, if five alternatives do well on a criterion receiving scale scores of 4.0, 4.3, 4.8, 4.9, and 5.0, then they would receive rank scores of 1,2,3,4, and 5. Rank scores lose information by operating on the assumption that pairs of adjacent alternatives are equally one rank apart. They do, however, have the advantage that some people find it easier to rank-order a set of alternatives than to score the alternatives even on a scale as simple as 1–5, which corresponds to −−, −, 0, +, and ++. In Table 13-2, providing for no right to counsel ranks lowest on acquitting the innocent and providing comprehensive right to counsel ranks the highest, with the opposite rankings on convicting the guilty.

With those alternatives, criteria, and relations, comprehensive right to counsel is the winning alternative with the highest summation score provided the goals are given equal weight. Its summation or overall score is 17 points. This is in contrast to limiting right to counsel only to the trial stage (although with all three types of crime severity), which receives only 16 points. Limiting right to counsel only to capital and felony cases receives 15 points. Limiting counsel only to capital cases receives 14 ponts, and limiting counsel only to hired counsel receives 13 points. Any alternative involving less than comprehensive right to counsel could, however, be the winner if enough extra weight is given to convicting the guilty and decreasing expense while the other three goals are held at weights of 1.00. For example, if we consider convicting the guilty and decreasing expense to be twice as important as acquitting the innocent, promoting respect for the legal system, and truth-finding under the adversary system, then one could justify only having a right to hired counsel. Most lawyers, however, would place more weight (not less) on acquitting the innocent, promoting respect, and determining truth under the adversary system.

One might then ask: Why was comprehensive right to counsel not adopted long ago or at least prior to the 1960s? One answer might be that lawyers and judges not only highly value acquitting the innocent and the other goals that favor right to counsel, but they also highly value a legal system that moves incrementally without unduly abrupt shifts from prior precedent. Thus, if one were to add a goal that refers to minimizing deviation from prevailing precedents, then as of 1932 the rule of having right to counsel for the indigent in capital cases could win over the rule of having right to counsel for all felony cases. This is so because the capital rule represents less of a deviation from precedent than the felony rule. As of 1963 and to some extent in the intervening years, the felony rule became less of a deviation from precedent because the Supreme Court kept finding exceptions and unusual circumstances that justified right to counsel in noncapital felony cases. Likewise by the 1960s, it was not such a big deviation from precedent to extend the felony trial rule to pretrial, posttrial, and misdemeanor cases. In other words, the values of lawyers about acquitting the innocent and conforming to precedent may not have changed that greatly from 1932 (at the time of the *Powell* case) to 1972 (at the time of the *Argersinger* case). Instead the facts were different concerning the extent to which the proposed policies deviated from prevailing precedent.[2]

CIVIL PROCEDURE

Private Practice: Damages Negotiation

Table 13-3 provides the data for an example of computer-aided negotiation in a damages case. The alternatives basically are either to go to trial or to settle out of court. This example is presented from a plaintiff's perspective, although it could have also been presented from a defense perspective. The example

Table 13-3
Civil Procedure: Damages Negotiation

A. The Alternatives of Trial Versus Settlement

Alternative
1. Go to Trial
2. Settle

B. The Criteria and Weights of the Benefits and Costs

Criterion	Meas. Unit	Weight
1.(L)Dams.if Won	$	0.22
2 (C)Dams.if Won		0.43
3 (L)Lit.Hours		-30.00
4 (C)Lit.Costs		-1.00
5 (L)Set.Offer		0.20
6 (C)Set.Offer		0.80
7 (L)Set.Hours		-20.00
8 (C)Set.Costs		-1.00

C. Scoring the Alternatives on the Criteria for Trial

	(L)Dams.	(C)Dams.	(L)Lit.H.	(C)Lit.C
Go To Trial	3000.00	3000.00	20.00	400.00
Settle	0.00	0.00	0.00	0.00

D. Scoring the Alternatives on the Criteria for Settlement

	(L)Set.O	(C)Set.O	(L)Set.H	(C)Set.C
Go to Trial	0.00	0.00	0.00	0.00
Settle	1000.00	1000.00	5.00	0.00

E. The Overall Results from the Lawyer's Perspective

	(L)Dams.	(L)Lit.H	(L)Set.O	(L)Set.H	Combined Rawscores
Go to Trial	650.00	-600.00	0.00	-0.00	50.00
Settle	0.00	-0.00	200.00	-100.00	100.00

F. The Overall Results from the Client's Perspective

	(C)Dams.	(C)Lit.C	(C)Set.O	(C)Set.C	Combined Rawscores
Go to Trial	1300.00	-400.00	0.00	-0.00	900.00
Settle	0.00	-0.00	800.00	-0.00	800.00

G. What It Would Take to Get the Client to Settle

	Go to Trial	Settle	Weight
(C)Dams. If Won	2769.23		0.400
(C)Lit. Costs	500.00		
(C)Set.Offer		1125.00	0.900
(C)Set.Costs		-100.00	

H. What It Would Take to Get the Lawyer to Trial

	Go to Trial	Settle	Weight
(L)Dams. If Won	3230.77		0.233
(L) Lit.Hours	18.33		-27.500
(L)Set.Offer		750.00	0.150
(L)Set.Hours		7.50	-30.000

involves a contingency fee arrangement, although it could have been shown with an hourly rate or a flat fee. Table 13-3B shows the criteria for deciding between trial and settlement from both the lawyer's perspective (L) and the client's perspective (C). The lawyer here happens to be a female, and the client is a male. The criteria can also be classified as those that involve benefits (positive weights) and those that involve costs (negative weights). They can also be classified in terms of whether the criteria relate to the trial alternative (1–4) or the settlement alternative (5–8).

The weights in Table 13-3B indicate the following:

1. The .22 shows that there is an estimated .65 probability of winning and that the lawyer gets .33 of what is won. That probability could also be discounted for time, using the time-discounting provisions of the P/G% program.
2. The .43 shows there is an estimated .65 probability of winning, and the client gets .67 of what is won.
3. The $30 indicates the lawyer feels her litigation hours are worth $30 an hour to her.
4. The −1 shows the client has litigation costs that are figured as a lump amount, not by the hour.
5. The .20 indicates the lawyer retains 20% of the settlement.
6. The .80 indicates the client retains 80% of the settlement.
7. The $20 indicates the lawyer feels her settlement hours are worth $20 an hour to her.
8. The −1 shows the client has settlement costs (if any) that are figured as a lump amount, not by the hour.

Table 13-3C and 13-3D show how each alternative scores on each criterion as follows:

1. The damages if won are estimated at $3,000.
2. The lawyer's litigation hours are estimated at 20 hours.
3. The client's litigation costs are estimated at $400.
4. The settlement offer thus far is $1,000.
5. The lawyer's settlement hours are estimated at 5.
6. The client's settlement costs are nothing.

In light of the above data, Table 13-3E shows the lawyer would do better to settle, rather than go to trial. For the lawyer, the $3,000 damages income (discounted by the .65 probability of victory and the .33 contingency fee rate) becomes $650. If she subtracts $600 in litigation costs ($30 times 20 hours), there is a net profit of $50. On the other hand, a $1,000 settlement means $200 income at 20%. If she subtracts $100 in settlement costs ($20 times 5 hours), there is a net profit of $100 for settling. Table 13-3F, however, shows the client would be better off going to trial, rather than settling. For the client, the $3,000 damages income (discounted by the .65 probability and the .67 complement of the contingency fee rate) is $1,300. If he subtracts $400 in litigation costs, there is a net profit of $900. On the other hand, a $1,000 settlement means $800 income at 80%. If he subtracts nothing in settlement costs, there is a net profit for settling that is $100 less than the estimated trial net profit.

The P/G% program is especially useful for computer-aided negotiation because it can so conveniently indicate what it would take to bring a second-place alternative up to first place. Table 13-3G, for example, shows that settlement would become more profitable to both the client and the lawyer than going to trial if the lawyer can get the insurance company to raise its offer from $1,000 to anything higher than $1,125. If the insurance company is unwilling to go higher than $1,125, then the lawyer has an ethical obligation to go to trial, assuming the estimated inputs are reasonably accurate. If, however, the estimated damages amount is as low as $2,769, then the lawyer should settle in the client's best interests, or if the client's litigation costs are more than $500. The lawyer should also accept the $1,000 settlement if the combination of victory probability and contingency complement are as low as .40 rather than .43, or if the client is allowed to keep 90% of the settlement rather than 80%, although then the lawyer may not be so enthusiastic about settling.

Table 13-3H shows from the lawyer's perspective what it would take to make going to trial more profitable than settling. There are eight answers plus combinations of them, as indicated by the eight break-even values shown in Table 13-3H. If any of the original scores change to the scores shown in Table 13-3H, then going to trial becomes more profitable. Those changes include increased damages, decreased litigation hourly rate, decreased settlement percentage, or increased settlement hourly rate. The table shows exactly what increase or decrease will generate a tie between the profitability of going to trial and the profitability of settling.

With that kind of information, the lawyer can negotiate better with the insurance company over the settlement offer and possibly with the client over the contingency fee. The lawyer can also see from these figures what margin of error there is on the estimates. Thus if it is better for the client's interests to go to trial with an estimated damages higher than $2,769, then the lawyer need not anguish over whether the damages are likely to be $3,000 or $5,000, since either figure is over $2,769, and likewise with the other estimates.[3]

Legal Policy: Juries in Civil Cases

Table 13-4 deals with evaluating the use of juries in civil cases. The basic alternatives are:

1. Abolish the civil jury as is the case in many countries of the world, including even England to a considerable extent where the civil jury originated.
2. Provide for limited civil juries with less than unanimous decisions, less than 12 people, and make the plaintiff pay to have a civil jury.

Table 13-4
Civil Procedure: Evaluating the Use of Juries in Civil Cases

A. THE ALTERNATIVES AND THE CRITERIA

ALTERNATIVES	CRITERIA	MEAS.UNIT	WEIGHT
1 No Civil Jury	1 Liability Determ.	1-5 Scale	1.00
2 Ltd.Civil Jury	2 -Delay and Cost		1.00
3 Full Civil Jury	3 Equal Treatment		1.00
	4 Const.Feasible		1.00
	5 Predictability		1.00
	6 Respect for Law		1.00
	7 Pub.op/Ambiquities		1.00

B. HOW EACH ALTERNATIVE SCORES ON EACH CRITERION

ALTERNATIVES	CRITERIA				
	Liability	-Delay	Equal Treatment	Const. Feasibility	Predictability
No Civil Jury	4.00	4.00	4.00	1.00	4.00
Ltd.Civil Jury	2.00	3.00	2.00	3.00	2.00
Full Civil Jury	2.00	2.00	2.00	5.00	3.00

	Respect	Pub.Op
No Civil Jury	2.00	2.00
Ltd.Civil Jury	3.00	3.00
Full Civil Jury	4.00	4.00

C. THE OVERALL SCORE FOR EACH ALTERNATIVE

ALTERNATIVES	COMBINED RAWSCORES
1 No Civil Jury	21.00
2 Ltd.Civil Jury	18.00
3 Full Civil Jury	22.00

D. WHAT IT WOULD TAKE TO BRING THE LIMITED CIVIL JURY TO THE DESIRABILITY OF A FULL CIVIL JURY

	ALTERNATIVES		
CRITERIA	Ltd. Civil	Full Civil	Weight
Liability Determ.	6.00	-2.00	??
-Delay and Cost	7.00	-2.00	5.000
Equal Treatment	6.00	-2.00	??
Const.Feasible	7.00	1.00	-1.000
Predictability	6.00	-1.00	-3.000
Respect for Law	7.00	0.00	-3.000
Pub.Op/Ambiguities	7.00	0.00	-3.000

3. Provide for full civil juries requiring unanimous decisions by 12 people as a matter of the plaintiff's constitutional right.

Basically the issue is one of should the legal system encourages less use of civil juries and thus more use of bench trials, which is the current trend in civil proceedings, or should the legal system seek to reverse or stabilize that trend. As a separate matter, one could discuss how to encourage or improve civil juries, as contrasted to the more basic issue of whether they should be encouraged.

The criteria (and roughly how well the alternatives score on them) include the following:

1. *Accuracy in determining liability in accordance with the law.* On that matter there is general agreement that judges are better in complying with prior precedent than juries are.
2. *Reducing delay and cost.* Picking and instructing juries do add some extra time, and time must be allowed for deliberation. That also means some extra costs, although juries are barely paid a minimum wage. The incremental time and cost, however, tend to be almost trivial in comparison to the long and costly trials in which juries tend to be present. In other words, if a case is tried by a jury, that tends to indicate it would probably be a long and expensive case even if it were not a jury trial.
3. *Equal treatment under the law.* When it comes to equality of treatment along economic class lines, juries can provide some offset to the upper-middle-class bias that judges tend to have. On the matter of equality along racial lines, however, judges may tend to be less biased, especially given their tendency to give more weight to precedent than to the characteristics of the litigants.
3. *Constitutional feasibility.* On this matter, totally abolishing the civil jury would be unconstitutional. The full civil jury is more in conformity with the spirit of the right to trial by civil jury in the seventh amendment than are the limitations that have been allowed on the civil jury.
5. There may be more *predictability* in bench trials than there is in jury trials because of the greater tendency of judges to comply with past precedent. Jurors are not so aware of past precedent and may be more influenced by the special circumstances of the present case. On the other hand, jurors do provide a kind of averaging across 12 or so people, whereas a judge could be a more unpredictable one-person sample. Even if the judge is idiosyncratic, his or her idiosyncracies are likely to be known by the lawyers who practice before him or her. The full civil jury may be more predictable than the limited civil jury because one can better predict the decisions of 12 people deciding unanimously than those of substantially less than 12 people who can go either way by just one vote.
6. Having jury trials may promote more *respect for the law* because people feel that the public is playing a part in the implementation of the law. Partly offsetting that may be a feeling that jury trials are not doing as well as bench trials at least in more technical cases.
7. The seventh criterion refers to the desirability of *relying on public opinion for resolving ambiguities* in the law, especially ambiguities that involve value judgements, rather than relying on the less-representative values of a single judge.

Given the rough scoring of each alternative on each criterion, the full civil jury comes out ahead of a system relying only on bench trials. This is so largely because the full civil jury does especially well on constitutional feasibility, stimulating public respect for the law, and injecting public opinion into the legal process to resolve ambiguous value conflicts. Bench trials, on the other hand, do better on liability determination, delay reduction, and predictability. Actually the margin of victory of the full civil jury over no civil jury is only 22 points versus 21 points if the criteria are given equal weight. One might therefore better conclude that there is a rough tie between those two alternatives.

Section D of table 13-4 indicates what it would take to bring the limited civil jury up to the desirability of a full civil jury. The limited jury is used here on the grounds that completely abolishing the civil jury is too lacking in constitutional feasibility to be considered a viable alternative. Looking at section D indicates that limitations in the civil jury could be justified if one places a high weight on reducing delay and cost or if one places a negative weight on constitutional feasibility, predictability, respect for the law, and the use of public opinion to resolve ambiguities. Likewise, the gap could be widened if one places a low weight on reducing delay and a higher positive weight on constitutional feasibility, predictability, and the other criteria on which the civil jury does relatively well.[4]

NOTES

1. For relevant literature on criminal procedure from a private practice perspective, see Wayne LaFave and Jerold Israel, *Hornbook on Criminal Procedure* (St. Paul: West, 1985); Frank Miller et al., *Criminal Justice Administration* (Mineola, N.Y.: Foundation, 1986); Jerold Israel and Wayne LaFave, *Criminal Procedure in a Nutshell* (St. Paul: West, 1980); and Richard Uviller, *The Processes of Criminal Justice: Investigation and Adjudication* (St. Paul: West, 1979).

2. For literature dealing with criminal procedure from a public policy perspective, see Richard D. Knudten (ed.), *Criminological Controversies* (New York: Meredith, 1968); Burton Atkins and Mark Pogrebin (eds.), *The Invisible Justice System: Discretion and the Law* (Cincinnati: Anderson, 1978); Harry More, *Criminal Justice Management* (St. Paul: West, 1977); S. Nagel (ed.), *The Rights of the Accused: In Law and Action* (Beverly Hills, Calif.: Sage, 1972); and Lester Orfield, *Criminal Procedure from Arrest to Appeal* (New York: New York University Press, 1947).

3. For relevant literature on civil procedure from a private practice perspective, see Jack Friedenthal, Mary Kane, and Arthur Miller, *Hornbook on Civil Procedure* (St. Paul: West, 1985); Robert Cover and Owen Fiss, *The Structure of Procedure* (Mineola, N.Y.: Foundation, 1979); Mary Kane, *Civil Procedure in a Nutshell* (St. Paul: West, 1986); Milton Green, *Text on Basic Civil Procedure* (Mineola, N.Y.: Foundation, 1979); and Maurice Rosenberg, Hans Smit, and Harold Korn, *Elements of Civil Procedure* (Mineola, N.Y.: Foundation, 1985).

4. For literature dealing with civil procedure from a public policy perspective, see Herbert Semmel (ed.), *New Approaches in the Law of Civil Procedure* (Mineola, N.Y.: Foundation, 1970); Herbert Jacob, *Justice in America: Courts, Lawyers, and the Judicial Process* (Boston: Little, Brown, 1984); Larry Berkson, Steven Hays, and Susan Carbon (eds.), *Managing the State Courts* (St. Paul: West, 1977); and Lawrence Baum, *American Courts: Process and Policy* (Boston: Houghton Mifflin, 1986).

CHAPTER 14

Legal Ethics and Microcomputers

This chapter will discuss some of the ethical aspects of using microcomputers as decision aids in law practice. This subject mainly refers to the fact that decision-aiding software requires lawyers or other decision-makers to be more explicit in the goals they are seeking to achieve than they otherwise would be if they made decisions on the basis of more traditional gut reactions. By requiring greater explicitness, decision-aiding software makes questions more visible that relate to whose goals should be considered and how. This includes the goals of the client, the attorney, other attorneys, the court system, and society. Decision-aiding software also has the capability of making those goals more reconcilable by being able to consider many goals simultaneously. It can thereby aid in arriving at mutually beneficial solutions where everyone involved comes out ahead of their best expectations.

There are some related ethical problems that this chapter does not deal with. For example, the use of microcomputers in law offices may generate new rules concerning lawyer malpractice. Those rules can relate to how careful lawyers should be in computerized document preparation, file management, litigation support, time and billing, and other computerized activities. To what extent can a lawyer use as a defense that something was wrong with the hardware, the software, or the operator? That is more a problem that relates to the law of computers, rather than to the role of computers in law.

There are various kinds of ethical problems that using microcomputers as decision aids in law practice might especially generate. They can be illustrated with examples from (1) deciding whether to go to trial or accept settlement, (2) deciding how much time to allocate to a case, (3) providing counsel to the poor and unpopular, and (4) being a lawyer who promotes the well-being of the legal system and society.

DECIDING WHETHER TO GO TO TRIAL OR ACCEPT A SETTLEMENT

Deciding whether to go to trial or accept a settlement is probably the most frequently mentioned decision when lawyers talk about the use of microcomputers as decision aids in law practice. Decision-aiding software can make more visible the conflict that may exist in such litigation strategy decisions between attorneys and clients.

Where Settling Is Best for the Client, but Not for the Lawyer

Table 14-1 provides a realistic example of where settling is best for the client but going to trial is best for the lawyer. This is a contingency fee case for which the lawyer gets paid nothing unless he or she wins, and then the lawyer receives a percentage of the settlement of the damages awarded. The lawyer does not bill the client for any hours worked. The reason for using this type of case here is partly because contingency fee cases are thought to involve less of a conflict of interest than other fee-paying arrangements since both the lawyer and the client are interested in maximizing victory and the damages collected.

If one follows across the *settlement* row of section A, we see:

1. A $5,000 settlement has been offered of which the lawyer gets 20%. This means $4,000 to the client and $1,000 to the lawyer.
2. The quantity of hours for settling is about 10. In this hypothetical data, we figure the lawyer's time is worth $30 an hour. That means the lawyer would be willing to pay no more than $30 an hour to have someone else take his or her place in the case. Thus the settlement cost is nothing to the client and $300 to the lawyer.
3. The net profit to the client is thus $4,000, which equals $4,000 in benefits minus $0 in costs. The net profit to the lawyer from settling is $700, which equals $1,000 in benefits minus $300 in costs.

If one follows across the *go-to-trial* row of section A, we see:

1. $10,000 is the average damages in a case like this where damages are awarded, but there is only a .60 probability of winning, giving this case a net value of $6,000.
2. The lawyer keeps 40% of the $6,000 since going to trial is more difficult than arranging for a settlement. This means $3,600 to the client and $2,400 to the lawyer.
3. The quantity of hours for going to trial is predicted to be about 25. The lawyer's trial time is worth $60 an hour since the lawyer would be willing to pay more to have someone take the lawyer's trial time. This is not the hourly rate at which clients are billed, since there is no client billing for hours worked in a contingency fee case. If there were, the client would probably be billed for more than $60 an hour. Another way of putting it is that for each hour the lawyer works in trial, he or she could be receiving $60 an hour that is being sacrificed by working in this case. Thus the litigation cost is $0 to the client and $1,500 to the lawyer.

Table 14-1

Data for Illustrating and Reconciling Some Attorney-Client Conflicts

GOALS / OPTIONS	BENEFIT ITEMS					COST ITEMS			NET ITEMS	
	(1) Average Damages If One Gets Them	(2) Probability of Receiving Damages	(3) Average Damages or Expected Value (1) x (2)	(4) Percentage Fee	(5) Total Benefits (3) x (4)	(6) Number of Hours	(7) Hourly Cost	(8) Total Costs (6) x (7)	(9) Lawyer B-C (5) - (8)	(10) Client B-C (3) x [1 - (4)]
A. THE ORIGINAL INPUT VALUES IN THE LITIGATION STRATEGY EXAMPLE										
Settle	$ 5,000	1.00	$5,000	20%	$1,000	10	$30	$ 300	$ 700	$4,000*
Go to Trial	$10,000	.60	$6,000	40%	$2,400	25	$60	$1,500	$ 900*	$3,600
B. TIE-CAUSING VALUES FROM THE LAWYER'S PERSPECTIVE										
Settle	$ 6,000*	1.20	$6,000	24%	$1,200	3.33	$10	$ 100	$ 900	
Go to Trial	$ 9,167	.55	$5,500	37%	$2,200	28.33	$68	$1,700	$ 700	
C. TIE-CAUSING VALUES FROM THE CLIENT'S PERSPECTIVE										
Settle	$ 4,500	.90	$4,500	28%	$3,600	--	--	--		$3,600
Go to Trial	$11,111	.67	$6,667*	33%	$4,000	--	--	--		$4,000

NOTES:

1. If any of the original input values in Table 14-1A change to its tie-causing value in Table 14-1B then the profit of the lawyer from settling will rise from $700 to $900, or the profit from going to trial will drop from $900 to $700
2. If any of the original input values in Table 14-1A change to its tie-causing value in 14-1C then the profit of the client from settling will drop from $4,000 to $3,600, or the profit from going to trial will rise from $3,600 to $4,000.
3. When one of the basic components changes to its tie-causing value, we assume the other basic components remain constant, although not the products or sums of the basic components. The basic components are shown in columns 1, 2, 4, 6, and 7. The products or sums of the basic components are shown in columns 3, 5, 8, 9, and 10.
4. The starred items are those most subject to change in order to bring the lawyer's interest and the client's interest together.

4. The net profit to the client is thus \$3,600, which equals \$3,600 in benefits minus \$0 in costs. The net profit to the lawyer is \$900, which equals \$2,400 in benefits minus \$1,500 in costs.

Thus the client comes out \$400 ahead by settling, whereas the lawyer comes out \$200 ahead by going to trial. If this were a flat fee case there could be a similar conflict since the arrangement might be that the lawyer gets paid \$5,000 if the case goes to trial but only \$1,000 if there is a settlement. Likewise, if this were an hourly rate case, there could be similar conflict since the arrangement might be that the lawyer gets paid \$100 an hour for gong to trial but only \$50 an hour for arranging a settlement.

Other Common Situations

At first glance it might look as if it is easier to have a conflict where settling is best for the client but not for the lawyer, since lawyers normally make more by going to trial than by settling. That, however, is not necessarily true. What may be needed at this point is to clarify with some simple formulas under what circumstances settling is best for the client but not for the lawyer, and vice versa, in contingency fee cases, hourly rate cases, and flat fee cases.

In a *contingency fee* case, the lawyer is better off going to trial if R_1D-L is greater than R_2S-A. The R_1 stands for the percentage rate for going to trial, the D stands for damages, and the L stands for the litigation costs. The R_2 stands for the percentage rate for arranging a settlement, the S stands for the settlement offer, and the A stands for the arrangement costs. On the other hand, if R_1D-L is less than R_2S-A, then the lawyer is better off settling. In Table 14-1, the left side of that inequality was greater than the right side. An example where the right side would be greater is where the damages are not so high, the litigation costs are high, or the settlement offer is relatively high. In a contingency fee case, no matter how high the damages are, if the litigation costs are going to eat up the lawyer's share of the damages, then the lawyer might be better off with the settlement.

In the contingency fee case, the client is better off going to trial if $(1-R_1)D$ is greater than $(1-R_2)S$. If, on the other hand, $(1-R_1)D$ is less than $(1-R_2)S$, then the client is better off settling. Note that the rate that the client receives is the complement of the rate that the lawyer receives, which explains the $1-R_1$ and the $1-R_2$. Also note that the client does not bear any of the litigation costs or arrangement costs, which explains why there is no L or R in the client formulas.

Thus we can predict there will be a conflict between the lawyer and the client in a contingency fee case if the above lawyer calculations result in trial being more attractive to the lawyer, and the above client calculations result in settling being more attractive to the client. There would also be a conflict if the calculations result in settling being more attractive to the lawyer and trial being more attractive to the client. The possibility of a conflict occurring is substantially increased if one recognizes that the lawyer's perception of the likely damages (D) may not be the same as the client's perception, especially when one considers that the damages component has two subjective subparts. One is damages received if the plaintiff wins, and the other is the probability of victory.

In an *hourly rate* case, the lawyer is better off going to trial if Q_1R_1 is greater than Q_2R_2, where Q_1 is the quantity of trial hours, R_1 is the rate per trial hour, Q_2 is the quantity of settlement hours, and R_2 is the rate per settlement hour. If the left-hand side is less than the right-hand side, then the lawyer is better off settling under an hourly rate. That is unlikely to occur because Q_1 is nearly always greater than Q_2 and R_1 greater than R_2. There is thus a need for constraints to keep lawyers who operate on hourly rates from billing excessive hours. The old constraints emphasized the Canons of Ethics, which were seldom enforced to protect clients except in extreme cases. The new constraints emphasize a more competitive legal profession whereby lawyers who bill excessively lose clients to lawyers who can do the job in less time at a lower rate.

In an hourly rate case the client is better off going to trial when $D-Q_1R_1$ is greater than $S-Q_2R_2$. Likewise, the client is better off settling when $D-Q_1R_1$ is less than $S-Q_2R_2$. Thus unlike the lawyer, the client is not consistently better off going to trial or settling in an hourly rate case. The decision depends partly on the values of D and S, which are not relevant to the lawyer's profit calculations. The lawyer may, however, be concerned with seeking to increase the value of both D and S as a matter of pride and good business. That raises the role of non-monetary considerations, which P/G% can take into consideration through its percentaging options if one wants them explicitly considered. That could include the usually greater anguish of either the lawyer or the client in going to trial, rather than settling. Some of that anguish can be considered by doing time-discounting, which P/G% allows for. Some of it, however, relates to the fact that going to trial is a more emotinal experience even if there is no delay.

In a *flat fee* case the lawyer is better off going to trial if F_1-L is greater than F_2-A, where F_1 is the flat fee for going to trial and F_2 is the flat fee for settling. The lawyer is likewise better off settling if F_1-L is less than F_2-A, as it could be if the litigation costs virtually wipe out the trial fee. If there is only one flat fee for resolving the case regardless of whether the case goes to trial or is settled, then the lawyer is better off going to trial if $F'-L$ is greater than $F'-A$, where F' is the overall flat fee. This reduces to saying the lawyer is better off going to trial if the litigation costs are less than the arrangement costs, which is not likely to be the case. Thus under this kind of a flat fee, the lawyer would probably have too strong an incentive always to settle, bearing in mind that the client does not cover the exact litigating or arranging costs.

In a flat fee case the client is better off going to trial if $D-F_1$ is greater than $S-F_2$, and is better off settling if $D-F_1$ is less than $S-F_2$. Note that in either the hourly rate situation or the flat fee situation, only the client's net profit depends on the size of the damages or the settlement offer, not the lawyer's net profit. If there is a single flat fee, then the client is better off going to trial if $D-F'$ is greater than $S-F'$. That reduces to saying the client is better off going to trial if the likely damages are higher than the settlement offer. That arrangement (like the contingency fee) gives the client no incentive to reduce the lawyer's expenses. This is unlike the hourly rate arrangement.

One should also note that although we have been talking about the perspective of the plaintiff lawyer and the plaintiff client, the analysis is also applicable to the *defendant* lawyer and the defendant client in a damages case. The only difference is that the defense side seldom operates on a contingency fee basis, although it could where the lawyer does not get paid unless the lawyer wins. The usual arrangement is an hourly rate, a flat fee, or a salary. All those arrangements can create a conflict of interest in terms of the lawyer wanting to go to trial or settle, and the client wanting to do the opposite. Under a salaried arrangement where the lawyer gets nothing extra for going to trial, there is a strong incentive to settle since settling is easier work. This may show up in salaried public defenders in criminal cases, although they have strong incentives to settle due to lack of investigative staff, trial staff, and other funding.

The analysis is also applicable to *criminal* defense in private practice, as well as the salaried public defender. A key difference, though, is that the defendant is likely to be operating under more nonmonetary considerations. That, however, does not lessen the possibility of a conflict over going to trial versus settling. On the prosecutor's side, the client can be considered as the victim who may always prefer to prosecute. The client could also be considered to be the taxpayers who may not always prefer to prosecute. The possibility of conflict is substantially increased when there are multiple clients involved.

Mutually Beneficial Solutions

When the situation is laid out in spreadsheet fashion as in Table 14-1, the conflict of interest becomes more visible. Some lawyers would say this is a disadvantage of spreadsheet-based decision-aiding software because it forces them to feel guilty when making decisions that might be motivated by the lawyer's goals more than the clients'. Other lawyers would say that making the conflict more visible is an advantage because it forces lawyers to think more explicitly in terms of maximizing their client's interests. Such decision-aiding software may be good or bad with regard to making the conflict more visible, depending on what is then done with that increased awareness.

How can those conflicting interests of Table 14-1 be resolved? Lawyers may rationalize by saying the client still comes out $3,600 ahead in comparison to never having filed a claim. Lawyers may also rationalize by saying that by going to trial, the client could have come out with $6,000 if the lawyer would have obtained $10,000 in damages and taken a 40% fee. Perhaps a typical lawyer resolves the conflicting interests by settling. Lawyers might then rationalize by saying that they still come out with a $700 profit in comparison to having never taken the case. Lawyers may also rationalize by saying that by settling, they thereby avoid the possibility of a total defeat in which they would collect nothing.

The Lawyer's Perspective

The main advantage in this context of decision-aiding software is that it enables the lawyer to see more clearly how the conflict can be reconciled to the mutual benefit of both the lawyer and the client. For example, section B of Table 14-1 shows the threshold or tie-causing values of all the inputs using the lawyer's goals. That part of the table shows what it would take to bring settling up to the desirability level of going to trial from the lawyer's perspective. More specifically, the lawyer makes a net profit of $900 by going to trial but only $700 by settling. We are thus asking what would it take to bring settling up to a net profit of $900. The answer is not simply to ask for $200 more from the insurance company as a settlement offer. That will only bring the $700 up to $740, since $160 of the extra $200 has to be given to the client under the 80%-20% arrangement.

We thus especially want to know how much the lawyer has to seek from the insurance company to make settling as attractive as going to trial. The P/G% software instantly shows that the answer is $6,000 instead of the $5,000 that the insurance company originally offered. As a matter of hindsight, the $6,000 makes sense because it means an extra $1,000. From that incremental amount, $800 goes to the client and $200 goes to the lawyer, bringing the original $700 up to $900. That, however, is only one of 16 inputs or combinations of inputs that are subject to change. Any one of the other 15 might be easier than getting the insurance company to offer an extra thousand dollars, or they might be more difficult. They are all worth looking at. The solution might be to get the insurance company to offer only another $500 and make up the rest of the difference through one or more of the other inputs.

More specifically, the threshold or tie-causing values in the *settlement row* of section B are:

1. Raising the $5,000 settlement offer to $6,000 as previously mentioned.
2. The next figure is to raise the probability of being paid when one accepts the settlement offer from 1.00 to 1.20. That is impossible since one cannot have a probability higher than 1.00 or certainty. One might, however, note that an important consideration in litigation strategy should often be the probability of getting paid. This is especially so in calculating the value of a damage award where one should discount it not only by the probability of winning, but also by the probability of collecting.
3. The $6,000 figure is not an input, but instead is the product of two input numbers. The two input numbers are not shown in the table since there are an infinite number of pairs of numbers representing damages multiplied by a probability figure that could equal $6,000. It could be $6,000 times 1.00, or $5,000 times 1.20, or any other combination that multiplies to $6,000. The $6,000 means that if the expected value of the settlement offer is $6,000, then the lawyer's net profit will be $900.
4. The lawyer could ask the client to raise the 20% contingency fee to 24%. The client

would have no legal obligation to do so, assuming the 20% fee was legitimately agreed to as part of a binding relation. More important, if the 20% figure were raised to 24%, then it is possible that we would simply reverse the conflict so that now the lawyer is better off settling and the client is better off going to trial. One does not reconcile conflicts by reversing them or by creating new ones that are equally intense. A related possibility is that the client could offer something from the client's business that would have substantial value to the lawyer, but not much loss to the client. That would be the case if the client were in the business of producing manufactured products for which the variable cost is low, but the market value is high.

5. If the total benefits (meaning the settlement offer multiplied by the settlement percentage fee) were to move up from $1,000 to $1,200, then the lawyer would be as well off settling as going to trial. This is about the same as saying that the settlement offer needs to go up from $5,000 to $6,000 if the percentage fee is going to remain constant at 20%.
6. If the lawyer can decrease the settlement hours from 10 to 3.33 hours, then the settlement will be worth $900 to the lawyer without having to get the insurance company to make a higher offer. This is so because at $30 an hour for settlement time, 3.33 hours is worth $100. If we then subtract $100 in cost from the $1,000 that the lawyer gets from the settlement, then the lawyer has a net profit of $900, which is just as good as going to trial. This option may be easier in whole or in part than getting the insurance company to offer an extra $1,000.
7. If the lawyer could deflate the value of his or her time from $30 an hour to $10 an hour, then the lawyer could still work 10 hours and have only $100 in cost. That seems unlikely in this case but is a possibility in some other cases where the lawyer is hiring someone at hourly rates and where it is possible to hire a less-expensive someone.
8. As already mentioned, if the costs can get down to $100, then the lawyer can take a $1,000 total benefits figure and come out as well as going to trial.

Looking now at the *go-to-trial row* of section B, we have eight more possible items that are subject to change that could make settling as profitable as going to trial from the lawyer's perspective:

1. If the estimated damages of $10,000 are being misestimated so that they are really about $9,167, then the lawyer could justify accepting the settlement that nets only $700 because with damages of $9,167, the trial profit would only be $700.
2. If the damage estimate is quite firm but the probability estimate might really be about .55 rather than .60, then the lawyer could also justify accepting the settlement because at a victory probability of .55, the average trial profit drops to $700.
3. Any drop in the damages estimate below $10,000 combined with a drop in the victory probability below .60 could yield an expected value product of $5,500. That would make going to trial as profitable or less profitable than accepting the insurance company's settlement offer that favors the client. The lawyer might therefore reexamine those two estimates to see if they may have been unduly high as a way of resolving the conflict.
4. If the lawyer is willing to accept only a 37% contingency fee instead of a 40%

contingency fee, then going to trial becomes no better than accepting the settlement. That option seems unlikely. Just as the client has no incentive to change upward from 20% to 24%, likewise the lawyer has no incentive to change downward from 40% to 37%. An imaginative possibility might be for the lawyer to offer the client a certain amount of free legal service that would be roughly the equivalent in market value to the $400 that the client could be losing on the average by going to trial. A complicating factor, though, is that if they do decide to go to trial in light of that side offer, they might win the case and then the client would come out substantially ahead as a result of going to trial. That, however, should not retroactively wipe out the side offer unless there was an agreement to that effect.

5. Any combination of the original 40% contingency fee multiplied by the expected value that yields total benefits of $2,200 would generate a tie between going to trial and settling. That, however, suggests reexamining those expected value estimates, as mentioned before.
6. If the lawyer decides that 25 hours is too low for litigation time and that it is really more like 28.33 or more, then grab the settlement as being at least as good or better than going to trial.
7. If the lawyer decides that trial time is worth at least $68 an hour rather than $60 an hour, then the settlement should look as good or better than the likely trial outcome.
8. If any combination of quantity of hours and rate per hour seems reasonable that is at or more than $1,700, then going to trial would not be cost effective.

The Client's Perspective

Actually there are ten more input values or combinations that are possibly subject to change that could reconcile the conflict, namely those from the client's perspective. Some people may not like to have so many options available. One big advantage of the P/G% software for many people, however, is that it does provide for so many different ways of reconciling conflicts in order to arrive at mutually beneficial agreements, including agreements or solutions that are better than the best original expectations of the parties involved. This is true not just with regard to the attorney-client relation but also to the plaintiff-defendant relation and any kind of conflict or dispute.

Looking at the *settlement row* of section C, the five tie-causing values there are:

1. If the insurance company changes its mind and decides to offer only $4,500, then both the client and the lawyer would be better off going to trial. This is so because 80% of $4,500 is $3,600, which means that the value of the settlement has dropped from the client's perspective to being no better than going to trial. The insurance company may not be so likely to change its mind. The situation, however, could involve one of trying to anticipate in advance what the settlement offer is likely to be, and deciding that $5,000 was too high an estimate.
2. If the $5,000 figure is in some way contingent on collecting the money and there is a .90 probability of collecting, then the expected value of the settlement drops to 90% of

$5,000, which is $4,500. When the client gets to keep only 80% of that, then the net to the client is the same $3,600 as going to trial would yield. At that point, both the lawyer and the client might be better off jointly agreeing to go to trial.

3. The third item is the $4,500 combination of the settlement offer and the probability of collecting it.
4. If the client were to somehow agree to give the lawyer 28% of the settlement instead of 20%, then the $5,000 would also drop to $3,600, making the client more likely to agree with the lawyer that they should go to trial. However, the client is not likely to agree with the lawyer to give the lawyer a 28% fee if they had previously agreed to a 20% fee for a settlement. As mentioned before, the client could through an in-kind payment make up the $200 that the lawyer would be losing by accepting the settlement. The multicriteria decision-making software thrives on multiple criteria like these, as indicated in chapter 4 on "Computer-Aided Mediation."
5. If the total benefits to the client are only $3,600 or less from settling, then the client would be better off going to trial. Note that none of the cost items listed apply to the client with regard to number of attorney hours, cost per hour, or total cost in terms of hours times the rate.

Looking at the *go-to-trial row* of section C, the tie-causing values there are:

1. If the lawyer can get the damages up from $10,000 to more than $11,111, then going to trial becomes better for both the lawyer and the client. That is the threshold damages figure because when it is discounted by the original .60 probability and the original 60% which the client gets to keep, then the net profit for the client is $4,000 from going to trial. That is just as good as accepting the $5,000 settlement from the insurance company, as indicated in the settlement row of section A.
2. Likewise, if the lawyer can get the victory probability up from .60 to more than .67, then the client will have more than $4,000 to take home as a result of the trial, which is better than the $4,000 take-home figure from the settlement offer.
3. Thus any combination of increased damages and increased probability of victory that adds up to more than $6,667 will make going to trial more profitable than accepting a settlement for either the client or the lawyer.
4. If the lawyer were willing to drop his trial contingency fee from 40% to 33%, then the client should be willing to go to trial. That, however, is another example of trying to reconcile a conflict by creating a new conflict. In this case it would mean that now the client will want to go to trial, but the lawyer may want to settle because the lawyer is not getting enough of a percentage of the damages. With other facts, however, lowering the contingency fee might reconcile the conflict. Perhaps everyone could come out ahead if the lawyer were to lower the contingency fee rate partly in response to the client offering an in-kind payment that would have substantial value to the lawyer, but little loss to the client.
5. The last of the 26 input items or combinations of them is the $4,000 in total benefits from the client's perspective. That number is saying that if any combination of increased damages, increased probability of victory, and decreased percentage fee could yield total benefits of $4,000 or more to the client, then the client should be

pleased to go to trial along with the lawyer as a mutually beneficial solution to their litigation strategy conflict.

Relevant Ethical Principles

The above analysis enables us to clarify better the ethical obligation of a lawyer operating under a contingency fee arrangement. It generates the following principles:

1. If it is more profitable to the lawyer to go to trial, but it is more profitable to the client to settle or vice versa, then the lawyer should seek to increase the settlement to make settling more profitable to both of them. The increase need go only as high as the threshold or tie-causing value of the settlement offer.
2. As an alternative, the lawyer should seek to increase the expected value of going to trial in order to make going to trial more profitable to both of them. The increase need go only as high as making the trial even more profitable to the client than settling. The lawyer need not push for still more profit for the client when it means operating at a decreased profit to the lawyer or even an increased loss.
3. If, in a rare situation, it is impossible to make settling or going to trial more profitable to both the client and the lawyer, then the lawyer should choose between settling and going to trial in light of the client's best interests.
4. Perhaps lawyers of the future should have an ethical obligation to systematically determine the relative profitability of settling and going to trial to the client and the lawyer at differing degrees of effort in order to be able to implement the above ethical principles to their mutual profit.[1]

DECIDING HOW MANY HOURS TO ALLOCATE TO A CASE

One of the most exciting aspects of the P/G% spreadsheet-based decision-aiding software for lawyers is that it can not only reconcile ethical conflicts between attorneys and clients by clarifying the numerous options that may be available for such reconciliation, it can also deal with problems that at first glance seem to involve inherent internal conflicts, like running faster than the speed of light while simultaneously running slower than molecules at minus 272 degrees Fahrenheit where nothing moves. To be more specific in the context of ethical problems between attorneys and clients, we should note that probably the main way the attorney can increase the damages or the victory probability in table 14-1 in order to make going to trial more attractive to the client is by putting more effort or hours into the case. Doing that, however, results in increasing the expenses of the attorney, thereby wiping out whatever may have been gained from increasing the damages or victory probability. Maybe there is some quantity of hours where the damages go up, but the lawyer expenses do not go up so much, and the lawyer and client somehow both come out ahead by going to trial, rather than by accepting the settlement.

Relating Input Hours to Output Achieved

It is common sense that working harder to prepare the case should result in more damages and a higher probability of victory, but how can one determine the quantitative nature of that relation between hours on the one hand and damages times victory probability on the other hand? One way to determine the relation is by obtaining information on lots of previous related cases showing how many hours were devoted to each case and the damages awarded. By inputting that information into a statistical calculator or an appropriately programmed microcomputer, one can determine the numerical parameters for a relation of the form $DP = A(H)^B$. In that equation, *DP* is the expected value to be predicted, *H* is the quantity of hours to be predicted from, *A* is the expected value when *H* is one hour, and *B* measures the degree of diminishing returns in the nonlinear relation between *DP* and *H.* Suppose we have only one case to predict from, like the case shown in row 2 of table 14-1A. One can assume a value for *B* of .50, since that is the simplest diminishing returns relation. This recognizes that as hours go up, *D* and *P* also go up, but at a plateauing rate. One can then solve for *A* in the equation, $\$6{,}000 = A(25)^{.50}$. Row 2 of Table 14-1A shows $6,000 expected value at 25 hours. The value of *A* is thus $6,000 divided by the square root of 25, if one divides both sides of that equation by $(25)^{.50}$. *A* is thus equal to $6,000/5, or $1,200. Any number raised to the .50 power is the same as the square root of the number.

An alternative approach to expressing the relation between expected value and hours is to assume the elasticity coefficient of *B* is .50 and the scale coefficient of *A* is 1. Doing so gives a relation of $DP = 1(H)^{.50}$. That means when there is a 1% increase in hours, there is a .50% increase in expected value. When there is a 100% increase in hours, there is a 50% increase in expected value. The expression $1(H)^{.50}$ also means that when hours are 1, the expected value is 1 monetary unit or $1,000. Another approach is to insert into a statistical calculator the data point of 25 hours and $6, and a second data point of 1 hour and $1. Doing so yields a production function of $1(H)^{.56}$, after one logs all the numbers. One need not argue over which approach is best among these, since they all produce approximately the same production functions when 1 monetary unit is $1,000.

Net Profit for the Lawyer and the Client

By substituting $A(H)^B$ or $\$1{,}200(H)^{.50}$ for *DP,* one can then express the lawyer's profit in terms of hours expended. The lawyer's profit can thus be expressed as $480H^{.5} - 60H$. The $480H^{.5}$ is equal to *DPF,* since *DP* equals

$1,200(H)^{.50}$ and F equals .40. The expression simplifies to $480H^{.5}$, since 1200 times .40 is 480. The $60H$ cost comes from $60 per hour. Likewise, one can express the client's profit as $720H^{.5}$ or 60% of $1,200(H)^{.50}$. One can then determine with a calculator the lawyer profit and the client profit for a variety of different hours, as is shown in table 14-2. Doing so indicates that the maximum lawyer profit is at 16 hours, whereas the maximum client profit is at infinity. The client does not directly pay any of the lawyer's costs, and thus increased hours mean increased net damages to the client, although at a plateauing rate.

At 31 hours, the lawyer is able to make going to trial more attractive to the client than accepting the $5,000 settlement. At that point the lawyer's profit of $813 is also greater than the settlement profit of $700. If, however, the lawyer puts in more hours, then at 64 hours the high total cost wipes out the total benefits. The total cost is increasing at a constant rate of $60 an hour for each additional hour. The total benefits, however, go up only 50% when the hours double or go up 100%.

Note the diminishing returns in the sense that from 50 hours to 75 hours, the client profit goes up by $1,144 (from $5,091 to $6,235), whereas from 75 hours to 100 hours, the client profit goes up by only $965 (from $6,235 to $7,200). Although the client profits rise at a plateauing rate, the lawyer losses rise at an increasing rate. Thus in going from 50 hours to 75 hours, the lawyer profit drops from a positive $394 to a negative $343 for a difference of $737. However, in covering the same 25 hours from 75 to 100 hours, the losses grow from a negative $343 to a negative $1,200 for a difference of $857. Perhaps more important to note is that with each successive hour starting from the very beginning, the client profits increase whereas with each successive hour after a relatively early peak is reached, the lawyer profits decrease and the losses increase. The key point is that under such a fee-paying arrangement, lawyers cannot be expected to maximize the profits of their clients because doing so would inherently bankrupt the lawyers.

So a different standard has to be developed for what constitutes promoting the best interests of one's client under these contingency fee circumstances. An appropriate standard might be to put in enough hours to optimize from the client's perspective whatever course of action one takes between going to trial or settlng. That results in choosing the best alternative with best being defined in terms of the client's interests, not the lawyer's. By proceeding in accordance with the analysis of table 14-2, the lawyer also comes out ahead since the analysis and the time allocation result in going to trial being the most profitable alternative for both the client and the lawyer.

Other Common Situations

On the matter of how many hours to allocate to a case, we should also look at the situations that involve hourly rates and flat fees. Under an hourly rate, the

Table 14-2
The Profits of the Lawyer and the Client at Different Hours Worked

HOURS	LAWYER PROFIT	CLIENT PROFIT	COMMENTS
0	0	0	Doing nothing generates nothing.
1	420	720	The starting point.
10	917	2,277	
15	959	2,789	
16	960	2,880	The lawyer's maximum.
20	946	3,210	
25	900	3,600	The trial row of Table 14-1A.
30	829	3,944	
31	813	4,009	Satisfying one's obligation to the client.
35	740	4,260	
50	394	5,091	
60	118	5,577	
64	0	5,960	Costs begin to exceed benefits for the lawyer.
65	-30	5,805	
75	-343	6,235	
100	-1,200	7,200	Profit is still rising for the client, but more slowly.

NOTES:

1. The average damages or expected value equals $1,200 times the square root of the trial hours. This is determined by observing the trial row of Table 14-1A and observing what has happened in other cases regarding the average damages and the trial hours.
2. The lawyer's profit equals DPF - HR, where D = damages, P = probability, F = % Fee, H = Hours, and R = Rate per Hour. That expression simplifies to $\$1,200(H)^{.5}(.40) - (H)(\$60)$, where $(H)^{.5}$ is equal to the square root of the trial hours. That expression further simplifies to $480H^{.5}-60H$.
3. The client's profit equals DP(1-F). That equation simplifies to $\$1,200(H)^{.5}(.60)$. That equation further simplifies to $720H^{.5}$.
4. All the profit figures in Table 14-2 can be calculated with any calculator that can handle exponents or square roots.
5. The optimum number of trial hours can be defined as the quantity that maximizes benefits minus costs from the lawyer's perspective, while making going to trial the more attractive alternative to both the client and the lawyer, not just the lawyer.

lawyer should put in as many hours as are needed to do the job properly. The lawyer should, however, be especially sensitive to a maximum time constraint since being paid by the hour can stimulate billing for an excessive number of hours. That sensitivity can be increased by doing a kind of spreadsheet analysis for hourly rate cases. Such an analysis would provide columns for the estimated or actual net profit of the client and the lawyer at various quantities of hours. It would also show the components that go into those profit figures. The main lawyer components are the fee received at the hourly rate and the time costs incurred at a lower hourly rate than one normally bills. The main client components are the benefits received from the lawyer's work or at least the quantity of output units. The fee paid by the client is the client's costs and the lawyer's income. The lawyer should bill for a quantity of hours that would satisfy a high percentage of clients, such that they are not likely to complain to the bar association or withhold referring the lawyer to other potential clients.

Under a flat fee, the lawyer should also put in as many hours as are needed to do the job properly. The lawyer should, however, be especially sensitive to a minimum time constraint since being paid a flat fee can stimulate working too few hours. That sensitivity can also be increased by doing a spreadsheet analysis for the flat fee cases. Such an analysis would include columns like those shown in table 14-2 and like those discussed above concerning the hourly rate spreadsheet. The lawyer should clock a quantity of hours that would satisfy a high percentage of clients such that they are not likely to complain to the bar association or withhold referring the lawyer to other potential clients.

The P/G% software can easily be used to show alternative quantities of hours on the rows. The columns show the lawyer and client profit and their components. The P/G% software would treat this type of problem as a mutually exclusive choosing problem. One cannot choose to put in both 20 hours and 30 hours in the same case. It is also an optimum level problem in the sense that doing too little or too much is undesirable. If a lawyer does too little, he or she may be guilty of malpractice and of missing the opportunity to make a bigger profit under either a contingency fee or an hourly rate. If a lawyer does too much, she or he may be guilty of overcharging under an hourly rate or of being inefficient to the detriment of the lawyer's profit by unduly incurring time expenses.

Just laying out the alternatives, goals, and estimated relations is helpful in planning time allocations. The software could be even more helpful by providing built-in formulas for calculating profit figures, profit components, and relations between input hours and the profit components. The software could ask the lawyer for estimates of the expected damages at different quantities of hours inputted in order to establish the relations between damages and hours worked. Actually, only one point in time would be sufficient to develop a relation, given assumptions about diminishing returns. However, two, three, or more points might be even better if they are representative.[2]

REPRESENTING THE POOR AND OTHER PROFESSIONAL RESPONSIBILITIES

Thus far we have been mainly discussing legal ethics and microcomputers in the context of private practice problems, rather than legal policy problems. The key private practice problems have been making choices, especially in litigation strategy, and allocating time, also mainly in the context of litigation situations. In this analysis, legal policy problems can also be subdivided in two parts. One part deals with the important matter of representing the poor. The other part deals with broader and more varied legal policy concerns.

Previous Legal Aid Issues

Microcomputers can be helpful in representing indigent clients, as part of a public defender program or a civil legal aid program. Those programs are traditionally starved or at least greatly lacking in funds for adequately servicing their clients. Microcomputers do have some capabilities for more efficiently using scarce resources. This includes microcomputers for office practice purposes such as word processing, file management, and citation retrieval. Citation retrieval, however, can be more expensive than traditional legal research unless there is a special rate to legal aid programs. Such retrieval may be more efficient in saving time, but not necessarily in saving money. Perhaps companies like WestLaw and Lexis should be more encouraged to supply low-cost help to legal aid programs. The encouragement could be provided by bar associations and government agencies without making it a legal requirement.

Microcomputers can help legal aid and public defender programs make decisions that are more effective, efficient, and equitable through the use of spreadsheet-based software like P/G%. An article in the *Software Law Journal* is devoted to that idea.[3] The article emphasized the use of the software for (1) computer-aided case analysis with welfare proceedings as an example, (2) computer-aided legal policy evaluation with alternative public aid programs as an example, (3) computer-aided advocacy with aid for low-income schools as an example, (4) computer-aided counseling with family disputes as an example, (5) computer-aided negotiation with plea bargaining as an example, and (6) computer-aided mediation with the legislative problem of how to provide legal services to the poor as an example.

This book has already discussed the application of P/G% analysis to providing legal counsel for the poor in civil cases in chapter 4 on "Computer-Aided Mediation." The main choices were salaried government lawyers versus volunteer attorneys. The salaried lawyers were considered better on accessibility and competency, whereas the volunteer attorneys were considered less expensive and more politically feasible. Liberals tend to favor the salaried government attorneys, partly because liberals put more weight on accessibility and competency than they do on inexpensiveness and political feasibility. The example was presented to illustrate partly the desirability of developing imaginative alternatives when there is a deadlock over the original alternatives. The new alternative involves working with salaried attorneys as the base, but bringing on volunteer attorneys in a well-organized manner to increase their accessibility and along with appropriate training to increase their competency. That kind of compromise turns out to be better than the best original expectations of either side.

The book has also already discussed the application of P/G% analysis to some aspects of providing legal counsel to the poor in criminal cases in chapter 13 on "Procedural Law." That analysis emphasized the circumstances under which attorneys should be appointed to represent indigent defendants. The analysis combined two related issues. One was how severe does the crime have to be. On that point, the U.S. Supreme Court began with capital crimes for which capital punishment is a possibility, and then proceeded to require court-appointed counsel for felony crimes in which a year or more in prison is a possibility. More recently, the Court has added misdemeanor crimes in which any time in prison is a possibility. The other issue was at what stage should attorneys be appointed. At first it was just the trial stage. Then the stage of pretrial interrogation and the stage of posttrial appeal. The expansion of the right to court-appointed counsel occurred in light of such goals as acquitting the innocent, convicting the guilty, decreasing government expense, increasing respect for the legal system, facilitating adversary truth-finding, and minimizing deviations from prior precedent.

How to Provide Counsel in Criminal Cases

Previous P/G% spreadsheet tables have dealt with *how* to provide counsel in *civil* cases (table 4-1), and *whether* to provide counsel in *criminal* cases (table 13-2). They have not dealt with the different but related issues of *how* to provide counsel in *criminal* cases, and *whether* to provide counsel in *civil* cases. Table 14-3 deals with deciding how to provide counsel in criminal cases. This is an important issue relevant to the professional responsibility aspects of legal ethics, since one of the most important lawyer responsibilities is seeing to it that people are properly represented in the legal system, especially the criminal justice system.

Table 14-3 shows five alternative ways of providing counsel to indigent defendants.

1. Provide public defenders for all counties in the state, with public defender defined as a salaried government attorney who represents the poor generally on a full-time basis, but on a part-time basis if there are not enough cases in the county.
2. Have assigned counsel, which generally means attorneys assigned in rotation order without pay except possibly for some court expenses.
3. Rely on volunteers to come forward to represent indigent defendants.
4. Have public defenders for big counties and appointed counsel for small counties, who could either be assigned or volunteer.

Table 14-3
Deciding How to Provide Counsel to the Poor in Criminal Cases

A. THE ALTERNATIVES AND THE CRITERIA

Alternative	Criterion	Meas.Unit	Weight
1 PD ALL COUNTIES	1 INEXPENSIVENESS	1-5	1.00
2 ASSIGNED COUNSEL	2 ACCESSIBILITY		1.00
3 VOLUNTEERS	3 POLIT.FEASIBLE		1.00
4 PD/BIG,APPTD/SMALL	4 COMPETENCE		1.00
5 PD/BIG,REGION PD'S	5 CONST.ADEQUACY		1.00

B. THE SCORES OF THE ALTERNATIVES ON THE CRITERIA

	INEXPENS	ACCESSIB	POLIT.FE	COMPETEN	CONST.A
PD ALL COUNTIES	1.00	5.00	3.00	5.00	5.00
ASSIGNED COUNSE	4.00	2.00	1.00	1.00	5.00
VOLUNTEERS	5.00	3.00	5.00	2.00	1.00
PD/BIG,APPTD/SM	3.00	4.00	4.00	3.00	5.00
PD/BIG,REGION P	2.00	1.00	2.00	4.00	5.00

C. THE TOTAL SCORES FOR EACH ALTERNATIVE

Alternative	Combined Rawscores	%
1 PD ALL COUNTIES	19.00	23.46
2 ASSIGNED COUNSEL	13.00	16.05
3 VOLUNTEERS	16.00	19.75
4 PD/BIG,APPTD/SMALL	19.00	23.46
5 PD/BIG,REGION PD'S	14.00	17.28

5. Have full-time public defenders for big counties, and then group small counties into regions for full-time regional public defenders.

Table 14-3 shows five criteria for judging among the five alternatives, although it is coincidental that there happen to be five alternatives and five criteria. The criteria are:

1. Inexpensiveness, meaning that if everything else is held constant, the least expensive program should be adopted.
2. Accessibility, meaning that the preferred program is the one where counsel is visible and easily reached in a central location such as the county courthouse, but with neighborhood or outlying offices if possible.
3. Political feasibility, meaning that the program should be one that is capable of being adopted by a state legislature, possibly over a governor's veto if necessary.
4. Competence, meaning likely to be associated with experienced lawyers who can represent their clients with a reasonable amount of aggressiveness.
5. Constitutional adequacy, meaning capable of providing enough lawyers so that all indigent defendants will be represented in light of the Supreme Court's requirements.

Section B of table 14-3 shows how each alternative roughly scores on each criterion. A 1–5 rank-order system is used on the first four criteria. This involves indicating for each criterion the alternative that does best, the alternative that does worst, and then filling in the middle ranks. For example, in inexpensiveness, volunteers are the best with 5 points and salaried government attorneys for all counties are the least inexpensive with only 1 point. On accessibility, public defenders for all counties are the best, whereas the regional arrangement is the least accessible, although it could be made more accessible by having circuit-riding regional public defenders. On political feasibility having volunteers arouses the least opposition, whereas assigned counsel arouses the most opposition. On competence, experienced full-time public defenders scores highest, and less-experienced assigned counsel and volunteers score the lowest. On constitutional adequacy, the scoring is basically just yes or no. All five systems are considered as being likely to satisfy the minimum constitutional requirements with the exception of relying exclusively on volunteers, especially in large counties.

Section C of table 14-3 shows the overall scores of each of the alternatives. Those overall scores indicate a tie between (1) having public defenders for big counties and appointed counsel for small counties, which is probably the prevailing system across the country, and (2) having public defenders for all counties, which is the system toward which the states and counties are moving as the work load becomes too much for assigned counsel and volunteers.

The best way to break the tie between those two leading alternatives is to observe that the mixed system does better on inexpensiveness and political feasibility, whereas the purer public defender system does better on accessibility and competence. Thus this problem reduces to value judgments that are similar to those involved in deciding between volunteer attorneys and salaried government attorneys in providing legal services in civil cases. If one places more weight on inexpensiveness and political feasibility, which tend to be somewhat conservative goals, then one is more likely to favor the mixed system. If, however, one places more weight on accessibility and aggressive competence, which tend to be somewhat liberal goals, then one is more likely to favor the salaried public defender system.

A key point to note is that regardless of ideological orientation, both conservatives and liberals on the Supreme Court and elsewhere within the legal profession favor counsel for the poor in criminal cases. They also favor inexpensiveness, accessibility, political feasibility, competence, and constitutional adequacy in providing counsel. Thus the differences are relatively minor, especially when one recognizes the trend toward salaried government lawyers for the poor in both criminal and civil cases.

Another subtantive point that relates to professional responsibility among American lawyers is that salaried government lawyers are endorsed by the American Bar Association (ABA) for criminal and civil cases, even in the capitalistic United States, whereas the British legal profession favors volunteer legal aid programs for both criminal and civil cases. This can be contrasted with salaried governmental medical services for the poor, which are opposed by the American Medical Association (AMA) but favored by the British Medical Association. The explanations that are offered for what otherwise might seem inconsistent include the following:

1. The United States has an explicit constitutional clause about right to counsel that has been interpreted broadly by the U.S. Supreme Court. There is no such clause in the amorphous British constitution and no British court with the judicial review powers that the U.S. Supreme Court has.
2. The American Bar Association and the American legal profession are more associated with immigrants than the British legal profession. That kind of demographic composition has stimulated American lawyers to be more sensitive to rights associated with the Bill of Rights than they otherwise would be.
3. With regard to health care, there is no constitutional right. Thus the AMA does not have to be as concerned with providing medical services to the poor as the ABA does regarding legal services to the poor.
4. Health care may be more essential to one's survival than legal care. Thus if a society is going to move from being capitalistic to being socialistic and there are no constitutional constraints, it may logically follow that Britain would adopt socialized health care before socialized legal care.

On a methodological matter, it is probably worth noting that table 14-3 does help provide insights that might otherwise be missed concerning the professional responsibility problem of how to provide counsel to the poor in criminal cases. On a high level of methodological generality, one might say that spreadsheet-based decision-aiding software helps provide insights that might otherwise be missed concerning any problem that relates to legal ethics or professional responsibility.

Whether to Require Free Counsel for the Poor in Civil Cases

As a concluding problem in this chapter and in this book, we might apply the software to the problem mentioned above of deciding whether to provide free counsel to the poor in civil cases, as table 14-4 does. This is still a somewhat controversial issue, even though the issue of whether to provide free counsel to the poor in criminal cases has been resolved in the affirmative at least since the 1960s. One might say that it looks like the civil side has also been resolved in the affirmative by virtue of the existence of the federal Legal Services Corporation since 1976 and the existence of the Legal Services Program of the Office of Economic Opportunity from 1965 to 1975. Those programs, however, are congressional programs, not constitutionally required programs. There was even some high-level opposition to civil legal services for the poor in the Reagan admin-

Table 14-4
Deciding Whether to Provide Free Counsel to the Poor in Civil Cases

A. THE ALTERNATIVES AND THE CRITERIA

ALTERNATIVES	CRITERIA	MEAS.UNIT	WEIGHT
1 No Civil Counsel	1 +Rightful Liab.	1-5 Scale	1.00
2 Special Cvl.Cases	2 -Wrongful Liab.		1.00
3 Any Civil Cases	3 Respect for Law		1.00
	4 Adversary Truth		1.00

B. THE SCORES OF THE ALTERNATIVES ON THE CRITERIA

ALTERNATIVES	CRITERIA			
	Rightful	Wrongful	Respect	Adversary
No Civil Counsel	1.00	5.00	1.00	1.00
Special Cvl.Cas	3.00	3.00	3.00	3.00
Any Civil Cases	5.00	1.00	5.00	5.00

C. THE TOTAL SCORES FOR EACH ALTERNATIVE

ALTERNATIVES	COMBINED RAWSCORES	PERCENTS
1 No Civil Counsel	8.00	22.22
2 Special Cvl.Cases	12.00	33.33
3 Any Civil Cases	16.00	44.44

istration, although it was usually carefully worded to refer to salaried government attorneys under the Legal Services Corporation rather than free civil legal services in general.

Table 14-4 can be considered as dealing with the constitutional question of providing civil legal services to the poor. The Supreme Court could say that the due process clauses of the fifth and the fourteenth amendments cover right to counsel in civil cases. Doing so would not be so contrary to prior precedent. One could argue that it is much worse to be wrongfully evicted from one's home, to have one's belongings repossessed, or to have one's children taken away than it is to spend a night in jail. The possibility of one night in jail, however, does guarantee right to counsel under the *Argersinger* case. One could also seek to extend the quasi-criminal, quasi-civil area of juvenile delinquency to serious civil cases. The Court has held that there is a right to counsel in all juvenile delinquency proceedings in *In Re Gault* even though many juvenile proceedings may be more like friendly family matters than is a civil case involving terminating welfare benefits, child custody, or one's status as a high school student. The average juvenile would probably much rather lose a minor juvenile delinquency proceeding than a paternity action that results in an 18-year child support judgment. Perhaps the Supreme Court could begin a constitutional right to counsel in civil cases by just talking in terms of the more serious civil actions, as it did with criminal cases.

The key point on the constitutional issue is that it would be possible to legitimately interpret due process as including counsel for the indigent in at least major civil cases like those mentioned above. The question then in part becomes whether it is socially desirable to provide free counsel to the poor in civil cases. Table 14-4 works with three alternatives: (1) no right to counsel in any cases where there is no provision for a jail sentence, (2) right to counsel in special civil cases that could be listed one at a time as they arise without necessarily seeking to establish general criteria, or (3) right to counsel for indigents in any civil case regardless of subject matter and regardless of whether the indigent person is the plaintiff or defendant.

The criteria in table 14-4 for judging among those alternatives are:

1. Increasing the establishing of rightful liability, analogous to convicting the guilty.
2. Decreasing the establishing of wrongful liability, analogous to not convicting the innocent.
3. Promoting respect for the law and the legal system.
4. Adversary truth-finding, which may require or at least benefit from having counsel on both sides.

Section B of table 14-4 shows roughly how the three alternatives score on the four criteria. The 1–5 scale allows for the use of 5 for highly conducive to the goal, 4 for mildly conducive, 3 for neither conducive nor adverse, 2 for mildly adverse, and 1 for highly adverse. However, only the numbers 1, 3, and 5 have been used. Thus the scale could be simplified to a 1–3 scale where 3 is conducive, 2 is neutral, and 1 is adverse. It could be further simplified to a 1–3 ranking where one simply asks which of the three alternatives does the best and which does the worst on each criterion. On establishing rightful liability, the alternative of full right to civil counsel scores highest on the grounds that without such counsel, poor people would have a difficult time bringing rightful suits, unless a contingency fee could be arranged or in other exceptional circumstances. On decreasing wrongful findings of liability, no civil counsel scores highest on the theory that anything that facilitates suing may facilitate the wrongful finding of liability. However, an indigent in a civil case may be wrongfully found liable, although they are not so likely to be sued in a damages action if they have no insurance. Respect for the law is promoted (especially on the part of poor people, but others as well) if counsel is available to legitimately sue or defend oneself. Adversary truth-finding is also promoted by having counsel on both sides in civil cases as well as criminal cases.

Section C of table 14-4 shows the overall scores for each alternative. Full civil counsel comes out the winner since it scores the best on three of the four criteria. If one were to do a sensitivity analysis for this problem, it might make good sense to think in terms of adding an additional criterion, namely that of monetary cost to society. That was initially overlooked in developing the criteria, although it was included in the analogous table 13-2 on right to counsel in criminal cases. Looking at the conclusion in this kind of decision analysis often causes one to recycle back and add additional alternatives or criteria, especially if the conclusion as to the best alternative seems to run so contrary to the alternative that has been adopted. In this situation, no civil counsel is the adopted alternative. Suppose, however, one adds a cost criterion and the three alternatives score 5, 3, and 1 on that criterion. Then the new overall scores are 13, 15, and 17, which brings the alternatives closer together. The middle alternative comes out the winner if we add a sixth criterion that relates to trying to be consistent with the prior precedents, including the trends in the prior precedents. If the three alternatives score 3, 5, and 1, respectively, then the new overall scores are 16, 20, and 18 favoring limited right to counsel in civil cases.[4]

BROADENING THE ANALYSIS

As we have seen before, this analysis can be used for advocacy as well as evaluation. Thus the analysis could enable us to improve our appellate advocacy arguments before the Supreme Court in a case dealing with providing free counsel to the poor in civil cases. In that regard, it might also be noted that by giving slightly more weight to minimizing the monetary cost to society, no civil counsel could be considered the winner. It can also come out the winner if one emphasizes prevailing precedent, rather than precedent trends, and one gives extra weight to prevailing precedent. In addition to evaluation and advocacy, this example could be used to help predict or explain existing or future alternatives concerning civil counsel for the poor. The example could also be used for purposes of counseling interested groups or mediating a legislative dispute between those proposing no civil counsel and those proposing full civil counsel.

One could also mention in the context of legal ethics and professional responsibility that attorneys should not only feel a responsibility when it comes to attorney-client relations, attorney-attorney relations, and attorney-court relations; they should also feel a responsibility for promoting legal policy at least in their fields of specialty with regard to developing laws that are more effective, efficient, and equitable and possibly that allow for more public participation, predictability, and procedural due process. Spreadsheet-based decision-aiding software can be helpful in analyzing legal policy alternatives in commercial law, property law, family law, torts, criminal law, constitutional law, economic regulation, international law, and other legal fields, as indicated in the legal policy examples or chapters 11, 12, and 13.

Table 14-4, like so many of the illustrative examples, tends to stimulate ideas for new alternatives, criteria, and relations. It also stimulates ideas for new uses that relate to lawyer skills and new applications that relate to fields of law. There is no limit to the number of uses and applications to which any of the illustrative examples can be put. There is especially no limit to the number of uses to which the general methodology can be put. The only limit is one's imagination, which almost by definition is an unlimited entity. It is hoped that this book has been as stimulating to its readers as it has been to its author in developing new and useful ways of using microcomputers as decision aids in law practice.

NOTES

1. For literature relevant to the subject of deciding whether to go to trial or accept the settlement, see Gerald Williams, *Legal Negotiation and Settlement* (St. Paul: West, 1983); Gerard Nierenberg, *Fundamentals of Negotiating* (New York: Hawthorn/Dutton, 1973); and Howard Raiffa, *The Art and Science of Negotiation* (Cambridge, Mass.: Harvard University Press, 1982.

2. For literature relevant to the subject of deciding how many hours to allocate to damages cases, see S. Nagel, "Allocating Attorney Time per Case" in *Microcomputers as Decision Aids in Law Practice* (Westport, Conn.: Greenwood-Quorum, 1987); F. MacKinnon, *Contingent Fees for Legal Services: A Study of Professional Economics and Responsibilities* (Hawthorne, N.Y.: Aldine, 1964); Murray Schwartz and Daniel Mitchell, "An Economic Analysis of the Contingent Fee in Personal Injury Litigation," 22 *Stanford Law Review* 1125 (1970); and Kevin Claremont and John Currivan, "Improving on the Contingent Fee," 63 *Cornell Law Review* 529-639 (1978).

3. S. Nagel, "Microcomputers as Decision Aids in Practice and Clinical Legal Education: The Poverty Law Perspective," 2 *Software Law Journal* 701-718 (1987).

4. For literature relevant to the subject of representing the poor and related professional responsibilities, see Joel Handler, Ellen Hollingsworth, and Howard Erlanger, *Lawyers and the Pursuit of Legal Rights* (New York: Academic Press, 1978); Legal Services Corporation, *The Delivery Systems Study* (Washington, D.C.: LSC, 1980); Arthur Berney et al. (eds.), *Legal Problems of the Poor: Cases and Materials* (Boston: Little, Brown, 1975), 499-588; Eli Jarmel (ed.), *Problems in the Legal Representation of the Poor: Cases and Materials* (New York: Matthew Bender, 1972); and Lee Silverstein, *Defense of the Poor* (Boston: Little, Brown, 1965).

Appendix: Visual Aids and Data Files

This listing shows for each table (or figure) five pieces of information in five columns: (1) the number, (2) the title, (3) the name of the file in the P/G% decision-aiding software that was used to generate the data, (4) the master file or umbrella file in which the specific data file is located, and (5) the page number on which the item appears.

Bibliography

ITEMS CITED

Abraham, Henry. *Freedom and the Court: Civil Rights and Liberties in the United States.* New York: Oxford, 1982.

Abrams, Norman. *Federal Criminal Law and Its Enforcement.* St. Paul: West, 1986.

Ackerman, Bruce (ed.). *Economic Foundations of Property Law.* Boston: Little, Brown, 1975.

Alperovitz, Gar and Jeff Faux. *Rebuilding America.* New York: Pantheon, 1984.

American Bar Association. *Standards Relating to Trial Courts.* Chicago: ABA, 1976.

American Enterprise Institute. *The New Consensus on Family and Welfare.* Washington, D.C.: American Enterprise Institute, 1987.

Areen, Judith (ed.). *Cases and Materials on Family Law.* Mineola, N.Y.: Foundation, 1985.

Atkins, Burton and Mark Pogrebin (eds.). *The Invisible Justice System: Discretion and the Law.* Cincinnati: Anderson, 1978.

Baldus, David et al. "Comparative Review of Death Sentences: An Empirical Study of the Georgia Experiences." 74 *Journal of Criminal Law and Criminology* 661 (1983).

Bardach, Eugene and Robert Kagan (eds.). *Social Regulation: Strategies for Reform.* San Francisco: Institute for Contemporary Studies, 1982.

Barron, Jerome and Thomas Dienes. *Constitutional Law in a Nutshell.* St. Paul: West, 1986.

Bartholomew, Paul. "Supreme Court and Modern Objectivity." 33 *New York State Bar Journal* 157-164 (1961).

Baum, Lawrence. *American Courts: Process and Policy.* Boston: Houghton Mifflin, 1986.

Benfield, Marian. *New Approaches in the Law of Contracts.* Mineola, N.Y.: Foundation, 1970.

Bergman, Paul. *Trial Advocacy in a Nutshell.* St. Paul: West, 1979.

Berkson, Larry, Steven Hays, and Susan Carbon (eds.). *Managing the State Courts.* St. Paul: West, 1977.

Berney, Arthur et al. (eds.). *Legal Problems of the Poor: Cases and Materials.* Boston: Little, Brown, 1975.

Bernhardt, Roger. *Real Property in a Nutshell.* St. Paul: West, 1981.

Boyer, Ralph. *Survey of the Law of Property.* St. Paul: West, 1981.

Brigham, John. *Civil Liberties and American Democracy.* Washington, D.C.: Congressional Quarterly, 1984.

Brightman, Harvey. *Problem Solving: A Logical and Creative Approach.* Atlanta: Georgia State University, 1980.

Buergenthal, Thomas and Harold Maier. *Public International Law in a Nutshell.* St. Paul: West, 1985.

Burns, John and Jim Hodde. "Decision Analysis: Using Computers to Make Better Choices." 6 *Attorney's Computer Report* 1-4 (February 1988).

Burris, Russell, Robert Keeton, Carolyn Landis, and Roger Park. *Teaching Law with Computers: A Collection of Essays.* Denver: Westview Press, 1979.

Burt, Robert. "Disorder in the Court: The Death Penalty and the Constitution." 85 *Michigan Law Review* 1741 (1987).

Calamari, John. *Hornbook on Contracts.* St. Paul: West, 1987.

Campbell, C. *The Reform of Educational Finance: A Selected Annotated Bibliography.* New York: New York State Library, 1981.

Carroll, S. and R. Park. *The Search for Equity in School Finance.* Cambridge, Mass.: Ballinger, 1983.

Catterall, James (ed.). *Economic Evaluation of Public Programs.* San Francisco: Jossey-Bass, 1985.

Claremont, Kevin and John Currivan. "Improving on the Contingent Fee," 63 *Cornell Law Review* 529-639 (1978).

Clark, Homer. *Hornbook on Domestic Relations.* St. Paul: West, 1968.

______. *The Law of Domestic Relations in the United States.* St. Paul: West, 1968.

Cohen, Neil and James Gobert. *Problems in Criminal Law.* St. Paul: West, 1976.

Conway, Richard et al. *Theory of Scheduling.* Reading, Mass.: Addison-Wesley, 1967.

Coons, John, W. Clune, and S. Sugarman. *Private Wealth and Public Education.* Cambridge, Mass.: Harvard University Press, 1970.

Cooper, George et al. *Law and Poverty: Cases and Materials.* St. Paul: West, 1973.

Cover, Robert and Owen Fiss. *The Structure of Procedure.* Mineola, N.Y.: Foundation, 1979.

Cribbet, John. *Principles of the Law of Property.* Mineola, N.Y.: Foundation, 1975.

Cunningham, Roger, Dale Whitman, and William Stoebuck. *Hornbook on the Law of Property.* St. Paul: West, 1987.

Dobbs, Dan. *Torts and Compensation: Personal Accountability and Social Responsibility for Injury.* St. Paul: West, 1985.

Dorsen, Norman, Paul Bender, and Burt Neuborne (eds.). *Political and Civil Rights in the United States.* Boston: Little, Brown, 1976.

Downs, Anthony. *Urban Problems and Prospects.* Chicago: Markham, 1970.

Easton, Allan. *Complex Managerial Decisions Involving Multiple Objectives.* New York: John Wiley, 1973.

Engdahl, David. *Constitutional Power: Federal and State in a Nutshell.* St. Paul: West, 1974.

Erickson, Jon and Charles Wilhelm (eds.). *Housing the Homeless.* New Brunswick, N.J.: Center for Urban Policy Research, 1986.
Erikson, Warren and Owen Hall. *Computer Models for Management Science.* Reading, Mass.: Addison-Wesley, 1986.
Falk, Richard and Saul Mendlovitz (eds.). *The Strategy of World Order.* New York: World Law Fund, 1966.
Frank, Jerome. *Courts on Trial: Myth and Reality in American Justice.* Princeton, N.J.: Princeton University Press, 1950.
Franklin, Marc and Robert Rabin. *Injuries and Remedies: Tort Law and Alternatives.* Mineola, N.Y.: Foundation, 1983.
Freedman, Leonard. *Public Housing: The Politics of Poverty.* New York: Holt, Rinehart, and Winston, 1969.
Friedenthal, Jack, Mary Kane, and Arthur Miller. *Hornbook on Civil Procedure.* St. Paul: West, 1985.
Friedman, Lawrence and Stewart Macaulay (eds.). *Law and the Behavioral Sciences.* Indianapolis: Bobbs-Merrill, 1977.
Gass, Saul, Harvey Greenberg, Karla Hoffman, and Warren Langley (eds.). *Impacts of Microcomputers on Operations Research.* Amsterdam: North-Holland, 1986.
Gellhorn, Ernest and Richard Pierce. *Regulated Industries in a Nutshell.* St. Paul: West, 1987.
Gellhorn, Ernest. *Antitrust Law and Economics in a Nutshell.* St. Paul: West, 1986.
Goodman, Martin. "United States as a Party in International Law Disputes." Bachelor's Thesis in the University of Illinois Law Library, 1964.
Grafton, Carl and Anne Permaloff, "Expert System Development Programs and Their Alternatives." 4 *Social Science Microcomputer Review,* 165-180 (1986).
Gramlich, Edward. *Benefit-Cost Analysis of Government Programs.* Englewood Cliffs, N.J.: Prentice-Hall, 1981.
Green, Milton. *Text on Basic Civil Procedure.* Mineola, N.Y.: Foundation, 1979.
Guthrie, J. (ed.). *School Finance Policies and Practices in the 1980s: A Decade of Conflict.* Cambridge, Mass.: Ballinger, 1980.
Haas, Kenneth and James Inciardi (eds.). *Challenging Capital Punishment: Legal and Social Science Approaches.* Newbury Park, Calif.: Sage, 1988.
Hafner, Carole (ed.). *Proceedings of the First International Conference on Artificial Intelligence and Law.* Boston: Northeastern University, 1987.
Handler, Joel, Ellen Hollingsworth, and Howard Erlanger. *Lawyers and the Pursuit of Legal Rights.* New York: Academic Press, 1978.
Harris, Clifford. *The Break-Even Handbook.* Englewood Cliffs, N.J. Prentice-Hall, 1978.
Harvard Board of Student Advisers. *Introduction to Advocacy.* Mineola, N.Y.: Foundation, 1981.
Hazen, Thomas. *Hornbook on the Law of Securities Regulation.* St. Paul: West, 1985.
Hill, David. *Landlord and Tenant Law in a Nutshell.* St. Paul: West, 1986.
Hornstein, Alan. *Appellate Advocacy in a Nutshell.* St. Paul: West, 1984.
Hovenkamp, Herbert. *Hornbook on Economics and Federal Antitrust Law.* St. Paul: West, 1985.
Huber, Peter. *Liability: The Legal Revolution and Its Consequences.* New York: Basic Books, 1988.
Humphreys, Patrick and Ayleen Wisudha. *Methods and Tools for Structuring and Analyz-*

ing Decision Problems. London: London School of Economics and Political Science, 1987.

Humphreys, Patrick and Janos Vecsenyi (eds.). *High Level Decision Support: Lessons from Case Studies.* Amsterdam: North-Holland, 1986.

Hwang, Ching-Lai and Kwangsun Yoon. *Multiple Attribute Decision Making: Methods and Applications.* Berlin: Springer-Verlag, 1981.

Iezzi, John G. "Partner Compensation: A Different Approach." 11 *Legal Economics* 29-34 (March-April 1985).

Israel, Jerold and Wayne LaFave. *Criminal Procedure in a Nutshell.* St. Paul: West, 1980.

Jackson, John and William Davey. *Legal Problems of International Economic Relations.* St. Paul: West, 1986.

Jacob, Herbert. *Justice in America: Courts, Lawyers, and the Judicial Process.* Boston: Little, Brown, 1984.

Jarmel, Eli (ed.). *Problems in the Legal Representation of the Poor: Cases and Materials.* New York: Matthew Bender, 1972.

Johnson, David and Paul Mode. *Improving Law Firm Productivity by Encouraging Lawyers' Use of Personal Computers.* New York: Harcourt Brace Jovanovich, 1985.

Jones, Harry, John Kernochan, and Arthur Murphy (eds.). *Legal Methods: Cases and Text Materials.* Mineola, N.Y.: Foundation, 1980.

Jones, Robert (ed.). *Programming the Process: An Examination of the Use of Computers in Dispute Resolution.* Washington, D.C.: National Institute of Dispute Resolution, 1988.

Kane, Mary. *Civil Procedure in a Nutshell.* St. Paul: West, 1986.

Kaplan, Martin and Gwen Kemmerick. "Juror Judgement as Information Integration: Combining Evidential and Nonevidential Information." *Journal of Personality and Social Psychology* 493-499 (1974).

Katz, Carol (ed.). *The Law and the Low Income Consumer.* New York: New York University School of Law, 1968.

Kerr, Norbert and Robert Bray (eds.). *The Psychology of the Courtroom.* New York: Academic Press, 1982.

Kim, Samuel. *The Quest for a Just World Order.* Denver: Westview, 1984.

Kingston, Charles. "Probability and Legal Proceedings." 57 *Journal of Criminal Law, Criminology, and Police Science* 93-98 (1966).

Kionka, Edward. *Torts in a Nutshell: Injuries to Persons and Property.* St. Paul: West, 1977.

Knudten, Richard (ed.). *Criminological Controversies.* New York: Meredith, 1968.

Kotler, Philip. *Marketing Decision Making: A Model Building Approach.* New York: Holt, 1971.

Krause, Harry. *Family Law in a Nutshell.* St. Paul: West, 1977.

Kripke, Homer. *Consumer Credit.* St. Paul: West, 1970.

Kronman, Anthony and Richard Posner (eds.). *The Economics of Contract Law.* Boston: Little, Brown, 1979.

LaFave, Wayne and Austin Scott. *Hornbook on Criminal Law.* St. Paul: West, 1986.

LaFave, Wayne and Jerold Israel. *Hornbook on Criminal Procedure.* St. Paul: West, 1985.

LaFrance, Arthur. *Law of the Poor.* St. Paul: West, 1973.

______. *Welfare Law: Structure and Entitlement in a Nutshell.* St. Paul: West, 1979.

Lee, Sang, Laurence Moor, and Bernard Taylor. *Management Science.* Dubuque, Iowa: Wm. C. Brown, 1981.

Legal Services Corporation. *The Delivery Systems Study.* Washington, D.C.: Legal Services Corporation, 1980.

Lempert, Richard. "Modeling Relevance." *Michigan Law Review* 1021-1057 (1977).

Levine, James, Michael Musheno, and Dennis Palumbo. *Criminal Justice: A Public Policy Approach.* New York: Harcourt Brace Jovanovich, 1980.

Lindsey, Peter and Donald Norman. *Human Information Processing.* Orlando, Fla.: Academic Press, 1972.

Llewellyn, Karl. *The Common Law Tradition: Deciding Appeals.* Boston: Little, Brown, 1960.

Lockhart, William et al. *Cases on the American Constitution.* St. Paul: West, 1986.

Loewy, Arnold. *Criminal Law in a Nutshell.* St. Paul: West, 1975.

MacKinnon, F. *Contingent Fees for Legal Services: A Study of Professional Economics and Responsibilities.* Hawthorne, N.Y.: Aldine, 1964.

Macneil, Ian. *Contracts: Exchange Transactions and Relations.* Mineola, N.Y.: Foundation, 1978.

Magaziner, Ira and Robert Reich. *Minding America's Business: The Decline and Rise of the American Economy.* New York: Harcourt Brace Jovanovich, 1982.

Malone, Wex. *Torts in a Nutshell: Injuries to Family, Social, and Trade Relations.* St. Paul: West, 1979.

Mason, Mary Ann. *An Introduction to Using Computers in the Law.* St. Paul: West, 1984.

McDougal, Myres and Michael Reisman. *International Law in Contemporary Perspective.* Mineola, N.Y.: Foundation, 1981.

McMillan, Claude. *Mathematical Programming: An Introduction to the Design and Application of Optimal Decision Machines.* New York: John Wiley, 1970.

Meier, Kenneth. *Regulation: Politics, Bureaucracy, and Economics.* New York: St. Martin's, 1985.

Miller, Frank et al. *Criminal Justice Administration.* Mineola, N.Y.: Foundation, 1986.

Mitra, Gautam (ed.). *Computer Assisted Decision Making: Expert Systems, Decision Analysis, Mathematical Programming.* Amsterdam: North Holland, 1986.

Moore, Christopher. *The Mediation Process: Practical Strategies for Resolving Conflict.* San Francisco: Jossey-Bass, 1986.

More, Harry. *Criminal Justice Management.* St. Paul: West, 1977.

Morris, Clarence. *Text on Torts.* Mineola, N.Y.: Foundation, 1980.

Nadel, Mark (ed.). *Consumer Protection Policy.* Urbana, Ill.: Policy Studies Organization, 1983.

Nagel, S. "Allocating Attorney Time per Case," in *Microcomputers as Decision Aids in Law Practice.* Westport, Conn.: Greenwood-Quorum, 1987.

______. "Alternative Predictive and Analytic Techniques Applicable to Multiple-Category Variables." In Nagel, *The Legal Process from a Behavioral Perspective.* Homewood, Ill.: Dorsey Press, 1969.

______. *Applying Microcomputers to Dispute Resolution.* Champaign, Ill.: Decision Aids, Inc., 1987.

______. "Attorney Time Per Case: Finding an Optimum Level." 32 *University of Florida Law Review* 424-441 (1980).

______. "Case Prediction by Staircase Tables and Percentaging." 25 *Jurimetric Journal* 169-196 (1985).

______. *Causation, Prediction, and Legal Analysis.* Westport, Conn.: Greenwood-Quorum, 1986.

______. "Computer-Aided Counseling, Negotiation, and Advocacy." *Connecticut Law Tribune,* January 5, 1987.

______. "Computer-Aided Law Decisions." 21 *Akron Law Review* 73-96 (1987).

______. "Dealing with Unknown Variables in Policy/Program Evaluation." 6 *Evaluation and Program Planning* 7-18 (1983).

______. *Evaluation Analysis with Microcomputers.* Greenwich, Conn.: JAI Press, 1989.

______. "Lawyer Decision-Making and Threshold Analysis." 36 *University of Miami Law Review* 615-642 (1983).

______. "A Microcomputer Program for Dealing with Evaluation Problems." 9 *Evaluation and Program Planning* (1987).

______. *Microcomputers as Decision Aids in Law Practice.* Westport, Conn.: Greenwood-Quorum, 1987.

______. "Microcomputers as Decision Aids in Practice and Clinical Legal Education: The Poverty Law Perspective." 2 *Software Law Journal* 701-718 (1987).

______. "Microcomputers, Risk Analysis, and Litigation Strategy." 19 *Akron Law Review* 35-80 (1985).

______. "Microcomputers and Improving Social Science Prediction." 10 *Evaluation Review* 635-660 (1986).

______. "New Varieties of Sensitivity Analysis." 9 *Evaluation Review* 772-779 (1985).

______. "Nonmonetary Variables in Benefit-Cost Evaluation." 7 *Evaluation Review* 37-64 (1983).

______. "Optimally Allocating Federal Money to Cities." 5 *Public Budgeting and Finance* 39-50 (1985).

______. "P/G% Analysis: An Evaluating-Aiding Program." 9 *Evaluation Review* 209-214 (1985).

______. *Policy Evaluation: Making Optimum Decisions.* New York: Praeger, 1982.

______. *Public Policy: Goals, Means, and Methods.* New York: St. Martin's, 1984.

______. (ed). *The Rights of the Accused: In Law and Action.* Beverly Hills, Calif.: Sage, 1972.

______. "Sequencing and Allocating Attorney Time to Cases." 13 *Pepperdine Law Review* 1021-1039 (1986).

______. "Using Microcomputers and P/G% to Predict Court Cases." 18 *Akron Law Review* 541-574 (1985).

______. *Using Personal Computers for Decision-Making in Law Practice.* Philadelphia: ALI-ABA, 1985.

Nagel, S. and Casimir Barczyk. "Can Computers Aid the Dispute Resolution Process?" 71 *Judicature* 253, 294-295 (1988).

Nagel, S., Mark Beeman, and John Reed. "Optimum Sequencing of Court Cases to Reduce Delay." 37 *Alabama Law Review* 583-638 (1986).

Nagel, S. and M. Mills. "Allocating Attorneys to Casetypes." 15 *Capital University Law Review* 223-242 (1986).

______. "Using Management Science to Assign Judges to Casetypes." 40 *Miami University Law Review* 1317-1336 (1986).

Nagel, S. and T. Stanton. "Using Framework Spreadsheets to Choose Among Alternatives." *Ashton-Tate Magazine* (1989).

Nierenberg, Gerard. *Fundamentals of Negotiating.* New York: Hawthorn/Dutton, 1973.

Nowak, John, Ronald Rotunda, and Nelson Young. *Hornbook on Constitutional Law.* St. Paul: West, 1986.

Nyhart, Don (ed.). *Computer Models and Modeling for Negotiation Management.* Cambridge, Mass.: MIT Conference Proceedings, November 1987.

Olson, Walter (ed.). *New Directions in Liability Law.* New York: Academy of Political Science, 1988.

Orfield, Lester. *Criminal Procedure from Arrest to Appeal.* New York: New York University Press, 1947.

Patterson, J. and David Zaretsky. *Contemporary Debate.* Boston: Houghton Mifflin, 1983.

Perkins, Rollin and Ronald Boyce. *Text on Criminal Law.* Mineola, N.Y.: Foundation, 1982.

Phelps, Glenn and Robert Poirier. *Contemporary Debates on Civil Liberties: Enduring Constitutional Questions.* Lexington, Mass.: Lexington-Heath, 1985.

Plager, Sheldon (ed.). *New Approaches in the Law of Property.* Mineola, N.Y.: Foundation, 1970.

Posner, Richard. *Economic Analysis of Law.* Boston: Little, Brown, 1987.

Prosser, William et al. *Hornbook on Torts.* St. Paul: West, 1984.

Quade, Edward. *Analysis for Public Decisions.* Amsterdam: North-Holland, 1982.

Rabin, Robert (ed.). *Perspectives on Tort Law.* Boston: Little, Brown, 1976.

Radcliff, Benjamin. "Multi-Criteria Decision Making: A Survey of Software." 4 *Social Science Microcomputer Review* 38-55 (1986).

Raiffa, Howard. *The Art and Science of Negotiation.* Cambridge, Mass.: Harvard University Press, 1982.

Rasmussen, Thomas (ed.). *System Science and Jurisprudence.* Lansing, Mich.: Spartan Press, 1986.

Remer, Daniel. *Computer Power for Your Office.* Berkeley: Sybex, 1983.

Richmond, Samuel. *Operations Research for Management Decisions.* New York: Ronald Press, 1968.

Rosenberg, Maurice, Hans Smit, and Harold Korn. *Elements of Civil Procedure.* Mineola, N.Y.: Foundation, 1985.

Saaty, Thomas. *Decision Making for Leaders: The Analytical Hierarchy Process for Decisions in a Complex World.* Belmont, Calif.: Wadsworth, 1982.

Sales, Bruce (ed.). *The Trial Process.* New York: Plenum, 1981.

Sawaragi, Yoshikazu (ed.). *Multiple-Criteria Decision Making.* Berlin: Springer-Verlag, 1987.

Schaber, Gordon. *Contracts in a Nutshell.* St. Paul: West, 1984.

Schubert, Glendon (ed.). *Judicial Behavior: A Reader in Theory and Research.* Chicago: Rand McNally, 1964.

Schum, David. "Contrast Effects in Inference: On the Conditioning of Current Evidence by Prior Evidence." 18 *Organizational Behavior and Human Performance* 217-253 (1977).

Schwartz, Alan and Robert Scott. *Sales Law and the Contracting Process.* Mineola, N.Y.: Foundation, 1982.

Schwartz, Murray and Daniel Mitchell. "An Economic Analysis of the Contingent Fee in

Personal Injury Litigation,'' 22 *Stanford Law Review* 1125 (1970).

Scott, Joseph and Travis Hirschi (eds.). *Controversial Issues in Crime and Justice.* Beverly Hills, Calif.: Sage, 1988.

Semmel, Herbert (ed.). *New Approaches in the Law of Civil Procedure.* Mineola, N.Y.: Foundation, 1970.

Silverstein, Lee. *Defense of the Poor.* Boston: Little, Brown, 1965.

Soroos, Marvin. *Beyond Sovereignty: The Challenge of Global Policy.* Columbia: University of South Carolina Press, 1986.

Spaeth, Harold. *Supreme Court Policy Making: Explanation and Prediction.* San Francisco: Freeman, 1979.

Sprowl, James. ''Editor's Note to Practical Tips on Using Microcomputers for Decision-Making in Law Practice.'' 2 ABA *Microcomputer Newsletter* 8-9 (Summer 1986).

Statsky, William and John Werner. *Case Analysis and Fundamentals of Legal Writing.* St. Paul: West, 1977.

Steiner, Henry and Detlev Vagts. *Transnational Legal Problems.* Mineola, N.Y.: Foundation, 1986.

Sundquist, James. *Constitutional Reform and Effective Government.* Washington, D.C.: Brookings, 1986.

Tessitore, John and Susan Woolfson (eds.). *Issues Before the 43rd General Assembly of the United Nations.* Lexington, Mass.: Lexington-Heath, 1981.

Thode, Wayne, Leon Lebowitz, and Lester Mazon (eds.). *Introduction to the Study of Law: Cases and Materials.* Mineola, N.Y.: Foundation, 1970.

Thompson, Mark. *Benefit-Cost Analysis for Program Evaluation.* Beverly Hills, Calif.: Sage, 1980.

______. *Decision Analysis for Program Evaluation.* Cambridge, Mass.: Ballinger, 1982.

Tribe, Laurence. *American Constitutional Law.* Mineola, N.Y.: Foundation, 1978.

Tullock, Gordon. *The Logic of the Law.* New York: Basic Books, 1971.

UCLA Moot Court Honors Program. *Handbook of Appellate Advocacy.* St. Paul: West, 1986.

Uviller, Richard. *The Processes of Criminal Justice: Investigation and Adjudication.* St. Paul: West, 1979.

Wadlington, Walter (ed.). *Statutory Materials on Family Law and Children in the Legal System.* Mineola, N.Y.: Foundation, 1981.

Walker, Samuel. *Sense and Nonsense About Crime: A Policy Guide.* Monterey, Calif.: Brooks/Cole, 1985.

Walter, Charles (ed.). *Computing Power and Legal Reasoning.* St. Paul: West, 1985.

White, W. *The Death Penalty in the Eighties: An Examination of the Modern System of Capital Punishment.* Ann Arbor: University of Michigan Press, 1987.

Wilkerson, Albert (ed.). *The Rights of Children: Emergent Concepts in Law and Society.* Philadelphia: Temple University Press, 1973.

Williams, Gerald. *Legal Negotiation and Settlement.* St. Paul: West, 1983.

Wilson, Donald. *International Business Transactions in a Nutshell.* St. Paul: West, 1984.

Wisudha, Ayleen. *Methods and Tools for Structuring and Analyzing Decision Problems.* London: London School of Economics and Political Science, 1987.

Zeleny, Milan. *Multiple Criteria Decision Making.* New York: McGraw-Hill, 1982.

SOFTWARE CITED

"The Art of Negotiating." Experience in Software, Inc., 2039 Shattuck Avenue, Suite 401, Berkeley, CA 97404.

"Computer Models for Management Science." Addison-Wesley, Reading, MA.

"Data Law." 6341 South Troy Circle, Suite E, Englewood, CO 80111.

"DBase II." Ashton-Tate, 20101 Hamilton Ave., Torrance, CA 90502.

"Estate Tax Planner." Aardvark-McGraw-Hill, 1020 North Broadway, Milwaukee, WI 53202.

"Evidence Master." 240 Stockton Street, Suite 400, San Francisco, CA 94108.

"Expert Choice." Decision Support Software, 1300 Vincent Place, McLean, VA 22101.

"Lexis." Mead Data Central, 9393 Springsboro Pike, P.O. Box 933, Dayton, OH 45401.

"Policy/Goal Percentaging (P/G%)." Decision Aids, Inc., 1720 Parkhaven, Champaign, IL 61820.

"SettleMate." Lawyers Technology, Inc., 339 15th Street, No. 200, Oakland, CA 94612.

"SPSS-PC." 444 North Michigan Avenue, Chicago, IL 60611.

"WestLaw." 50 West Kellogg Blvd., St. Paul, MN 55164.

"WillWriter." Nolo Press, 950 Parker Street, Berkeley, CA 94710.

"WordStar." MicroPro Corporation, 33 San Pablo Avenue, San Rafael, CA 94903.

Name Index

Llewellyn, Karl, 109
Lockhart, William, 194
Loewy, Arnold, 193

Subject Index

About the Author

STUART S. NAGEL, Professor of Political Science at the University of Illinois, is Secretary-Treasurer and Publications Coordinator of the Policy Studies Organization and an active member of the Illinois bar. Among his most recently authored books are *Policy Studies: Integration and Evaluation* (Greenwood Press/Praeger, 1988), *Causation, Prediction, and Legal Analysis* (Quorum Books, 1986), *Law, Policy, and Optimizing Analysis* (Quorum Books, 1986), *Microcomputers, Evaluation Research, and Policy Analysis*, and *Public Policy: Goals, Means, and Methods.* His major edited books include *Law and Policy Studies, Public Policy Analysis and Management*, and *The Policy Studies Field: Its Basic Literature.* His articles have appeared in the *American Bar Association Journal, American Political Science Review*, and other law and professional journals.

www.ingramcontent.com/pod-product-compliance
Ingram Content Group UK Ltd.
Pitfield, Milton Keynes, MK11 3LW, UK
UKHW020257051026
15470UKWH00020B/870

9 780899 303826